"Author Darrell Fields takes you on a j[o]... [Ameri]ca to uncover the momentous and often trag[ic] ... ethical foundation for the social experimen[t] ... his work is gripping, provocative, insightful, and relevant as 21ˢᵗ century America seeks to emerge as a just and caring multicultural society not prone to repeating the injustices of the past. *The Seed of a Nation* communicates William Penn's vision for a new nation in which the values of justice, liberty, and equality would prevail and describes why that vision is yet to be fulfilled."

Dr. William J. Brown
College of Communication and the Arts
Regent University, Virginia Beach, VA

"Now is the time to cleanse and heal the foundations. God has been restoring our understanding of priestly mediation over nations and peoples, a clear word has come from the prophets and Bible teachers, the only question is, will we obey God? The first step is an encounter with God's heart, the second is to honestly uncover and appraise the story of the land in His presence. Everything now depends on the work of godly researchers.

"In *The Seed of a Nation*, Darrell Fields has given us an outstanding example of scholastic integrity combined with prophetic passion. Understanding the story of Pennsylvania is profoundly important when considering the spiritual battle for America as a whole. This small state contains redemptive potentials in its foundations like few others and a story of modern heroism and sacrifice is beginning to unfold that could instruct us all."

John Dawson
Founder, International Reconciliation Coalition
Author, *Healing America's Wounds*
Ventura, CA

"*The Seed Of A Nation* is an excellent book that opens up a rich well of American history. It is a key to opening the blessings of God on a whole nation. From the root of William Penn and the land where my forefathers landed in the 1700's, a shoot will spring up. Read the book and dig the well."

Lou Engle
President, The Call
Author, *Digging the Wells of Revival*

"It is my firm conviction that the destiny of this nation lies in the commission given to William Penn. The Lord has raised up Darrell Fields for such a time as this to research and bring forward these truths. As you read this great book you will be inspired to dig the wells of destiny as found in *The Seed of a Nation*."

James W. Goll
Ministry to the Nations
Author, *The Lost Art of Intercession,*
Wasted On Jesus, and 20 other books and study guides

"*The Seed of a Nation* is a thoroughly researched and fascinating account of William Penn's efforts to establish a "Holy Experiment" in Pennsylvania—a vision of governance grounded in faith and operating on the principles of tolerance and respect for all. Darrell's focus on Penn's relations with the early inhabitants of Penn's Woods does not shortchange the Native American perspective. Unlike other histories of the period, this book is informed with a faith that must be very close to the faith that guided Penn himself."

Pennsylvania Senator Stewart J. Greenleaf

"Excellent book! *The Seed of a Nation* is a must read for every Pennsylvanian and for everyone who cares about the future of our nation. May we take responsibility before the Lord and truly repent for not honoring the covenants of our ancestors. I encourage you to read each page prayerfully with an open heart before the Lord. Thank you Darrell, for this timely book."

Larry Kreider
International Dir. of DOVE Christian Fellowship Intl.
Author, *House to House; The Cry for Spiritual Fathers and Mothers*
Ephrata, PA

"*The Seed Of A Nation* is an incredible look at an almost forgotten chapter in America's spiritual and national heritage—the founding of Pennsylvania. Darrell Fields' incisive analysis of this states origins and their affect on American history, is essential reading for anyone who takes seriously their responsibility to pray for the United States."

Jim Laffoon
Every Nation Ministries
Nashville, TN

"Broken covenants result in curses (2 Samuel 21). More than 800 treaties (solemn covenants) with American Indians were made. Not one was kept! How much repentance, by how many, will be required to set America free? Repentances must become concrete and specific. Darrell Fields' book details, in historical clarity, what needs repentance in Pennsylvania and the surrounding states, and thus America. Whoever reads can not help but shed tears of guilt and shame—godly sorrow that produces earnestness and zeal for repentance and restitution (2 Corinthians 7:11). On the other hand *The Seed of a Nation* rings a clarion bell of celebration, for it reveals not only seeds of evil for repentance but the historical fact that the seed of faith, with all the wondrous fruits of the Spirit—love, respect, trust, admiration, gentleness and forgiveness—is just as deeply rooted in the foundations of our country. The questions of the book resound—who will respond? And which foundation shall be allowed to stand as that which governs our destiny? Only the readers' replies can tell."

John Sandford
Elijah House, Inc.
Author, *Transformation of the Inner Man*
Hayden, Idaho

"*The Seed of a Nation* is a wake up call to America. Over the last several years the Church has been repenting for the iniquitous ways of our unrighteous forefathers. The question Darrell Fields is asking, "Do we have the courage and faith to walk in the ways of America's righteous fathers?" William Penn understood his covenant with God and could therefore be God's ambassador of extending His covenant to the indigenous people of this land. Darrell has made it clear that God's blessings upon America depend upon keeping our covenant with Him. The evidence of which is reflected in our keeping covenant with others. The blood of innocent people through breaking covenant with God and those He created in His image defiles this land. The Native Americans know that more than their white brothers. Our hope now lies in the ever living and powerful blood of Christ to reconcile and restore."

Jean Steffenson
President, Native American Resource Network
Castle Rock, CO

"Darrell Fields' book is a 'must read' for intercessors and all who are pursuing national revival. It uncovers important yet neglected dynamics in the spiritual and ethical history of Pennsylvania. Much of America's destiny has found its inception or turning points in the Keystone State of Pennsylvania. Philadelphia, Valley Forge and Gettysburg are well known crucibles in our history. Lesser known is the treacherous and unredressed treatment of the Native American peoples. As you read this tragic story, you cannot help but wonder if some of the keys to national revival and healing of racial injustices may hinge on God's agenda for Pennsylvania. This book will inspire you to cry out to God for mercy and justice to come together."

Charles Stock
Senior Pastor, Life Center
Harrisburg, PA

"As a Lakota man, I was encouraged to read how William Penn lived a life that truly reflected the person of Jesus Christ and Biblical faith to the First Nations people of North America. His genuine love for Jesus and for Native people stands in stark contrast to the greed, injustice and genocide that so often reflected the motives and attitudes of his fellow European immigrants. It inspired hope in my heart for a better tomorrow. *The Seed of a Nation* will help you feel the painful journey we have been on as co-inhabitants of this land. Darrell Fields does a beautiful job painting pictures of what the "founding of America" was really like from a First Nations perspective. I highly recommend this book. It is a book of healing. My heart was touched in a very deep way and I now understand better the purpose that God had in mind for the inhabitants of these lands called America and Canada."

Richard Twiss
Rosebud Lakota/Sioux
President, Wiconi International
Author, *One Church Many Tribes*

"Darrell started on a journey that captures the heart of God in understanding the power of covenant. Although it is applied to William Penn and his godly receiving of the Native Americans as equals, the principle has a universal application of the effects of broken covenants on all societies. He brings the application that can help bring healing and a release of true freedom for all peoples. A masterful work that provides answers for the deep racial wounds of our nation and world."

Sam A. Webb
Every Nation Ministries
Honolulu, HI

THE
SEED
OF A
NATION

Rediscovering America

DARRELL FIELDS
WITH LORRIE FIELDS

NEW YORK

The Seed of a Nation
Rediscovering America

Unless otherwise indicated, all Scripture quotations are from the authorized King James Version. References marked NKJV are from the New King James Version of the Bible, copyright © 1979, 1980, 1982, by Thomas Nelson, Inc., Nashville, Tennessee. References marked NLT are from the New Living Translation of the Bible, copyright © 1996 by Tyndale House Publishers, Inc., Wheaton, Illinois. References marked NIV are from the *New International Version* of the Bible, copyright © 1973, 1978, 1984 by International Bible Society, Colorado Springs, Colorado.

THE SEED OF A NATION: Rediscovering America

ISBN: 978-1-60037-204-9 (Paperback)
ISBN: 978-1-60037-212-4 (Hardcover)

Healing the Land Publishers
an imprint of Morgan James Publishers
P.O. Box 73
Scotland, PA 17254
Phone: 717-263-9106
Fax: 760-874-9874
info@healingtheland.com
www.healingtheland.com

Morgan James Publishing, LLC
1225 Franklin Ave Ste 325
Garden City, NY 11530-1693
Toll Free 800-485-4943
www.MorganJamesPublishing.com

Habitat for Humanity®
Peninsula
Building Partner

Design and Layout by Tony Laidig, www.thecoverexpert.com

For Worldwide Distribution

TABLE OF CONTENTS

Foreword ix

Introduction xi

Part One: Promise . . . .**xix**
1   Into the Light 1
2   The Architect of Freedom 15
3   The Seed of a Nation 25
4   Born of Covenant 39
5   William Penn Removed 57

Part Two: Broken Trust **75**
6   The Gathering Storm 77
7   The Disgrace of the Colonies .93
8   The French Make Their Move 107
9   Distant Thunder 117

Part Three: A Time for War **129**
10   Forlorn Hope 131
11   Lightning Strikes 149
12   The Fury of the Storm 165
13   The Final Dispossession 179

Part Four: Reconnecting **199**
14   Rediscovering America 201
15   Putting an End to Hostility .215
16   Keeping Covenant 233
17   Replanting the Seed 247

America especially will forever be indebted to him (William Penn). If there is anything permanently abiding in America's history, it is the respect for human dignity and human rights. That tradition may lose its force and currency or be sacrificed on the altar of security, but the memory of it must surely endure. The Holy Experiment of Pennsylvania was the first notable modern application of that ageless search for human freedom within the bounds of a benevolent governmental discipline. The experiment was the product of a great mind whose radiant energy, in a fog-bound transitional age, revealed basic principles by which western civilization, America particularly, could find its way to freedom. Jefferson may have been the perfect product of that evolution, but Penn was its herald angel.

Tolles, Frederick B., Alderfer, E. Gordon, *The Witness of William Penn,* (The Macmillan Company, New York, 1957), pg. x

FOREWORD

I like Darrell Fields, had the Lord begin to sneak up on me where His heart for America was concerned. While growing up I was never very interested in history, including America's, and would have been likely to fall asleep in any Civics or Government class. Talk about boring! But God began His stalking of my heart and now I hardly recognize myself. I love history!

With me, it started as a simple fascination concerning America's roots. Quotes from founding fathers began to captivate my thoughts, stories of God's sovereign intervention in our birthing and preservation began to intrigue my mind, and national holidays like Thanksgiving and Independence Day grew in their significance. A God-given, yet previously unseen, love for America was beginning to manifest. I believe it was there all along, but like the dormant fruit of an immature tree, could not yet be seen. Perhaps my development was similar to that of America's—seeds planted by the hand and heart of God were waiting for time to catch up with their destined purpose. Sooner or later time always reveals what is in the seed.

Darrell became captivated by the words of William Penn who asked that God make Pennsylvania the seed of a nation. No finer seed could have been found than that planted by Penn, who was a covenant keeping lover of God and his fellow humans. A man of integrity and humility, his desire was to always "do the thing that is truly wise and just." These seeds are in the soil of America, and though hidden by much sin, selfish ambition and pride, time will reveal that the seed planted by William Penn and other godly individuals, still lives. Through repentance and turning we can see the power of the seed perform again.

That is why I believe so much in this book, *The Seed of a Nation*. As few have, Darrell tapped into a precious vein of revelation, a vein that touches more than a nerve; it touches a heart—God's heart. He looked past the hull, inside the seed and saw that God's plan was for America to become more than a place of abundant provision and a launching pad for freedom and democracy. It was to become a representation of the heart and character of God to all nations of the earth. Hidden in the seed he saw God's heart for all peoples, not just the European settlers. The "melting pot" really was there in the seed.

But just as with our great icon of freedom, the Liberty Bell, this melting pot has been cracked. Our sins against God and one another have been grievous. So Darrell teaches us how to grieve over our sins against Native Americans, just as Penn would have, and also over the many other injustices we Americans have perpetrated against each other.

Thankfully, however, he does more than grieve. Sorrow is a necessary part of the repentance process but Darrell also has great revelation concerning God's redeeming heart. Therefore, he leaves us with a hope that the fruit of the seed, though damaged, yet lives.

You will be fascinated, intrigued, enlightened and deeply moved as you read this journey – America's journey. And who knows, like Darrell and me, God might just sneak up on you and awaken something that will allow you to dream His dream with Him. If so, you'll agree with us: the seed is still alive, and its fruit can be good again.

Dutch Sheets

INTRODUCTION

During the 9/11 Commission Hearings, former National Security Advisor, Condoleezza Rice, was challenged about the viability of freedom in Iraq. As an African American she reminded the Commission that the founding fathers "hadn't thought of her" in light of our nation's long struggle for freedom. But William Penn had—a century before our founding fathers wrote the Constitution of the United States. So brilliant was Penn's contribution to America's liberties that Thomas Jefferson named him, "the greatest lawgiver the world has produced."[1] And he was, not only because Penn's Charter of Privileges provided the framework for the United States' government, but also because of the underlying potential freedom it provided *all* people.

Yet I knew none of this when my family and I moved to Pennsylvania in January of 1995. Claiming only a casual interest in American history, I was thrilled to know that I was standing where much of our nation's history began. As novel as that was, however, all I knew was that I was excited and ready to begin a new chapter in my life.

During that first summer we traveled down to Virginia Beach to visit some good friends of ours who had moved to the East Coast from Hawaii only a couple years before we did. I returned home from our trip alone, leaving my wife, Lorrie, and our three children for a brief vacation. On the six-hour drive home I had an unusual experience.

While driving on the beltway around Washington, D.C., my thoughts unexpectedly returned to my first visit to the state capitol building in Harrisburg, Pennsylvania. I remembered reading a quote there by William Penn that hadn't left much of an impression, then, but was now strangely affecting me with an overwhelming sadness. I wasn't quite sure what was happening as I suddenly was filled with a deep-seated anguish that rose to the surface in waves of brokenness. I began wiping away the many tears, now streaming down my face. It was all I could do to keep my eyes focused on the road before me. I somehow sensed that a divine purpose regarding our nation had been tragically lost. For many miles this brokenness consumed me as I cried out to God for our nation and whatever part Pennsylvania had played.

No sooner had I arrived home that I excitedly called Lorrie and said, *"You won't believe what just happened to me."* I thought if I dialogued with her about the experience it might help trigger some answers, or at least help me make better sense of it. It seemed odd to have been touched so deeply without any foreknowledge of what might have caused this pain. Unable to produce any results, we finally said goodbye. Filled with a desire to know more, I was determined to solve the mystery. It reminded me of the scene from the movie, *Field of Dreams*, where, in the middle of his Iowa corn field, Ray Kinsella, hears a mysterious voice say, "If you build it, he will come." As confused as Ray was, at least he was given a few signs. For me, however, there was no voice, no vision and, thankgoodness, no ghost. Yet, like Ray, I had, without a doubt, an encounter that profoundly and substantially provoked me for reasons that were eluding me.

I tried to go to bed that night but had become so disturbed that I couldn't sleep. And the more I reflected the more burdened I became. Was William Penn the connection to the experience I had gone through? If so, why was I being drawn to a man I knew absolutely nothing about? I paced the floor all night until the morning sun compelled me to visit the state capitol in Harrisburg once again. As I entered the building and stepped into the rotunda I couldn't help but agree with President "Teddy" Roosevelt when he said at its 1906 dedication, "This is the handsomest State Capitol I have ever seen ... and I don't believe there is a finer on earth." It was also magnificent to me, quite possibly the most beautiful building I had ever seen. The architect, Joseph Huston, accomplished his goal when he designed it to be a "Palace of Art." I then looked up and there before me, twice encircling the arch of the rotunda's ceiling, was the mosaic of Penn's words. However, with all the angles in the ceiling, it was difficult to read in its entirety. I asked the woman at the information desk if she had the quote on any literature, she was happy to comply. It read:

There may be room there for such a
Holy Experiment.
For the nations want a precedent
And my God will
Make it the Seed of a Nation.
That an example may be set up to the Nations.
That we may do the thing
That is truly wise and just."

As I stood there and read them, a new sensitivity swept over me, connecting me with my highway experience and filling me with even more questions. What was the legacy following this powerful statement? Were they just a memoriam to honor a great man? What was the Holy Experiment? What was the seed? Did the nations really want a precedent? Do they still? I was trembling as the ache I had experienced the day before rushed over me again. I felt myself being drawn across the threshold into a historical discovery far greater than any romanticized glance into America's past I may have ever entertained. I couldn't refuse. I was awestruck. I didn't know what else to do so I walked across the rotunda, laid my hands on the wall, and prayed, *"Oh God, what are you saying? What are you doing?"*

That day changed the direction of my life as my attention was turned to Pennsylvania and its enduring contribution to this nation. I knew enough history to know that many of the events that formed our nation took place here in Pennsylvania. But I wondered how, and if these events had any connection to the passion I experienced.

Historically, Pennsylvania has been dramatically used, as a seed, in defining her as the "Birthplace of our Nation." Many documents and events that outlined what this country would become were birthed in Pennsylvania. On July 4, 1776, the *Declaration of Independence* was signed in Philadelphia. Four days later the Liberty Bell rang out, declaring our freedom. The inscription upon the surface of the bell is a passage from Leviticus 25:10, "Proclaim Liberty throughout all the land unto all the inhabitants thereof." In 1777-1778, Valley Forge became the turning point of the Revolutionary War. The drafting and signing of the *Constitution*, ratifying our first frame of government, happened here. The separation between the North and the South was decisively altered here at the Battle of Gettysburg in July 1863. President Abraham Lincoln brought closure to that terrible battle with his now esteemed speech, *The Gettysburg Address*.

Alone or summed together these events can only be factors as they are combined with the viable faith, humility and dedication of men and women who lived beyond them.

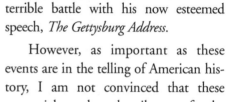

However, as important as these events are in the telling of American history, I am not convinced that these memorials are the only milestones for the freedom we proclaim. Alone or summed together these events can only be factors as they are combined with the viable faith, humility and dedication of men and women who lived beyond them.

Initially, as Lorrie and I began pouring over the available recorded history, the thoughts of writing a book had never entered my mind. It wasn't until others began suggesting the idea did we begin thinking of its possibility. So, as I began the process of putting my thoughts and facts down on paper, Lorrie began applying the connective tissue to it all, helping to flesh out the reality of this book. She added the "color" to my "play-by-play." It became remarkable how our combined effort, as husband and wife, began to flow throughout the pages of this writing. I couldn't have done it without her. Together, we were able to see more objectively why the message entrusted to this nation still speaks to us today and tells more about who we are than its obvious chronological evolution. We were convinced others would respond if the story could be told again in light of present day realities. People want answers and are more ready to consider that God may have something to say about world events. The debate over how God fits into our culture is portrayed almost daily in our secular media.

The validity of my interstate encounter with God became more real to me than ever. I saw that my heart had been broken because I believe God's heart is. I began to grasp the magnitude of our nation's history as it relates to people today. The painful implications have kept me on my knees.

History is not merely dated events from the past. For those who will hear, it speaks. Identifying with our history recounts our heritage, but more importantly it reveals hidden impulses lingering from our past that keep us from truly being free. Historically, we have followed in the footsteps of the decisions made by those who have gone before us. That's a fearful thing. Many of us continue uninformed, accepting the status quo, whether we like it or not, submitting to generational mind-sets that tell us, *"That's just the way it is."* Yet, over the last several years legitimate questions are being asked. *"How do we define America?" "What about her message of freedom being proclaimed around the world?" "How much authority do we have?"* If it weren't so serious, the mad race to redefine America would be comical. America doesn't need to be redefined as much as rediscovered. Rediscovering America means we must come to see her, all of her, for who she is and how she arrived. Winston Churchill, Great Britain's prime minister during the Second World War, had a firm understanding of this truth when he said,

Historically, we have followed in the footsteps of the decisions made by those who have gone before us. That's a fearful thing.

> The greatest advances in human civilization have come when we recovered what we had lost: when we learned the lessons of history. We cannot say 'the past is past' without surrendering the future. The farther backward you can look, the farther forward you can see.

It is not a mistake that America is in an exposed position before the entire world. Many are feeling the insecurity and are being tempted to despair. Less are able to shrug away their disappointment with cynicism and indifference. But what are we to do?

As Jesus' ministry attracted large crowds, He, at one point, challenged them to make a greater commitment. Many, if not all, turned and left. Turning to His disciples, Jesus asked, "You do not want to leave too, do you?" (John

6:67) Peter said what I believe needs to resonate in every American heart, "Lord, to whom shall we go?" (John 6:68)

Everyone is being asked this same question. Our commitment to "in God we trust" is being challenged; world events tell us so. But, like Peter, is there the same desperate cry and acknowledgement from us that there is no turning back and no other resource but God?

The Lord is raising up a people who will not turn back from the necessary greater commitment. This is an exciting time to live! I pray that those who take the time to read this book will allow it to create a compassion for people and a passion for the glory of God to be made known in this generation, in this land and for the sake of the whole world. Because of its governmental importance to the founding of our nation, I believe that hidden in the heart of Pennsylvania are keys needed to unlock this land and bring the precious seed Penn planted out of dormancy. Could it be that God could use us to bind the wounds of the precious people of this nation, participate in their healing and introduce them to the wonder of the free gift of God? What a privilege! It is also entirely possible that the message of freedom will be heard again around the world with new meaning. For our children's sake it is necessary that it be so.

So, with my heart and mind filled with more wonder and questions than could be answered by my limited knowledge, I began my discovery of the person of William Penn and his enduring contribution to this New World. This book chronicles many detailed events and written records of William Penn's life and heart, but *only* as they relate to the vital role he played in the first hundred years of America's history and government. It also accounts for the subsequent events after his death that forced into dormancy the seed he carried. These events shaped our nation long before the American Revolution and long before men like Washington, Jefferson and Franklin took their place in our minds as the founding fathers of freedom.

ENDNOTE

1. See Chapter Five, Endnote 10.

Part One

PROMISE

1

INTO THE LIGHT

*See to it that no one takes you captive through hollow and deceptive phi-
losophy, which depends on human tradition and the basic principles of this
world rather than on Christ.*

Colossians 2:8

The idea of freedom has never ceased to be vitally important to any age, in any culture. However, the inherent realities of freedom are forever dependent on its continuance and application. America prides herself in the promise of freedom. But there is a problem; our interpretations and prejudices can contrive a freedom that changes in definition from generation to generation (sometimes from circumstance to circumstance). As freedom changes by the perspectives in which it is viewed, some gain, and tragically, some lose.

The enormous task of making freedom available is God-sized. The historical evidence you are about to read makes the conclusion irrevocable: men alone cannot create or sustain it. The mystery, amazingly, is that God wants and waits to use people to introduce the kind of freedom that only He can offer. William Penn was one of those persons. Through divine guidance and his indomitable spirit Penn founded the colony of Pennsylvania on a grass roots government so powerful that it became the building blocks of a new nation. This story of his life and contributions are presented herein not as a biography to elevate Penn or Pennsylvania, but as historical proof that God limits Himself to people and is yearning for the continuation of "His"story to any who would ask in any place and any time.

Because of William Penn's precursory guidance in American liberties, it becomes imperative, if our judgments are to be accurate regarding our present culture, to look carefully into the world that produced such a man. What he meant by freedom and the Separation of Church and State may surprise you, and is addressed in later chapters. For now, I pray that as you peek into the seventeenth and eighteenth centuries, the spark that ignited Penn for his life purpose may help you—and all of us—sort through the realities of this new millennium and prepare us for what lies ahead.

The late Dr. George P. Donehoo, foremost authority on the history of Pennsylvania (former Secretary of the Pennsylvania Historical Commission, State Librarian) explains why grasping the historical context of William Penn's life and times is vital today when he said:

> In order to comprehend the character of William Penn, and to understand, with any degree of completeness the government which he founded, one should have a knowledge of the various elements which produced such a character, and of the conditions then existing, not only in England, but throughout the civilized world which made Penn's "Holy Experiment" a real experiment in government. The inherited traits, the environment, the training of any man has much to do with the part which he plays in the world. Every student of biography must take into consideration not only the character of the particular subject of his study, but also the causes which produced such a character, and the environment in which it was developed.[1]

FROM OUT OF DARKNESS

October 31, 1517, marked a significant date in world history as men and women were consequently brought nearer to God when Martin Luther nailed his *Ninety-Five Theses* on the door of Castle Church in Wittenberg, Germany, sounding the trumpet for the Reformation, bringing an end to the thousand-year reign of the Dark Ages. Simply put, the Light was being proclaimed as the Roman Catholic Church, Europe's central religious authority was being called to return to repentance not works and end its religious abuses upon the people.

As a result of Luther's actions the Reformation came in like a flood and created such a religious upheaval that the entire political system of Europe felt its torrent. As many powers struggled for a foothold, England's monarchy, ruled by King Henry VIII, England's king from 1509 to 1547, had become all the more determined to secure its position using fear and manipulation for control. Yet the transformation continued and there arose such groups as the Diggers, Levelers, Baptists, Seekers, Muggletonians, Fifth Monarchists and more creating the most powerful spiritual renewal since the birth of the Church after Christ's resurrection. Religious factions like the Puritans rose up from within the Church and called for reform of the monarchy and the Church.

Like a violent earthquake, the Reformation, and other events of the sixteenth and seventeenth century, shook all of Europe. Political upheaval and social unrest prevailed, devastating England with war, civil and foreign. The thinking of the Dark Ages was proving a contemptible foe against reform. Actions from both sides begged to forfeit the very freedom the Reformation was trying to bring. Tradition, as we shall see, tenaciously resisted change.

POWER STRUGGLE

Reform was in the air but so was the will of the king. And in 1534 decisions were made that set into motion a powerful chain of events—events so powerful that they would not only challenge the Reformation, but also forever challenge the way we look at Church and Government and their involvement, one with the other. King Henry VIII wanted a divorce from his first wife. When the Pope of the Roman Catholic Church refused to grant the king his divorce the King exerted power of his own and annulled the marriage himself. The Pope excommunicated King Henry from Rome. King Henry then broke off relations with Rome and quickly established an autocracy that consolidated the spiritual and political power of England. He then passed the *Act of Supremacy*. The *Act of Supremacy* established King Henry as the Supreme Governor of his new church, the Church of England. This political doctrine, which was soon to become known as *The Divine Right of Kings,* or the *Right to Rule,* held that

Kings and Queens were appointed by God, and therefore, not answerable to any man. Having a divine right gave the king certain privileges and governing the Church was one of them.

After King Henry's death England's political *Right to Rule* supremacy over her Church continued into the seventeenth century. Queen Elizabeth I ruled England from 1558 to 1603, and when she died she left no heir apparent to succeed her to the throne. King James VI of Scotland, a Stuart and distant relative to the queen was chosen, and in 1603 became King James I of England, thus uniting Scotland with England. King James had reigned as Scotland's king for thirty-six years and continued the rule upon England by *The Divine Right of Kings*.

King James also took on the role of Supreme Governor of the Church. Under King James' rule, England's religious and political structure became so closely woven together that the monarchy became intolerant of those who would not conform to the Church. Enemies of the Church became enemies of the State, and therefore, a threat to national security.

Many, including Parliament, were beginning to feel that too much power lay in the hands of the king. The Puritans wanted to see the Church purified from within (thus their name). King James was initially sympathetic towards them, for he too had been raised a Calvinist. He appeased their grumbling by authorizing the first printing of the English translation of the Bible in 1611. Many Puritans, however, fled to the New World to escape persecution, and founded the Massachusetts Colony of Plymouth in 1620.

King James died in 1625, and his second son, Charles, was made king over England. Ascending to the throne of his father, King Charles I also took upon himself *The Divine Right of Kings*. He too brought both Scotland and Ireland under English rule and pushed them both to conform to the Church of England. In 1642 rivalry between Parliament and the king's monarchy broke out in one of the greatest upheavals in British history. Led by Puritan General Oliver Cromwell, the Puritans, along with the Scots, sided with Parliament and revolted against the Irish-backed monarchy, thereby starting the English Civil War.

King Charles lost the war, was captured by the Puritans and beheaded in 1649. Cromwell rose to the throne, taking the title, Lord Protector of the Commonwealth. His rule, however, was short-lived; he died in 1658. Weary of Puritan restrictions, many were ready for a return to the monarchy. The year 1660 brought the dawn of the Restoration, bringing back to the throne of

England the Stuarts. King Charles II, a Stuart and son of the deceased, ascended to the throne of his father.

The Stuarts had come back into power during the emergence of the Age of Reason where secularism had penetrated its way into the religious mainstream. As early as 1648, schools of thought were asking questions like, "Who needs God? Does man need to answer to an invisible creator?" The Restoration subsequently became a free-spirited, pleasure loving time in which theatre, fanciful dress, music and dance, poetry and romance flourished. Some let their inhibitions go wild, giving rise to brawling and dueling, seduction and scandal, and the king was no exception.

In 1665 war broke out between England and the Dutch as the Bubonic Plague (the Black Death) besieged London. The plague claimed the lives of more than one hundred thousand within one year, taking as many as seven thousand lives a week. Corpse-haulers pushed open carts through the cobble stoned streets of London, crying, "Bring out your dead." Immediately following the plague, in September of 1666, four-fifths of London was destroyed as the "Great Fire" swept through the city. Many believed that God was punishing the city for its sins.

Within this chaotic environment William Penn was raised, the eldest of three children, born October 14, 1644 to the affluent Vice-Admiral, Sir William and Lady Margaret Penn.

THE CALL

Amid these turbulent times, at the age of twelve, profound disillusionment began to touch the young William. Probing for answers to great injustices he could not reconcile, he found a great storm in his own conscience beginning to unravel the English traditions to which he was being groomed. That would comprise a difficult plight for any pre-teen—on the one hand groomed to continue the values and traditions of a wealthy responsible heritage, and on the other impelled by his conscience to challenge and resist that very life he was to inherit. In the midst of this turbulence, God visited William in a dramatic way. Listen to Dr. Donehoo as he relates this revealing account of twelve-year-old William Penn while he was alone at school.

He was suddenly surprised with an inward comfort; and, as he thought, an external glory in the room, which gave rise to religious emotions, during which he had the strongest conviction of the being of God, and that the soul of man was capable of enjoying communication with Him. He believed also, that the seal of Divinity had been put upon him at this moment, or that he had been awakened or called upon to a holy life.[2]

Donehoo suggests it must have been the same sort of experience:

As in the case of the vision of the Apostle Paul, when on the way to Damascus, (because) no matter what it was or how it was brought about, it was something which changed and then moulded the boy's whole after life, as the vision did that of the Apostle. The difference in the two is that one came to a man of mature life and experience, and the other came to a boy without experience in life. The "vision" of the Apostle has changed the history of the world, and the more I (Donehoo) study the life and influence of William Penn the more I am inclined to believe that it also, in a different way, has changed the history of America, if not the civilized world.[3]

How unusual Penn was, in his day, to experience God so personally, acutely, at that tender age. For the remainder of his youth he pursued the God Who was much more manifest to him than the life of affluence and advantage he was inheriting.

THE TRADITIONS OF MEN

At age sixteen, in 1660, William Penn entered Christ Church College, Oxford. It was here that William first heard, and was stirred, by the preaching of the Quaker,[4] Thomas Loe, never realizing then how Loe would be used to speak into his life seven years later, finally and forever altering his destiny.

At Oxford young William learned of the Quaker's desire to have a refuge in the New World to escape persecution for not conforming to the State's prescribed form of worship.

By May of 1661, Parliament passed a total of four laws collectively known as the Clarendon Code, sharply restricting the free exercise of religion. The Corporation Act required all municipal officers to participate in the sacraments of the established Church. In May of 1662, Parliament also passed the Quaker Act, making it illegal for Quakers to gather in groups of more than five members under the pretense of worship. The second stage of the Clarendon Code declared the Act of Uniformity, which required all clergy to follow without variation the prescribed Prayer Book in the services they conducted.[5]

Penn...knew first hand that God personally interacts with men.

These rules, acts, laws and codes greatly impacted William Penn, who by his own irrefutable testimony knew first hand that God personally interacts with men. He was greatly disturbed. He wondered how any man could dictate or prescribe the way others could or couldn't worship God. Such control was a violation of his conscience. For Penn, the rhetorical question was, "Fear men or choose God?" Penn's actions to choose God became clear and unequivocal.

A FATHER'S DETERMINATION

After two years at Oxford, William Penn was expelled for being too religious and a non-conformist. This was a severe blow to the vanity of Penn's father, Sir William Penn, who was a highly favored knight of the king, served as the Admiral of Ireland, Governor of Kinsdale, commissioner in the British Navy, and held a seat in Parliament's House of Lords. He became indignant over his son's expulsion because he knew it was due, in short, for his consorting with Quakers, a common and vulgar class of people, as they were then regarded. This was not the true aristocrat his father was trying to produce and he could not tolerate this kind of behavior. William Penn's return home in 1662 was met with "whipping, beating, and turning out of doors," as Penn would later write.

In an effort to separate him from the influence of these religious fanatics, Sir William then sent his son on a two-year stay to Paris with a company of young noblemen from the best of society, and as much money as he could spend. Sir William thought he could liberate his son from his over-religious ways by "baptizing" him in the "ways of the world."

In August of 1664, Sir William brought Penn back from Paris to London, happy to see a change of attitude and appearance taking shape in his son. It appeared to Penn's father that the two years in Paris had distanced his son from the fascination of his earlier "religious" experiences and that he was finally succumbing to the established social order. From outward appearances, Paris had indeed made its mark on young Penn. It is written by Samuel Pepys (Peeps), a diarist who lived next door to the Penns, that William Penn portrayed, "A great deal if not too much of the vanity of the French garb, and affected manner of speech and gait."[6]

Listen to Penn defending himself years later, in a trial, regarding allegations of the same,

'I make this bold challenge to all men, women and children upon earth, justly to accuse me with ever having seen me drunk, heard me swear, utter a curse, or speak one obscene word…I speak this to God's glory, that has ever preserved me from the power of those pollutions, and that from a child begot an hatred in me towards them.'[7]

A FAITH THAT OVERCOMES

In February 1665, Admiral Penn enrolled his son at the London law college, Inns of Court, in its prestigious law school, Lincoln's Inn, to study law and rub shoulders with other sons of the rich and powerful. But William's time at Lincoln's Inn would be short-lived. In the spring of that same year, the school was closed due to the outbreak of the plague.

William Penn in Armor

Courtesy Pennsylvania Historical and Museum Commission

In the spring of 1666, Admiral Penn sent William to Ireland, first to Dublin, and then to Shanagarry Castle to manage the Penn estate. While in Dublin, William, now a trained and accomplished swordsman, voluntarily joined a military force that helped put down an insurrection that occurred among the English soldiers. With the taste of battle running in his veins, William Penn contemplated following his father's military footsteps and was eager to take command of the company at Kinsdale, Ireland. His father, however, feeling William was too young to move into such a position, denied his request. Moreover, Sir William was angered at his son's continued association with Quakers, even in Ireland. This decision caused the Admiral to play into the hands of eternal destiny for his son.

William Penn, now twenty-two, aware of the world's attempt to overtake his faith, learned that Thomas Loe was preaching in nearby Cork. He had to hear this man again. Attending the meeting, Penn heard a message that released the conviction he had held inside which harmoniously confirmed the vision he had received as a twelve-year-old boy.

The title of the text he heard from Loe that night was: "There is a faith that overcometh the world, and there is faith that is overcome by the world."

Loe's message that day was the final wedge that separated Penn from the temptations with which he had wrestled. Penn had been submitting himself to the expectations of the world around him in an effort to please his father, rather than to the convictions he knew to be true. Now, Loe's message would produce the Quakers' greatest convert and revolutionize Penn's entire life, causing him to adopt the Quaker way of life. William Penn had made up his mind; from this time on he would lay hold of the faith that overcomes the world.

In spite of Penn's many struggles and the rejection of his father, he remained strong. Ten years later, while visiting other Quakers in Holland and Germany, William Penn shared his testimony regarding these early struggles of his life and his desperate search for the truth.

'Of my persecution at Oxford...Of my being banished the college; the bitter usage I underwent when I returned to my father; whipping, beating, and turning out of doors in 1662. Of the Lord's dealings with me in France, and in the time of the great plague in London. In fine, the deep sense He gave me of the vanity of this world; of the irreligiousness of the religions of it: Then of my mournful and bitter cries to Him, that He would show me His own way of life and salvation, and my resolutions to follow Him, whatever reproaches or sufferings should attend me, and that with great reverence and brokenness of spirit. How after all this, the glory of the world overtook me, and I was even ready to give up myself unto it, feelings as yet no such thing as the primitive spirit and church on the earth: And being ready to faint concerning my hope of the restitution of all things.

It was at this time that the Lord visited me with a certain sound and testimony of His eternal word, through one of those the world calls Quakers, namely Thomas Loe.'[8]

A NEW FIRE

The Quakers believed,

> ...that the teachings of Christ were meant to be obeyed, not just discussed or agreed to in a passive manner. The Sermon on the Mount was not an ideal towards which a person might gaze, but an actuality to be achieved. Furthermore, Quakers were filled with the conviction that God still spoke to them and that they were to be constantly in communion with divine authority. These were people on fire with a divine spark.[9]

Freedom of religion, however, was nonexistent in seventeenth century England. The Church of England, ruled by the autocratic monarchy of King Charles II, considered the Quakers, Congregationalists, and others, a threat to the State. Worshipping outside the king's established order was a treasonous act. Penn and his newly adopted Friends, who could hear from God themselves, were considered dangerous. Imprisonment, banishment and sometimes death were the sentences for those who would not conform.

Parliament began tightening the noose. They passed the Conventicle Act, which prohibited any gathering for worship except under the auspices of the Church of England. Not far behind was the Five Mile Act, banning any nonconformist preacher from coming within five miles of any corporation or town. And when they did, a new oath of allegiance to the Crown and the Church of England was required.

Although Penn was well respected and admired among the civil leaders of his day, the monarchy remained unmoved. If it had not been for the reputation and prestige of Penn's father, the King's conciliation of Penn may have expired long before. Penn, however, had not involved himself with the Quakers to rebel against England. He believed and advocated that England's transformation was needed and a reasonable possibility.

Others of less advantage suffered far greater consequences than Penn for propagating the same kind of radical thinking. Penn learned very early in life that a new discourse suggesting change could bring persecution by those protecting the divine right of the monarchy.

How Penn responded to these opposing forces rigidly set the course for the rest of his life. And he knew that would happen. If he had held any doubts regarding his relationship to the truths he was experiencing, or his part in disclosing it to the world, he would have needed to distance himself from these "rebellious" Quakers. As in every "Red Sea" experience, there would be no turning back. Penn knew the authorities would not relent forever.

CHRONOLOGICAL TABLE

1517	October 31. Martin Luther posts his *Ninety-Five Theses* on the door of Castle Church at Wittenberg, starting the Reformation.
1509-1547	King Henry VIII rules England.
1534	King Henry VIII passes the *Act of Supremacy*, breaks from Rome, establishes the Church of England and elects himself as the Supreme Governor of the Church.
1558-1603	Queen Elizabeth I rules England.
1603-1714	Stuart dynasty rules England.
1603-1625	King James VI of Scotland becomes king of England under *The Divine Right of Kings*.
1611	King James I prints the first Authorized English translation of the Bible.
1620	Puritans found Plymouth Colony in Massachusetts.

1625	King Charles I ascends to the throne of England.
1642	English Civil War breaks out.
1644	October 14. William Penn is born in London.
1647	Quakers founded by George Fox.
1649	King Charles I is beheaded by the Puritans; Puritans take throne of England.
1658	Oliver Cromwell dies, ending the rule of the Puritans.
1660	(1) Restoration of the Stuarts (King Charles II) to the throne of England. (2) William Penn enters Christ Church College, Oxford. (3) Admiral William Penn knighted by King Charles II.
1661-1665	May. Parliament passes four laws collectively known as the *Clarendon Code*, restricting the free exercise of religion.
1662	(1) May. Parliament passes the *Quaker Act*, restricting Quakers to meet in worship in groups of no more than five members. (2) Sir William sends Penn to Paris.
1664	August. William Penn returns to London from Paris.
1665	(1) February. Sir William enrolls Penn at Lincoln's Inn. (2) Bubonic Plague hits London killing seventy-thousand within the year.

1666   (1) Sir William sends Penn to Ireland to manage his Shanagarry Castle estate.

(2) September. The Great Fire destroys four-fifths of London.

At twenty-two, William Penn becomes a Quaker.

ENDNOTES

1. Donehoo, Dr. George P., *Pennsylvania: A History*, five vols., (Lewis Historical Publishing Company, Inc., New York, Chicago, 1926), p. 136-139

2. *Ibid.* p. 143.

3. *Ibid.*

4. The Quakers, who called themselves the Children of the Light or Friends of the Truth, were founded by a young man by the name of George Fox in 1647. They were scornfully given the name Quakers because they "Trembled at the word of the Lord." Late in the eighteenth century they were called the Society of Friends, which name has remained to this day. The Quakers had come into existence after George Fox sought the Lord over a three-year period for the revealed will of God regarding his internal doubts and questions. In 1647, the answer suddenly came to him. "When all my hopes in them and in all men was gone, so that I had nothing outwardly to help me, nor could tell what to do, then, O then I heard a voice which said, 'There is one, even Christ Jesus, that can speak to thy condition.' And when I heard it, my heart did leap for joy." Bronner, Edwin B., *William Penn's "Holy Experiment," The Founding of Pennsylvania*, (Greenwood Press, Westport, Connecticut, 1978), p. 7.

5. Trussell, John B. B., *William Penn Architect of a Nation*, (Pennsylvania Historical And Museum Commission, Harrisburg, PA 1994), p. 8,9.

6. Donehoo, Dr. George P., *Pennsylvania: A History*, five vols., (Lewis Historical Publishing Company, Inc., New York, Chicago, 1926), p. 149.

7. *Ibid.*

8. *Ibid.*, p. 20-21.

9. Bronner, Edwin B., *William Penn's "Holy Experiment," The Founding of Pennsylvania*, (Greenwood Press, Westport, Connecticut, 1978), p. 7.

10. Trussell, John B. B., *William Penn Architect of a Nation*, (Pennsylvania Historical And Museum Commission, Harrisburg, PA 1994), p. 13.

2

THE ARCHITECT
OF FREEDOM

America did not come out of New England.

—President Woodrow Wilson

England's oppressive reign was quickly producing in William Penn a conviction regarding man's need and right to be free. He yearned for others to have access to the life-giving message of God's Word. Yet many were denied the opportunity by the political and religious climate. Convinced by his own transformation, Penn began traveling throughout England, Holland and Germany preaching the gospel, openly confessing Christ could be the shining light in the heart of every man who was willing to receive and obey His light.

However, Penn's conversion and public testimony put his life in jeopardy with the ruling majority. This type of free expression was forbidden in England, and her Church; both of which having sharply restricted the free exercise of religion, was not about to accept this new itinerant preacher. The Crown had already suffered incalculable damage when overthrown by the Puritans and was not about to make the same mistake twice. No more would

England risk the nation's security on religious zealots bent on bringing reform to the established order and were all the more guarded against them.

For Penn's new freedom to be real in a world dominated by fear and tradition meant an impending collision with the well-established strongholds of England's Church. Nevertheless, he had determined it was worth the risk, even if his father, the king and the king's Church were against him. To be found in Christ gave Penn a great boldness and personal freedom to pursue those convictions.

He said:

'The truest end of life is to know the life that never ends. He that makes this his care will find it his crown at last...

'He that lives to live ever, never fears dying...For though death be a dark passage, it leads to immortality, and that's recompense enough for suffering of it.

'For death is no more than a turning of us over from time to eternity...Death then being the way and condition of life, we cannot love to live, if we cannot bear to die.'[1]

The Quaker faith was evangelistic in nature. It hung on two scriptural realities: That Jesus was the light of the world come into the hearts of men—"The true light that gives light to every man was coming into the world." (John1:9), and that they were to be an expression of that light—"You are the light of the world." (Matthew 5:14)

Penn said:

'Religion is the fear of God, and its demonstration good works; and faith is the root of both: For without faith we cannot please God; nor can we fear what we do not believe...

'To be like Christ, then, is to be a Christian. And regeneration is the only way to the kingdom of God, which we pray for...'[2]

WILLIAM PENN, THE EVANGELIST

Thomas Loe continued to speak into William Penn's life, and in 1668, on his deathbed, parted with one last exhortation, which would later be the theme for one of Penn's most important written works:

'Bear thy cross, and stand faithful to God; then He will give thee an everlasting crown of glory, that shall not be taken from thee. There is no other way which shall prosper, than that which the holy men of old have walked in. God hath brought immortality to light, and life immortal is felt. Glory, Glory to Him! For He is worthy of it. His love overcomes my heart, nay, my cup runs over: glory be to His name forever.'[3]

William Penn held true to Loe's words and acted upon them. He couldn't keep silent. Penn reasoned that if *he* could receive divine revelation, others could receive as well. Penn wrestled with the prevailing deception that truth was limited to priests and theologians. *All* could receive, and so Penn began to preach that God's revelation was continuous and direct to the heart of *every* believer. His stand quickly gained him recognition as a spokesman and defender of the faith; but at the same time, it also brought him, and his hearers, severe persecution as their message collided with the established order. Penn remained undaunted and as a result became a prolific writer. He published a total of 157 written works in his lifetime— nearly four treatises a year from 1668 to 1712— approximately one and a half million written and printed words.[4] Many of his writings declared that people could hear from God for themselves.

No doubt there were some in high places of religious authority who felt threatened.

The monarchy, and its Church, opposed Penn repeatedly. No doubt there were some in high places of religious authority who felt threatened.[5] And though Penn never posed a threat to the Crown with rebellion, force or manipulation, his favored position with the King quickly expired. He became regarded as a rebel by his superiors and was arrested and thrown into prison on six different occasions for preaching the message of Christ from street corners. He had to be silenced.

A PRISONER FOR THE LORD

See, I have refined you, though not as silver; I have tested you in the furnace of affliction.

Isaiah 48:10

Penn could have been a seventeenth-century courtier. His education—tutors, Oxford, a stay at the French court, and a year of law at Lincoln's Inn—followed the proper course for the son of a rich admiral and knight. But Penn became a seventeenth-century man of religion. The world's debt to him is that he spent more time in jails than in courts, that he preached to the people instead of flattering princes, that he followed his conscience more than his ambition.[6]

On December 12, 1668, William Penn was imprisoned in the Tower of London where many good thinkers with noble intent spent their last days. Penn was confined to the Tower for publishing a book, *The Sandy Foundation Shaken,* challenging the established order and defending his right to freedom of conscience. The Bishop of London charged Penn with heresy and blasphemy against the Church of England and offered him an opportunity to recant, or face imprisonment for life, to which Penn replied, "My prison shall be my grave before I will budge a jot."[7] If preaching the gospel meant imprisonment, then so be it, he reasoned.

While in prison Penn became more determined than ever. He made good use of his captivity by putting his thoughts on paper, producing one of his greatest apostolic works, entitled, *No Cross, No Crown,*[8] which since then has become one of the standards of the Quaker faith. After seven and a half months, on July 28, 1669, he was released without recantation after pleading his own case.

NO CROSS, NO CROWN

'Christ's cross is Christ's way to Christ's crown.'[9]

Penn was very conscious of Divine guidance in his writing of *No Cross, No Crown.* Not only did he make the above powerful statement in the Preface but also continued to say,

'But thou wilt say, What is Christ and where is He to be found? And how received and applied in order to this mighty cure. I will tell thee then: First, He is the Great Spiritual light of the World, that enlightens everyone that come into the world; by which He manifests to them their deeds of darkness and wickedness, and reproves them for committing them. He is not far away from thee. Behold (says Christ himself) I stand at the door and knock; if any man hear my voice, and open the door, I will come in to him, and sup with him, and he with me.[10] What door can this be, but that of the heart of man.'[11]

'O, this shows to every experience, how hard it is to be a true disciple of Jesus. The way is narrow indeed, and the gate very straight, where not a word, no not a thought, must slip the watch, or escape judgement: Such circumspection, such caution, such patience, such constancy, such holy fear and trembling. This gives an easy interpretation to that hard saying, Flesh and blood cannot inherit the Kingdom of God[12]:

'...they that cannot endure the cross, must never have the crown. To reign, 'tis necessary to suffer.'

Those that are captivated with fleshly lusts and affections; for they cannot bear the cross; and they that cannot endure the cross, must never have the crown. To reign, 'tis necessary to suffer.'[13]

THE DEATH OF SIR WILLIAM

In the summer of 1670 Penn was again arrested for preaching in the streets of London after soldiers had seized, padlocked and placed under guard their newly built Quaker meetinghouse. He was again thrown into prison. When the case went to Court it became clear to Penn that he wasn't going to receive a fair trial. He appealed to the Court that the civil rights of all English citizens were protected by the fundamental laws of that age-old English charter, the Magna Carta. He argued that the Magna Carta had established a precedent for English Government which predated the English Church and guarded against their assault on the Liberty of Conscience. Therefore, the persecution the Crown was inflicting upon the Quakers, and others, was legally unfounded. After four days of deliberations his pleas continued to fall upon deaf ears and Penn was thrown back into prison.

Knowing his father would pursue his release, Penn wrote him refusing his assistance, telling him, "I entreat thee not to purchase my liberty." He would not ask for leniency. However, Penn's father, Sir William, was quickly failing in health and desired to see and receive the consolation of his son before his death. Penn's release was quickly secured. In spite of all their differences and opposing points of view, Sir William had come to admire the heroic and enduring spirit of his son and had become sympathetic with his ideals. Calling his son to his side, the father looked him steadfastly in the eyes, and said:

'First, let nothing in this world tempt you to wrong your conscience; so you will keep peace at home, which will be a feast for you in the day of trouble. Secondly, whatever you design to do, lay it justly and time it seasonably, for that gives security and despatch. Lastly, be not troubled at disappointments; for if they may be recovered, do it; if they cannot, trouble is vain; if you could not have helped it, be content; there is often peace and profit in submitting to providence, for afflictions make wise; if you could have helped it, let not trouble exceed your instruction for another time. These rules will carry you with firmness and comfort through this inconsistent world.'[14]

Having been reconciled to his son, the forty-nine year old admiral breathed his last on September 16, 1670. After his father's death, Penn was bequeathed the entire family fortune, which included estates both in Ireland and England.

In the same year of his father's death, at the age of twenty-eight, Penn found solace from his grief when he met and became acquainted with a beautiful, talented, sweet-tempered girl, Gulielma Maria Springett. Guli, as she was called, also a Quaker, was fully supportive to the calling on Penn's life. Penn's heart was captured. Their love for each other quickly grew and they were married in the spring of 1672. In the company of his beautiful new bride, William Penn found rest, peace and happiness.

LIBERTY OF CONSCIENCE

Penn was a true pioneer when it came to the principles of religious liberty. Penn reckoned on what Jesus said in John 8:36, "If the Son sets you free, you will be free indeed," and believed that God made this truth available to all men. Of the many tracts, pamphlets and letters he wrote, none was so highly regarded as *The Great Case of Liberty of Conscience*. In it Penn argued that true faith must be free, not forced, and certainly not controlled by the monarchy. He said,

'That man cannot be said to have any religion, that takes it by another man's choice, not his own.'[15]

Penn best defined Liberty of Conscience when in 1674, while serving one of his prison terms, he wrote a letter to some magistrates. In part, William Penn said:

'The nature of body and soul, earth and heaven, this world and that to come, differs. There can be no reason to persecute any man in this world about anything that belongs to the next. Who art thou (saith the Holy Scripture), that judgeth another man's servant? He must stand or fall to his master, the great God.[16] Let tares and wheat grow together till the great harvest.[17] To call for fire from heaven was no part of Christ's religion, though he reproved zeal of some of his disciples.[18] His sword is spiritual, like his kingdom. Be pleased to remember that faith is the gift of God; and what is not of faith, is sin.[19] We must either be hypocrites in doing what we believe in our consciences we ought not to do, or forbearing what we are fully persuaded we ought to do.

He dreamed of a government in which freedom of conscience was not only permitted but also substantive.

'Either give us better faith, or leave us with such as we have, for it seems unreasonable in you to disturb us for this that we have, and yet be unable to give us any other.'[20]

The monarchy continued to prevent any tangible opportunity for Penn's philosophy of religious and civil freedom from being realized. Penn reasoned that in order to enjoy Liberty of Conscience, which was to him the true basis for political liberty, people must be guaranteed these three essential rights: the right to life and property, the right to representative government, and the right to trial by jury. The idea that the people had rights, much less a voice, was forcing Penn into a battle with centuries of the State's heavy-handed religious legalisms and traditions. Faced with this ongoing persecution, Penn and the Quakers became seriously interested in establishing a colony of their own in the New World. Their first opportunity arose when they (with Penn acting as trustee) purchased a share in the charter for New Jersey[21] on March 18, 1674.

21

A SPIRITUAL FORCE

Penn wanted to see his dreams realized in a land where men and women could serve God freely without hindrance. He dreamed of a government in which freedom of conscience was not only permitted but also substantive. He knew that God concerns Himself in the affairs of men and that man's response to His voice brings the only true freedom. He believed that it was a possibility not because he wished it but because he experienced it, not only in his own life but also in the sum of ages past. Penn's English government was a product of countless generations of men ineffectively and brutally attempting to make life work outside of God.

The birthing of Pennsylvania would be unique among the other colonies established in the New World. From her founding she would prove to be more definitive of the nation as a whole than her own geographic, cultural and political boundaries. President Woodrow Wilson, our twenty-eighth President, said, in speaking of the phenomenon of Pennsylvania, "America did not come out of New England."[22]

Dr. Donehoo gives an awesome commentary to the elements that make up Pennsylvania when he says,

> Pennsylvania is more than a territory with certain boundaries; that it is more than a Commonwealth, with certain laws for its government, and that it was in every sense an 'Holy Experiment,' and that it is an epic, a spiritual thing and force which cannot be defined, and whose history, as such, can never be written by any mortal man with any degree of completeness.
>
> In the history of Pennsylvania is included not only the facts of its conception and development, but also the hopes and dreams of humanity from the time when fallen man started on his weary and blood-stained pathway from the Garden of Paradise. Pennsylvania is a result of all the struggles of humanity from the time when law first became a factor in the life of man.
>
> It takes almost unlimited ages of development in an environment in which mere brute strength is the only real law, to bring man to the place where he can even see such a vision of human government as that which the founder of Pennsylvania, not only saw, but realized. A

dominant force, such as that of Alexander, or Caesar, or Nero, or Napolean, or Pontiac, and hundreds of other leaders of men, is the result of merely physical and political evolution. But, the production of such a character and the evolution of such a force as that which lies back of William Penn and Pennsylvania, is brought about by nothing merely physical and political. In the individual character, and in the Commonwealth produced by it, it is a spiritual force.[23]

CHRONOLOGICAL TABLE

1668	(1) Quaker Thomas Loe passes away.
	(2) William Penn imprisoned for eight months in the Tower of London and writes *No Cross, No Crown*.
1670	September 16. William Penn's father, Sir William Penn, Admiral in the English Navy, passes away.
1672	April 4. William Penn marries the "love of his youth," Gulielma Maria Springett.
1674	March 18. The Quakers, with Penn acting as trustee, purchase the charter for West New Jersey.

ENDNOTES

1. William Penn Tercentenary Committee, The, *Remember William Penn 1644-1944*, (Harrisburg, PA, 1944), p. 29.

2. *Ibid.* p. 28.

3. *Ibid.* p. 24.

4. Hull, William I., *William Penn, A Topical Biography*, (Oxford Universtiy Press, London, New York, Toronto, 1937), p. 155.

5. People who are fearful of losing their place or position are capable of many atrocities as we see by the Pharisees's plot to kill Jesus. "If we let him go on like this, everyone will believe in him, and then the Romans will come and take away both our place and our nation." (John 11:48)

6. William Penn Tercentenary Committee, The, *Remember William Penn 1644-1944*, (Harrisburg, PA, 1944), p. xv.

7. Wallace, Paul A. W., *Pennsylvania, Seed of a Nation*, (Harper & Row Publishers, New York and Evanston, 1962), p. 37.

8. Penn, William, *No Cross, No Crown*, (Friends United Press, Richmond, Indiana, 1981).

9. William Penn Tercentenary Committee, The, *Remember William Penn* 1644-1944, (Harrisburg, PA, 1944), p. 155.

10. Rev. 3:20

11. William Penn Tercentenary Committee, The, *Remember William Penn 1644-1944*, (Harrisburg, PA, 1944), p. 156.

12. 1 Corinthians 15:50

13. William Penn Tercentenary Committee, The, *Remember William Penn 1644-1944*, (Harrisburg, PA, 1944), p. 156.

14. Donehoo, Dr. George P., *Pennsylvania: A History, Five Vols.*, (Lewis Historical Publishing Company, Inc., New York, Chicago, 1926), p. 155.

15. William Penn Tercentenary Committee, The, *Remember William Penn 1644-1944*, (Harrisburg, PA, 1944), p. 53.

16. Romans 14:4

17. Matthew 13:24-30

18. Luke 9:51-56

19. Romans 14:23

20. William Penn Tercentenary Committee, The, *Remember William Penn 1644-1944*, (Harrisburg, PA, 1944), pp. 53-54.

21. When the Quakers purchased a share in New Jersey it became divided and governed as two distinct provinces, with the Quakers owning West New Jersey. The whole of the province came under Quaker control when they purchased East New Jersey in 1682. In 1702, the two provinces were united under a royal, rather than a proprietary, governor.

22. Sipe, C. Hale, *The Indian Wars of Pennsylvania*, (originally published, Harrisburg, PA, 1931., reprinted, Gateway Press, Baltimore, MD, for Wennawoods Publishing, Lewisburg, PA, 1995), p. 67.

23. Donehoo, Dr. George P., *Pennsylvania: A History, Five Vols.*, (Lewis Historical Publishing Company, Inc., New York, Chicago, 1926), p. 138.

3

THE SEED OF A NATION

...my God that has given it me through many difficulties, will, I believe bless and make it the seed of a nation.

—William Penn

P enn formally petitioned King Charles II for a grant of land in the New World on June 1, 1680. William Penn's father owned large estates in England and Ireland and had lent the Crown substantial amounts of money in England's war with the Dutch. And yet, in spite of the admiral's financial support, the price of war had taken an exhaustive toll upon England's treasury. By granting Penn's request, the King saw how he could not only be released of the 16,000 pound debt he owed the Penns but how he could also rid himself of the Quakers.

The King granted Penn's request and insisted that the province be named Pennsylvania[1] in honor of William Penn's father. However, Penn thought the name Pennsylvania would appear as an attempt at his own self-glorification. He offered to have the name changed to Sylvania or New Wales, but the King's instructions stood.

The King affixed his signature and seal on the document on March 4, 1681. Known since as *The Charter*, this document gave Penn full governmental authority in Pennsylvania. William Penn, at the age of thirty-six, became the sole proprietor of more than 28,000,000 acres. This was the largest territory owned entirely by any single British citizen in history, second only in size to England itself. Eleven of America's original Thirteen Colonies had already been settled leaving only Georgia as the remaining colony to be founded.

King Charles II
Courtesy National Portrait Gallery, London

The next day, on March 5, Penn closed a letter to his friend, Robert Turner,[2] with these words.

'...**My God** that has given it (Pennsylvania) me through many difficulties, **will**, I believe bless and **make it the seed of a nation**. I shall have a tender care to the government, that it be well laid at first. No more now, but dear love in the truth.*

Thy true friend, Wm. Penn'[3] (emphasis mine)

"NATIONS WANT A PRECEDENT"

Pennsylvania was more than just another colony offering asylum for the religiously persecuted. Unlike England, whose government trumped individual freedom with its perverted mixture of Church and State, "the seed of a nation," that Penn spoke of, was a revelation about government so enormous that he intuitively knew it would be nation forming. Penn's government framed an environment that honored God and used its powers to protect individual freedom, generously weighing its inhabitants with individual choice as well as contribution. It would set a precedent for the rest of the world.

---

* The bold text in the above quote and the two quotes on pages 27 and 28 are the words that were combined and used to grace the rotunda's ceiling in the state capitol building in Harrisburg, Pennsylvania.

Who could have comprehended the disillusionment Penn suffered at the hands of English tradition? It would dawn a new era and the "Holy Experiment," as Penn would call it, was the answer to the questions that drove him to intercession and divine wisdom. The seed of a new nation was about to be born on the principles of liberty of conscience, whose broad scope far exceeded that of the Quakers and the confines of Pennsylvania's borders. Pennsylvania's government became a keystone that would hold together America's fledgling colonies and eventually change the way the world thinks leading men and women to sacrifice their lives in the American Revolution.

> *The elements for the experiment were the God who never changes and human beings plagued with variables.*

These facts are evidenced in 1681 when Penn wrote a letter in this regard. He said:

> 'And because I have been somewhat exercised at times about the nature and end of government among men, it is reasonable to expect that I should endeavor to establish a just and righteous one in this province, that others may take example by it—truly this my heart desires. **For nations want a precedent**, and till vice and corrupt manners be impartially rebuked and punished, and till virtue and sobriety be cherished, the wrath of God will hang over nations. I do, therefore, desire the Lord's wisdom to guide me, and those that may be concerned with me, **that we may do the thing that is truly wise and just**'[4] (emphasis mine).*

THE HOLY EXPERIMENT

On August 25, 1681, William Penn wrote these words to a Quaker friend, James Harrison,[5] regarding Pennsylvania:

> 'For my country, I eyed the Lord, in obtaining it; and more was I drawn inward to look to him, and owe it to his hand and power, than to any other way; I have so obtained it and desire to keep it; that I may not be unworthy of his love; but do that, which may answer his kind

Providence, and serve his truth and people: **that an example may be set up to the nations: there may be room there**, though not here, **for such an holy experiment**[6] (emphasis mine).*

In this letter we find Penn's first mention of a Holy Experiment. The elements for Pennsylvania's experiment were the God who never changes and human beings plagued with variables. The experiment was, therefore, dependent on men putting their trust in a holy God.

William Penn stated in simple fashion his deepest feelings in regard to Pennsylvania. First, he believed that God had been instrumental in granting him the magnificent province in the New World. Secondly, and growing naturally out of his gratitude, he desired to use the gift from above to the glory of God. Finally, he hoped that the operation of his colony in accordance with the highest Christian ethic might serve as a model for mankind, to indicate by example what men may achieve on earth if they would but put themselves into the hands of God.

Thus to William Penn, the word "holy" was the more important word of the two. He expected the "experiment" to be permeated with the Spirit of God. He was certain that if the province were filled with virtuous persons, who not only knew God's will, but who lived according to His Light, his "holy experiment" could not fail.[7]

Gaining Pennsylvania was Penn's crowning achievement for the cross he had borne and the choices he had made up to this time in his life. Donehoo gave further thought and insight to the founding of Pennsylvania when he correlated the lives of William Penn and Moses.

The author (Donehoo) has often thought of the resemblance between the experiences and training of the great Lawgiver and Founder of the Israelites, as a Nation, and that of the first real Lawgiver and Founder of Pennsylvania. Moses was brought up as an Aristocrat at the court of the Ruler of Egypt. His whole early life was spent in touch with the luxury and the honors which belonged to the court of a Pharaoh. And yet, because of the vision at the Burning Bush, he threw himself with the suffering and afflicted, and 'refused to be called the son of Pharoah's daughter; choosing rather to share ill treatment with the people of God, than to enjoy the pleasure of sin for a season; accounting the reproach of Christ greater riches than the treasures of Egypt.'⁸ He turned his back upon all of the opportunities, which Egypt had to offer, and started out on his mission to lead the oppressed bondservants to a Land of Promise. So, William Penn turned away from all of the honors which were directly in his pathway, to take up the cause of the persecuted and ill treated, to be persecuted and ill treated with them, because he was not disobedient to the vision which came to him as a boy, and which was deepened in the visions which Thomas Loe gave to him at Oxford and at Cork. And, like the great Founder of the Commonwealth of Israel, he sought to lead the afflicted and persecuted, not only out of England, but of the whole World into a land of Promise, in which he could lay the foundations of a commonwealth, which would grant to men and women a real liberty of soul to worship God, without let or hindrance.⁹

GOD, GOVERNMENT AND THE PEOPLE

It is impossible to write about Penn and the government he established without acknowledging the sovereign grace that enabled him. Penn believed and was careful to observe Proverbs 14:34— "Righteousness exalts a nation." Upon gaining Pennsylvania, his first order of business was to give God precedence in the establishing of a suitable government for his new colony. And he did just that. For more than a year after receiving his charter, Penn spent his time writing and drafting a constitution for Pennsylvania, entitled, *The First Frame of Government.*

Penn knew that men were created to be free. In an unprecedented move, in a world where political democracy was an unknown factor, he framed the *Preface* of his constitution to say, "Government is free to the people under it, whatever be the frame, where the laws rule and the people are a party to those laws." But for Penn democracy alone did not offer true freedom. It was more than just creating a government of the people, though, that in itself was a distinct accomplishment. It was about a government that would allow God to intervene in the affairs of men. This was Penn's basic tenet on the Liberty of Conscience. Only God could set the conscience free and, thus, govern the hearts of men. Without the Spirit of God permeating their hearts Penn knew, by virtue of the persecution he suffered under English rule, the awful advantages governmental powers had when left in the hands of ambitious and self-serving men. But this is not to be mistaken for Penn's thoughts about the separation of Church and State: that is, the governing control of the Church, not the removal of God from the government. In other words, the separation should be jurisdictional not relational. He was convinced for any system of government to work it would have to be God-centered, but that could only happen if men were centered *in* God. For in the continued writing of the *Preface*, Penn declared, "Government seems to me to be a part of religion itself, a thing sacred in its institutions and end."[10] Without this vital and key ingredient he knew his best ideas about government could only replace the tyranny of England with the tyranny of fallen humanity, subject not to one king but the fleshly impulses of many men.

He was convinced for any system of government to work it would have to be God-centered, but that could only happen if men were centered in God.

Penn realized that he could not legislate a hunger for God nor could he ever manipulate the people of his province to obey his laws. The big question then was, *"Could a government run by men be established on the principles laid in scriptures?"* Penn sadly knew the liberties that would be taken by those who would abuse the religious freedoms written into his constitution. But what other system could he trust? He knew it must be tried. His final and most logical conclusion, then, was to put his trust in the sovereignty of God's grace and the people's desire to choose Him. Thomas Jefferson would later say that Penn was, "the first, either in ancient or modem times, who has laid the foundation of government in the pure and unadulterated principles of peace, of reason and right."[11]

Since the light of God shone spontaneously or not at all, it followed that liberty of conscience must be a first consideration in any well-ordered state. On that principle William Penn founded democracy in Pennsylvania.[12]

…Penn and the Quakers asked for themselves only what they were prepared to give to all men. Penn put this philosophy into memorable words: 'We must give the liberties we ask."[13]

The *Preface* expressed Penn's strong conviction for the effectual operation of any government. Within the *Preface* Penn quoted the Apostle Paul from Romans 13:1-2.

> Everyone must submit himself to the governing authorities, for there is no authority except that which God has established. The authorities that exist have been established by God. Consequently, he who rebels against the authority is rebelling against what God has instituted, and those who do so will bring judgment on themselves.

Not only was submission to the authority that God established a priority, but Penn reasoned that there should be no separation between God and government. Unless tempered by the Lord, Penn knew that every man's tendency is to become a conscience, even a law, to himself. Penn's life demonstrated that if one trusted God, then good government increased naturally out of that trust.

THE BUILDER OF THE HOUSE

Unless the Lord builds the house, its builders labor in vain.

Psalm 127:1

Penn wanted to give the people of his province the ability to be ruled by laws of their own making but knew, all too well, the limits men have in governing themselves without the sublime intervention of God. Understanding that good government was limited in itself to those men who ran that government, he continued to lay a strong foundation within the writing of the *Preface*. Penn said,

> 'Governments, like clocks, go from the motion men give them, and as governments are made and moved by men, so by them they are mined too. Wherefore governments rather depend upon men, than men upon governments. Let men be good, and the government cannot be bad; if it be ill, they will cure it. But if men be bad, let the government be never so good, they will endeavor to warp and spoil it to their turn.'[14]

31

Penn was not saying that "good men" could not make wrong choices or misuse their authority. What he was saying is that "good men" or godly men who walk in humility would have the courage to face the error of those choices, for the common good. He proposed that "bad" men, with self-serving interests, would "spoil" and "warp" the government, again, reiterating that "the shining light of God's truth" would spontaneously give understanding and wisdom to those who would make it their habit to listen to God's voice. Otherwise God's truth would not shine at all, making men mere subjects in the shadows of their own uninspired laws. In the closing paragraph of the *Preface* Penn states, "Liberty without obedience is confusion, and obedience without liberty is slavery."[15] In this statement alone Penn clearly illustrated the delicate balance he knew was necessary to maintain the Holy Experiment. The people of his province would always enjoy their liberties so long as they did not abuse the powers from above that established these liberties. Penn's government was modeled after the first demonstration of government founded through Christ at the advent of His birth.

> *For to us a child is born, to us a son is given, and the government will be on his shoulders... Of the increase of his government and peace there will be no end.*
>
> Isaiah 9:6-7

Penn believed that God established government to rest on His (God's) shoulders, and if His government were allowed to continue, then of His peace there would be no end, *or no end to its increase.* It was Penn's desire to see the glory of God revealed throughout the earth through a people who actually and literally knew this peace.

After the *Frame* was completed and adopted in England on April 25, 1682, Penn drafted an additional set of forty *Laws* as part of the constitution. These were adopted on May 5, 1682. Two of these Laws upheld his ideals of the "Holy" Experiment. In them Penn ruled that all those who held public office had to declare an honest faith in Jesus Christ, and he further ruled that the freedom of religion would be mandatory. The two *Laws* were written as follows:

XXXIV. All Treasurers, however, Judges, Sheriffs, Justices of the Peace, and all whatsoever in the service of the government, and all members elected to serve in provincial council and general assembly, and all electors, were to be such as professed faith in Jesus Christ...

XXXV. All persons who confessed the one almighty and eternal God to be the Creator, Upholder, and Ruler of the world, and who held themselves obliged in conscience to live peaceably and justly in society, were in no ways to be molested for their religious persuasion and practice, nor to be compelled at any time to frequent any religious place or ministry whatever.[16]

On December 7, 1682, Penn wrote a provision within the *Frame*, what he called the *Great Law*. In its opening sentence Penn said, "Whereas, the glory of Almighty God and the good of Mankind, is the reason & end of government, and therefore, government in itself is a venerable ordinance of God."[17]

"COME, LET US FOLLOW HIM"

In his book, *No Cross, No Crown*, William Penn compared the exploits of other great leaders and the establishing of their kingdoms to that of the Kingdom established by Christ.

'Come, let us follow Him, the most unwearied, the most victorious captain of our salvation. Compare Him to the great Alexanders and mighty Caesars of the world. They were great princes of their kind and conquerors too but on very different principles. For Christ made himself of no reputation to save mankind. But these worldly conquerors plentifully ruined people to augment their kingdoms. They vanquished others, not themselves. Christ conquered self, that ever vanquished them. They advanced their empires by plunder and blood, but he by suffering and persuasion. He never by compulsion, they always by force prevailed. Misery and slavery followed all their victories. Christ's victory brought greater freedom and felicity to those he overcame. In all they did, they sought to please themselves. In all he did he aimed to please the Father.'[18]

It is very difficult for us to realize in these days and in this country, where the principles which are laid down by William Penn in his Frame of Government and Laws have been in force for more than two centuries, what a drastic change these made from the conditions which then existed in England and in every other government of the world. Democratic government and religious liberty are now established facts. When William Penn wrote these immortal documents, from which many of the principles in the Constitution of the United States have been taken, both democracy and religious liberty were unknown factors in human government. Penn knew by sad experience how little of religious liberty there was in England. He was living in a period of persecution, when men were not allowed to make the laws for their own government, nor to decide for themselves anything regarding their religious beliefs or methods of worship. One has but to read the history of England during the reigns of Charles I, Cromwell, Charles II, James, and William and Mary to realize how little there was of either democratic government or religious liberty during this period in which William Penn was planning and then making his Holy Experiment in human government. William Penn had supreme faith, not only in God, but also in man, and both of these are essential for the building of a government such as that which he planned to erect on the shores of the Delaware. A man who has faith in God and no faith in man may build a nation, but it takes a man who has faith in both God and man to build a Commonwealth such as Penn wished to build.[19]

William Penn speaks to the condition of our times.

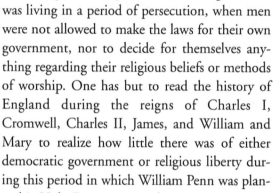

In all of his work, as in the case of Pennsylvania, he was putting into practice his basic faith in God and man. In his conception Pennsylvania was not founded as a possible success or failure—for he was depending upon the leading of God's Spirit and man's response to it, to make it a success.[20]

If he had done nothing else, William Penn would be remembered today as one of the great architects of freedom. But that was, of course, only the beginning. He advanced from the mere redressing of individual grievances to the creation of a whole society in which freedom should be mandatory.[21]

A fitting epitaph for the founder has been written by Catherine Owens Peare in *William Penn: A Biography*:

'He is eternally our contemporary, holding before us the finest traditions of Anglo-Saxon law, showing us the fruits of liberty of conscience, pointing the way to lasting freedom through individual dignity and endowing us with the example of a workable peace among men. William Penn speaks to the condition of our times.'[22]

CHRONOLOGICAL TABLE

1680	June 1. William Penn formally petitions the Crown for a grant of land in the New World.
1681	(1) March 4. King Charles II grants William Penn, age thirty-six, the *Charter* for Pennsylvania. (2) March 5. William Penn, in a letter to Robert Turner, believes that Pennsylvania will be the "seed of a nation." (3) August 25. William Penn, in a letter to James Harrison, calls Pennsylvania a "Holy Experiment."
1682	(1) April 25. *The First Frame of Government* for Pennsylvania is adopted in England. (2) May 5. Penn writes an additional forty laws for his constitution and are adopted on this date. (3) December 7. The *Great Law* enacted.

ENDNOTES

1. *Pennsylvania* in Welsh meant "Head Woodlands."

2. "Robert Turner (1635-1700) was a Quaker cloth merchant in Dublin who bought land in both New Jersey and Pennsylvania and recruited Irish purchasers of Pennsylvania land for WP." Soderlund, Jean R., *William Penn and the founding of Pennsylvania*, (University of Pennsylvania Press, Philadelphia, PA, 1983), p. 55.

3. *Ibid.*, pp. 54-55.

4. Cope, Thomas P., *Passages from the Life & Writings of William Penn*, (Friends' Book-Store, Philadelphia, PA, 1882), p. 237.

5. James Harrison, a Quaker minister in Bolton, Lancashire, in northern England, helped William Penn promote the sale of lands in Pennsylvania and later became the steward of William Penn's home, Pennsbury Manor.

6. Bronner, Edwin B., *William Penn's "Holy Experiment," The Founding of Pennsylvania*, (Greenwood Press, Westport, Connecticut, 1978), p. 6.

7. *Ibid.*

8. Hebrews 11:24-26

9. Donehoo, Dr. George P., *Pennsylvania: A History, Five Vols.*, (Lewis Historical Publishing Company, Inc., New York, Chicago, 1926), pp. 151-152.

10. Dunn, Richard S., & Dunn, Mary Maples, *The Papers of William Penn*, (University of Pennsylvania Press, 1982), p. 212.

11. Comfort, William Wistar, *William Penn And Our Liberties*, (The Penn Mutual Life Insurance Company, Philadelphia, Pennsylvania, 1947), p. 131.

12. Wallace, Paul A. W., *Pennsylvania, Seed of a Nation*, (Harper & Row Publishers, New York and Evanston, 1962), p. 36.

13. *Ibid.*, p. 38.

14. William Penn Tercentenary Committee, The, *Remember William Penn 1644-1944*, (Harrisburg, PA, 1944), p. 81.

15. Dunn, Richard S., & Dunn, Mary Maples, *The Papers of William Penn*, (University of Pennsylvania Press, 1982), p. 214.

16. Cornell, William Mason, D. D., LL. D., *The History of Pennsylvania*, (Quaker City Publishing House, Philadelphia, 1876), p. 96

17. William Penn Tercentenary Committee, The, *Remember William Penn 1644-1944*, (Harrisburg, PA, 1944), p. 85.

18. Penn, William, *No Cross, No Crown*, (Friends United Press, Richmond, Indiana, 1981), p. 23.

19. Donehoo, Dr. George P., *Pennsylvania: A History, Five Vols.*, (Lewis Historical Publishing Company, Inc., New York, Chicago, 1926), pp. 164-165.

20. William Penn Tercentenary Committee, The, *Remember William Penn 1644-1944*, (Harrisburg, PA, 1944), p. 144.

21. Wallace, Paul A. W., *Pennsylvania, Seed of a Nation*, (Harper & Row Publishers, New York and Evanston, 1962), p. 38.

22. *Ibid.*, p. 55.

4

BORN OF COVENANT

I will consider you as the same flesh and blood with the Christians, and the same as if one man's body were to be divided into two parts.

—William Penn

For the better part of the seventeenth century Europeans had been arriving and settling America's shores. By the time William Penn received his colony the two colonies of Jamestown, Virginia, settled by English Cavaliers in 1607, and Plymouth, Massachusetts, settled by the Pilgrims in 1620, were well underway. Close on their heels were the Dutch, who, in 1624, settled the island of Manhattan,[1] naming it New Amsterdam.

However, long before Europe had considered settling the New World, America's indigenous population, the American Indian, had already made it their home. And, as the arrival of more and more Europeans continued, the Powhatan[2] tribes of Virginia, and the Pequot,[3] Wampanoag,[4] and Narragansett[5] tribes of New England challenged the expansionist activities of their new European neighbors. The colonists were unyielding. And while many Europeans claimed their colonies in the name of "religious freedom," many also showed primitive levels of faith. Religious freedom was in the early stages of its development and many were still infected with *Right to Rule* values, refusing to grant Indians any part of *their* New World. This put the Native people in a very strained and increasingly difficult situation. In fact, with brief exceptions made by Pocahontas and Squanto, from the arrival of the first Europeans to America, these relations were met with disaster. Unrestrained violent conflict soon followed and settlers and Indians alike, died.

None of his best ideals would compare to the impact his Holy Experiment would have if his attempt to gain favor of the Indians were to fail.

A TIME FOR COVENANT

William Penn was fully aware of Pennsylvania's Native population and the abuses that had been taken by other colonies. After he had done everything necessary to secure Pennsylvania from England Penn established a precedent that became one of his greatest accomplishments—a true testament to the legacy of Pennsylvania's Indian relations. Penn's approach to the Indians would prove to be different than that of his European predecessors. Even before he met them, he was determined to love them and show them a genuine respect, making his attempt to colonize Pennsylvania extraordinary. He would see to it that they too were treated with the same equality that he would give to his colonists. He believed that, while that would be morally required of him in keeping with a clear conscience, it would also be the most thrilling and adventurous part of the Holy Experiment. William Penn's message in the New World was to establish a godly government and within the same framework of that government create an environment that could include and embrace Native Americans. It would put everything he believed on the line, and would make him totally dependent on God for the outcome. None of his best ideals would compare to the impact his Holy Experiment would have if his attempt to gain the favor of the Indians were to fail.

More important to William Penn than the working of a good government was the foundation on which such a government could endure. Penn's conviction was that God is the Creator of good government and that it rests on His shoulders for the benefit of all. Within that premise is the belief that *all* men, created in the image of God, are worthy of that equality and privilege. God makes no distinctions, nor did Penn.

William Penn's Holy Experiment was more than just an experiment in government; it was also an earnest trust in God's ability to draw men unto Himself. Penn desired all men to know God, and he knew that the survival of his colony depended upon God's blessings. He founded Pennsylvania on the revelation that if the increase of God's government were allowed to flourish, Pennsylvania would be blessed and an atmosphere would be created for men and women to find and know God. Penn had said, "Government seems to me a part of religion itself," but in that, he believed that good government, created by God, was to transcend for the good of all men, not just a select few. It was upon this conviction that William Penn would greet the Native inhabitants of Pennsylvania and set forth a new colony.

William Penn's language, of Pennsylvania being a seed, cannot be fully understood or appreciated if we perceive what he meant as pertaining to political government alone. Penn's understanding of government was far greater than that. If the God-head (Father, Son and Holy Spirit) expresses the government of God, and within the Godhead is perfect unity, then every expression of the Kingdom of God on earth, if the scriptures are true about the "increase of God's government bringing peace," should express divine unity—from the smallest unit of God's government, the family, to the Church, to the civil government, all the way to the Godhead himself. That was not a mere ideal. It was God or it was not. It would bring peace or it would not. That's why Penn could not separate God from Government or His Government from a people, including Native Americans.

HOW GOOD AND PLEASANT

The principle of goodwill and friendship toward all men lay at the very root of Quaker belief, and in this context it is not difficult to understand why Penn's treatment of the Indians differed from that of his predecessors. He was determined, even before he left England or had seen his first Indian, to treat them as brothers and win their confidence and friendship. This sprang from his deep sense of humanity and a conviction that the Indians, no less than the whites, were children of God, entitled to love and respect. Before coming to Pennsylvania, Penn sent a letter, (dated October 18, 1681), to his commissioners[6] who preceded him, to be translated into the Algonkian dialect and read to the Indians.[7]

'My Friends

There is one great God and power that has made the world and all things therein, to whom you and I and all people owe their being and well being, and to whom you and I must one day give an account for all that we do in this world. This great God has written his law in our hearts, by which we are taught and commanded to love and help and do good to one another, and not to do harm and mischief one unto another. Now this great God has been pleased to make me concerned in your parts of the world, and the king of the country where I live has given unto me a great province therein, but I desire to enjoy it with your love and consent, that we may always live together as friends, else what would the great God say to us, who has made us not to devour and destroy one another, but to live soberly and kindly together in the world.

'...I desire to enjoy it with your love and consent, that we may always live together as friends...'

'Now I would have you well observe, that I am very sensible of the unkindness and injustice that has been too much exercised towards you by the people of these parts of the world, who have sought themselves, and to make great advantages by you, rather than be examples of justice and goodness unto you; which I hear has been matter of trouble to you and caused great grudgings and animosities, sometimes to the shedding of blood, which has made the great God angry. But I am not such a man, as is well known in my own country. I have great love and regard toward you, and I desire to win and gain your love and friendship by a kind, just, and peaceable life; and the people I send are of the same mind, and shall in all things behave themselves accordingly. And if in anything any shall offend you or your people, you shall have a full and speedy satisfaction for the same by an equal number of honest men on both sides, that by no means you may have just occasion of being offended against them.

'I shall shortly come to you myself, at what time we may more largely and freely confer and discourse of these matters. In the meantime, I have sent my commissioners to treat with you about land and a firm league of peace. Let me desire you to be kind to them and the people, and receive these presents and tokens which I have sent to you as a testimony of my good will to you and my resolution to live justly, peaceably, and friendly with you. I am your friend.

Wm. Penn'[8]

WITH LOVE AND CONSENT

Clinton Weslager, in his book *The Delaware Indians*, says this about William Penn's treatment of the Native Americans:

So much has been written about Penn's exemplary treatment of the Indians that it would appear little more remains to be said; still, I do not believe the significance of the word *Consent*, as he used it, has been fully explained or appreciated. The use of this one word signified a radical change in Indian colonial policy; and used in connection with the word *Love*, which was also applied in a new connotation in relation to the "savages," had a deep meaning in Indian affairs.

The British Crown, long fortified with its traditional divine power, completely ignored and, in fact, denied the Indian tribes any ownership rights to lands in the New World "discovered" by English navigators or explorers, or navigators in English employ. Basic in the territorial concepts of the Stuarts, who occupied the throne during the critical period of American settlement, was that land not yet discovered nor yet in the possession "of any Christian Prince, County or State" belonged to its discoverer, irrespective of its native population. If the savages living on land discovered by Englishmen made any effort to oppose the exploitation of their country, they were to be treated as enemies of England. To Charles II the idea that he should demean the throne to obtain the consent of heathen savages so that Englishmen might occupy land belonging to the crown by right of discovery was preposterous. To deny the right of the King to newly discovered land…"is in Effect denying his *Right to Rule* there."

Under this legalistic concept, the Delaware Indians had no more right to the lands on which they had lived for many years than did birds flitting in the trees or wild animals roaming the forests. When Penn insisted that the Indians give their "Consent" to his occupation of lands in Pennsylvania, he recognized their prior right as legal owners.[9]

William Penn said the soil of Pennsylvania was theirs (the Indians) by *jus gentium* (Latin: *Law of the People*), and no one had a right to seize it. Penn did not come with the *Right to Rule* supposition. He came instead to serve, bear friendship and live at peace. This was radical thinking for his day.

SETTING SAIL

Holding his dream in his heart, William Penn continued to make preparations

Penn's First Sight of the Promised Land
Brian Hunt & Pennsylvania Capitol Preservation Committee

for its fulfillment, but it would not come easily. While making last minute preparations for his departure to America, Penn received devastating news when his mother, Lady Margaret Penn, whom he dearly loved, passed away. Grief stricken, Penn was unable to continue for a time. Finally, on August 31, 1682, when all was made ready for the long and dangerous voyage, one hundred brave souls said farewell to their English homeland and boarded the ship *Welcome*. Filled with more wonder than their hearts could imagine, William Penn and his Quaker pioneers set out for the distant shores of the Delaware River to establish their new colony.

Hardship, suffering and affliction often accompanied such voyages, and Penn's was no exception. Their nine-week passage was met with peril, as small pox broke out among the passengers. Penn, who had been exposed to the deadly disease as a child, did all within his power to offer sympathy, comfort and consolation to help alleviate the affliction of the sick, the suffering and the dying. Of the one hundred passengers on board, thirty-one perished before ever seeing the Holy Experiment realized on the shores of the New World.

William Penn sighted the Delaware Bay on October 24, 1682, and arrived at New Castle, Delaware, on October 28, where he was greeted by its inhabitants.[10] The next day he sailed up the Delaware River into Pennsylvania to Upland, a settlement the Swedes had established in 1628. Penn renamed the town Chester.

THE LENAPE

The Indians whom William Penn encountered on his arrival on the shores of the Delaware River were a people of three different clans belonging to the greater Algonquin linguistic family, the largest Indian family in North America (measured by the extent of territory occupied). They called themselves the Lenape, (lenah'-pay) meaning the Original People or Real People. The Lenape were considered a Grandfather tribe whose presence and power in the region served to settle disputes among rival tribes. The English commonly called them the Delaware for the river[11] on which they dwelt. They greeted and welcomed William Penn and began negotiating with him about the purchase of land along the Delaware River where he would soon lay out the city of Philadelphia.[12]

The three clans of the Lenape were the Unami (Turtle clan), "down river people," who dwelt on both sides of the Delaware River from the mouth of the Lehigh River to the line dividing the colonies of Pennsylvania and Delaware. The Unalachtigo (Turkey clan), "people living near the sea," occupied the land on the lower reach of the Delaware River and Delaware Bay. The Munsee (Wolf clan) lived in the mountain country, from the mouth of the Lehigh River northward into New York and New Jersey, embracing the territory between the Blue or Kittatinny Mountains and the sources of the Susquehanna and Delaware Rivers. The Lenape called all this land, *Lenapehoking*, or, Home of the Lenape.

THE WHITE TRUTHTELLER

Though William Penn received the territory of his province by royal charter of the king in payment for the 16,000-pound debt, William Penn recognized the Delaware as the host inhabitants and owners of Pennsylvania. This recognition would be the gateway to his realizing and receiving the full blessings of the land. Between 1682 and 1684 he formed ten treaties with them, in which he purchased, with their willing consent, the greater part of southeastern Pennsylvania. These were not treaties of peace by surrender or forced submission or the result of conflict and war. The treaties between Penn and the Delaware were treaties of covenant agreement over the purchase of land for the *cohabitation* of their two nations.

> *...Penn was the first to go towards them with hands empty of weapons. He treated them as equals before God, not as blood-thirsty savages...*

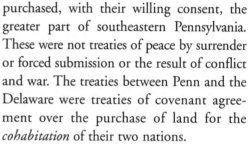

It was not that he was the first to buy their land; others had done that with excellent results in other colonies. But Penn was the first to go towards them with hands empty of weapons. He treated them as equals before God, not as bloodthirsty savages, and on no account would he fight them. He would put the Quaker doctrine to the test; he would have courage to go among them unarmed. The faith, and the valiance of faith, needed to do this were stupendous. His approach is perhaps his highest achievement as a religious leader, and it was politically successful. But politics were not in his mind; here he was the primitive Christian.[13]

During the first years of Pennsylvania history, when the government of the Province was administered on the Christian principles of the preservation of peace, which consisted of doing justice and using patience and forbearance, there were no garrisons, forts, soldiers or muskets to be seen within all of the boundaries. None were needed. The Indians were aware of this and, they too, mixed with the inhabitants, carrying neither bows, arrows, nor tomahawks. All implements of war were laid aside in perfect confidence that neither the natives nor the settlers would harm each other.

Pennsylvania soon became a colony to excite the admiration of the whole world. Without war, conquests, revolution or struggle, Penn had accomplished a model settlement. The natives were won by the love and tact of the Quaker proprietor, and everywhere began to pay tribute to his methods.[14]

For Penn, even in contact with the Indians, and not merely as an idea, treated them humanely, rationally, as fellow-creatures; he walked with them, joined in their sports, learned their language, sympathized with their troubles…he was always scrupulously fair with them, putting them on an equality with his own people.[15]

'I have made it my business to understand it (speaking of their language), that I might not want an Interpreter on any occasion,' he wrote. 'And I must say, that I know not a language spoken in Europe that hath words of more sweetness in Accent and Emphasis, than theirs.'[16]

Penn was so duly impressed and committed to knowing his new Lenape friends that he wrote his own account of their people, called, *William Penn's Own Account of the Lenni Lenape or Delaware Indians,* which is still referenced to this day.

Returning Penn's love and respect, the Delaware made William Penn a chief among their people and devised their own name for him; they called him *Miquon,* which to them meant feather or quill (the Iroquois equivalent was *Onas*). For ages to come Penn would be remembered with endearing affection by the Delaware as "the white truthteller."

THE GREAT TREATY

In June of 1683 William Penn and the Delaware met together at Shackamaxon,[17] the capitol city of the Delaware, for what has become one of the most historically celebrated treaties between Native American and white men. This meeting was not to sell or purchase any land but to celebrate and confirm a friendship of love and commitment. Next to the flowing waters of the Delaware River and underneath the outstretched boughs of a great elm tree was celebrated what has traditionally been called the *"Great Treaty."*

Shackamaxon was the Delaware's principal city where they held their Council Fire, and where Penn would eventually lay out the city of Philadelphia. In the Algonquin tongue Shackamaxon meant, "the place where chiefs are made." The

Susquehannocks, Seneca and other tribes also held their conferences with the Delaware here.

William Penn entered into the *Great Treaty* with Tamanend—the Great Sachem, or chief, of the Turtle Clan. He was a chief of great influence. The

chief of the Turtle Clan always presided as head-chief over the Delaware Nation and therefore represented all three clans in all councils. Tamanend, admired and respected among the Indians and Colonists alike, had been given the name, "Saint Tamanend."

Tamanend and his people, adorned in feathers and paint as was their custom, but all unarmed, gathered underneath the elm and sat in their traditional half circle to hear

The Great Treaty

Courtesy Pennsylvania Historical and Museum Commission

what Penn had come to say. In front were the chiefs, with their counselors and elders on either side. Behind them sat the young men. Represented also were the tribes of the Mingoe and Shawnee.

Great excitement and celebration filled the air because of what these two great chiefs, Penn and Tamanend, had come to exchange.

When all had assembled, Tamanend placed his chaplet on his head, the emblem of kingly power, approached Penn and through an interpreter announced that the nations were now ready to hear him.

THE SAME FLESH AND BLOOD

Penn approached Tamanend and said,

'The Great Spirit, who made me and you, who rules the heavens and the earth, and who knows the innermost thoughts of men, knows that I and my friends have a hearty desire to live in peace and friendship with you, and to serve you to the utmost of our power. It is not our custom to use hostile weapons against our fellow-creatures, for which reason we have come unarmed. Our object is not to do injury, and thus provoke the Great Spirit, but to do good.

'We are met on the broad pathway of good faith and good will, so that no advantage is to be taken on either side, but all to be openness, brotherhood, and love. I will not…compare the friendship between us to a chain, for the rain may rust it, or a tree may fall and break it; but I will consider you as the same flesh and blood with the Christians, and the same as if one man's body were to be divided into two parts.'[18]

With these few words, not many were needed, Penn expressed the very heart of the Holy Experiment. It was their unity, and mutual trust, that was the necessary seed that would be the building blocks for a new nation. Penn was entirely trusting God to work out the details. He was, however, just as committed as ever, and so were his Native friends. God's kingdom, and His government, that Penn was so earnestly expressing, was dependant upon the success of their covenant.

The value that this covenant placed upon the Delaware and the sequential trust that followed brought Tamanend great honor. Tamanend had no reference for falsification and received Penn's words as gospel. Chief Tamanend declared,

'We will live in love with William Penn and his children as long as the creeks and rivers run, and while the sun and moon and stars endure.'[19]

Tamanend confirmed the covenant with words that were as equally eternal—as long as the creeks and rivers run, and the sun, moon, and stars endure. As long as the earth and heavens functioned, the covenant would continue to exist.

Witnessed before heaven and earth, these two nations, represented by their respective leaders, made a covenant of peace, friendship and love, one with the other. Before God and man, a powerful commitment was exchanged face-to-face and heart-to-heart. It was the necessary ingredient required for keeping both these nations together in a lasting bond of mutual respect and love.

Of this great treaty, Voltaire, the French writer said, 'the only league made between those nations and the Christians, which was never sworn to by oath, and never violated.'[20]

49

In a letter to the Free Society of Traders, Penn said that another chief in attendance at the treaty turned and addressed his people,

'…to charge and command them to love the Christians, and particularly live in peace with me, and the people of my Government; that many Governors had been on the River, but that no Governor had come himself to live and stay here before; and having now such an one that treated them well, they should never do him or his any wrong. At every sentence of which they shouted and said Amen in their way.'[21]

At the great elm tree treaty at Shackamaxon the Lenape presented William Penn with a large belt of wampum, as seen on the cover of this book, declaring their eternal friendship. This belt is now on display at the Historical Society of Pennsylvania in Philadelphia.

Wampum comes from the Algonquin word, *wampumpeak*, meaning, "strings of white shell beads" and was made from the white, blue, purple and black part of the Quahog Shell. The Quahog Shell and the beads that were shaped from them were highly esteemed by America's Eastern Seaboard Indians as an important medium of exchange. The beads were also strung together and designed in various patterns to form 'belts' that held a record of the culture and history of the Indian people: many of them telling stories, traditions and treaties such as our history books do today. Wampum belts were very sacred and used in making declarations of war, peace or friendship. When the speaker held the belt in his hand, it was the equivalent of the white-man's placing his hand on the Bible and taking an oath.

You can see a presentation of a belt in the 1992 movie, *The Last of the Mohicans*, where Hawkeye, played by Daniel Day-Lewis, adopted son of the Mohicans, presents his tribe's belt to the chief of the Huron while pleading for the lives of Colonel Monroe's two daughters who were taken captive at the fall of Fort William Henry during The French and Indian War.

A TIME TO SING, DANCE AND CELEBRATE

Arthur Quinn, from his book, *A New World*, relates this story about the covenant made between these two nations:

There survives only the general oral tradition about the great elm, and the specific memories of an old woman who claimed to have witnessed the event as a young girl. She remembered it vividly not because she understood at the time its historical significance; parleys with the Indians were common occurrences on the frontier in those days. She remembered it vividly because Penn was the handsomest man she had ever seen, before or since. She also told of the celebration after the treaty formalities concluded. The handsome Penn was joyous, his spirits overflowing. He ate the Indian dishes with relish, and resolved to learn their language so he could communicate with his new friends directly.

Then something extraordinary happened that made the evening even more memorable to the young girl. The Indians began to dance in celebration, to jump and hop with the throb of the drums, and to whoop and chant their weird songs. Finally Penn could contain himself no more. This was no time for gloomy sternness. Then there he was, unbelievably, there was Governor William Penn, proprietor of all Pennsylvania, friend of King Charles, William Penn up dancing with the Indians, leaping and shouting and shaking as if trying to be more Indian than the Indians.

Failure to maintain relationship with the "Original People" would set precedence for many yet-to-arrive and yet-to-be Americans.

Turning from the wonder of the girl at this handsome man dancing with abandon, we can only imagine the shock of Penn's party at this breach of decorum. Had Penn entirely taken leave of his senses? For a fleeting moment some must have worried that Penn would strip off his clothes to free his limbs.

And what would Penn have said if his friends on the way back to Philadelphia had gently admonished him for succumbing to carnal frivolity? Since they had not been fully moved by the moment, he would have to cite authorities they respected. They did remember— didn't they?—that on the great judgement day we will all dance and take hands. Had his friends forgotten Psalm 149? It bids us now to sing a new song unto the Lord, and to praise His name in dance. Penn was only praising the Lord of the Dance, for He surely must take pleasure in His people, as with every step they are delivered further into heavenly purity and bliss. Let everything that breathes, let every breath be full of praises of the Lord. There was a time for dignity, and a time for ecstasy. So he could warmly exhort his dear friends not to be like haughty Michal looking down from her high window in disdain.

And what could these dear friends say in rebuttal? Perhaps they could remind him that they were now returning to a careful quadrille of streets called Philadelphia. Now was a time for dignity, and also discreet silence. No one should have to explain to King Charles what happened under the great elm. Let the event be forgotten, or at least unrecorded. So they all agreed, not realizing that this event would never be forgotten by one impressionable young girl.[22]

It is this treaty, the covenant made between these two nations, that became a witness, proving the Holy Experiment. Pennsylvania became an example to the nations (or as the Bible defines nations—ethnic groups) when these two people groups embraced each other underneath the great elm on the banks of the mighty Delaware River: the American Indian and the white man. It was a powerful precedent that held within its DNA a value of all people. It spoke of faith and unity. It spoke of hope. It was the building blocks of freedom.

Failure to maintain relationship with the "Original People" would set precedence for many yet-to-arrive and yet-to-be Americans. In the next few chapters we'll look at the tragic progression of events that forfeited the opportunities America had to be an expression of divine love and real hope. The importance of these lost opportunities cannot be underestimated; the health of our conscience[23] as a nation and the validity of the freedom we proclaim depended upon what happened next.

CHRONOLOGICAL TABLE

1681	October 18. William Penn sends a letter of greeting to the Indians of Pennsylvania.
1682	(1) March. William Penn's mother, Lady Margaret Penn, passes away. (2) August 31. William Penn sets sail for the New World and Pennsylvania with one hundred passengers aboard the ship *Welcome*. (3) October 24. William Penn sights the Delaware Bay. (4) October 28. William Penn arrives in New Castle. (5) October 29. William Penn sets foot in Pennsylvania.
1683	June 23. Penn enters the *Great Treaty* with the Delaware.

ENDNOTES

1. The Dutch bought Manhattan Island from the local Indians for 60 guilders (about $24) and named it New Amsterdam (present New York). Between the years 1641 and 1664, the Dutch mercilessly massacred sixteen hundred Indians on the lower reaches of the Hudson. The Dutch also migrated south and settled on the Delaware River in 1655 and in 1660 sold much liquor to the Indians causing the murders of both Indians and whites.

2. The Powhatan War started no sooner after the arrival of the English and the establishing of Jamestown in the Tidewater country of eastern Virginia in 1607, and lasted until 1646. Two separate massacres, one on Good Friday, March 22, 1622, and the other on April 18, 1644, cost the lives of nearly 850 colonists.

3. The Pequot War, lasting from 1636 until 1638, was the first Indian war in New England.

4. King Philip's (Metacom, or Metacomet, chief of the Wampanoag) War picked up where The Pequot War left off and lasted from 1640 until 1676, and was the costliest Indian war in New England. During King Philip's War nearly 600 colonists lost their lives as Western Massachusetts, Maine, and New Hampshire had been nearly swept clean of all its white settlers.

5. The Narragansett's, who were at first neutral during King Philip's War, were drug into the war when their principal village was attacked by whites in December of 1675. Three hundred of their braves were killed along with four hundred of their women and children. In the spring of 1676 the Narragansett's joined the Wampanoag's and wrought much devastation and death to the colony of Rhode Island.

6. William Penn commissioned his cousin, William Markham, as his deputy-governor on April 10, 1681. Markham reached Pennsylvania that summer and served until Penn's arrival in 1682.

7. Weslager, C. A., *The Delaware Indians A History*, (Rutgers University Press, New Brunswick, New Jersey, 1972), p. 156.

8. Soderlund, Jean R., *William Penn and the founding of Pennsylvania*, (University of Pennsylvania Press, Philadelphia, PA, 1983), p. 88.

9. Weslager, C. A., *The Delaware Indians A History*, (Rutgers University Press, New Brunswick, New Jersey, 1972), pp. 156-157.

10. Most of the European inhabitants Penn greeted upon his arrival to Pennsylvania were Dutch and Swedish. The Swedes settled on the west shore of the Delaware River in 1638 and started the colony of New Sweden. The Dutch overthrew New Sweden in 1655 and ruled on the Delaware River from then until the English took possession of the settlements in 1664.

11. Before William Penn arrived on the Delaware River, this great river had gotten its name in 1610 from the Governor of the English Colony at Jamestown, Lord De La Warre. Oddly enough, this lord had never set eyes upon the famous river that bears his name. However, the Indian name for this river was, Lenapewihittuck, "river of the Lenape," long before the European ever thought to immortalize it with his own.

12. According to Egle's, *History of Pennsylvania*, a portion of Philadelphia was on the site of an Indian village called Coquanoc. Other villages in the county near the city were "Passyunk, which lay on the east bank of the Schuylkill, south of Grey's Ferry road; Wicaco, east of Passyunk, and near the Delaware; Cackamensi, modernized into Shackamaxon, between

Gunner's run and Frankford creek, on the Delaware; Nittabaconk, on the Schuykill, near the falls; Poquessing, on the banks of the creek flowing into the Delaware, which forms the north-eastern boundary of the city; Pennypacka, or Pennypack, near the creek still bearing the latter name; Wequiaquenske, the site of which is not known." p. 1017.

13. Dobree, Bonamy, *William Penn Quaker and Pioneer*, (Riverside Press, Cambridge, Mass. 1932), p. 126.

14. William Penn Tercentenary Committee, The, *Remember William Penn 1644-1944*, (Harrisburg, PA, 1944), p. 140.

15. Dobree, Bonamy, *William Penn Quaker and Pioneer*, (Riverside Press, Cambridge, Mass. 1932), p. 146.

16. Weslager, C. A., *The Delaware Indians A History*, (Rutgers University Press, New Brunswick, New Jersey, 1972), p. 166.

17. Shackamaxon was situated within the present sight of Kensington, a short distance from the business part of Philadelphia. The historical site of this treaty is now called Penn Treaty Park in Philadelphia, located on the Delaware River on Cecil B. Moore (Columbia) Ave.

18. Janney, Samuel M., *The Life of William Penn*, (Philadelphia, Friends' Book Assoc., 1851), p. 214.

19. Sipe, C. Hale, *The Indian Wars of Pennsylvania*, (originally published, Harrisburg, PA, 1931., reprinted, Gateway Press, Baltimore, MD, for Wennawoods Publishing, Lewisburg, PA, 1995), p. 71.

20. Dobree, Bonamy, *William Penn Quaker and Pioneer*, (Riverside Press, Cambridge, Mass. 1932), p. 145.

21. Sipe, C. Hale, *The Indian Chiefs of Pennsylvania*, (originally published, Butler, PA, 1927., reprinted, Gateway Press, Baltimore, MD, for Wennawoods Publishing, Lewisburg, PA, 1995), p. 62

22. Quinn, Arthur, *A New World*, (Berkley Books, New York, New York, 1994), pp. 346-347.

23. The scriptures show us that the conscience is real, affects the entire body and can be seared. Without a clear conscience one loses their ability to be a witness (can't call sin, sin,) and conquer temptation. Every friendship and relationship is affected. Every decision is warped as it is bounced off guilt stored in the conscience. People without a clear conscience react instead of respond. People without a clear conscience cannot hear God clearly and lose authority. (1 Timothy 1:5, 3:9, 4:1-2; Acts 23:1, 24:16; 1 Peter 3:21; 2 Corinthians 1:12, 7:1-12; 1 John 3:19-21)

5

WILLIAM PENN
REMOVED

I desire fervent prayers to the Lord for continuing my life, that I may see Pennsylvania once more before I die...

—William Penn

Tragically, in 1684, after just two years in his province, unable to complete his own home, Pennsbury Manor,[1] along the Delaware River, William Penn was forced to return to the courts of England to settle border disputes that were arising between Lord Baltimore of Maryland and Pennsylvania. Confusion existed on the part of King Charles II as to the running of the true fortieth degree latitude marking the boundary (Mason-Dixon Line[2]) between these two colonies. It was a dispute that, after much bloodshed between the colonists, did not end until long after Penn's death. Remarkably, this boundary line would become the symbolic demarcation in the United States between the North and the South.

Before returning to England, Penn had every reason to look on his colony with pride at the end of its first two years. There was no reason to suspect that the Holy Experiment was not launched successfully. In fewer than two years he not only laid a prosperous and healthy government, but he also created a colony that could remain unfortified and undefended because of its friendly relations with the Lenape.

PENN'S FAREWELL TO PENNSYLVANIA

Of all the letters written by Penn, none have been so well remembered as the one written on August 12, 1684 to the people of his beloved province on his return to England aboard the ship *Endeavour*. He closed the letter with a compassionate prayer for Philadelphia.

'Dear Friends and people,

My love and my life are to you and with you, and no waters can quench it nor distance wear it out or bring it to an end. I have been with you, cared over you, and served you with unfeigned love, and you are beloved of me and near to me beyond utterance. I bless you in the name and power of the Lord, and may God bless you with His righteousness, peace, and plenty all the land over. Oh, that you would eye Him in all, through all, and above all the works of your hands, and let it be your first care how you may glorify God in your undertakings; for to be a blessed end are you brought hither and if you see and keep but in the sense of that providence, your coming, staying, and improving will be sanctified. But if any forget God and call not upon His name in truth, He will pour out His plagues upon them and they shall know whom it is that judges the children of men.

'Oh, now you are come to a quiet land, provoke not the Lord to trouble it. And now liberty and authority are with you and in your hands, let the government be on His shoulders, in all your spirits, that you may rule for Him, to whom the princes of this world will one day esteem it their honor to govern under and serve in their places. I cannot but say, when these things come weightily into my mind, as the apostle (Peter) did of old, what manner of persons ought we to be in all godly conversation. Truly the name and glory of the Lord are deeply concerned in you as to discharge of yourselves in your present stations, many eyes being upon you. And remember that as we have been belied about disowning the true religion, so of all government. And that to behold us exemplary and Christian in the use of that, will not only stop our enemies, but minister conviction to many on that account prejudiced. Oh, that you may see and know that service and do it for the Lord in this your day.

'And thou Philadelphia, the virgin settlement of this province, named before thou was born, what love, what care, what service, and what travail have there been to bring thee forth and preserve thee from such as would abuse and defile thee. Oh, that thou may be kept from the evil that would overwhelm thee, that faithful to the God of thy mercies in the life of righteousness thou may stand in the day of trial, that thy children may be blessed of the Lord and thy people saved by His power. My love to thee has been great and the remembrance of thee affects my heart and my eye. The God of eternal strength keep and preserve thee to His glory and thy peace.

'So dear friends, my love again salutes you all, wishing that grace, mercy, and peace with all temporal blessings may abound richly among you. So says, so prays,

Your friend and lover in the truth, Wm. Penn'³

It was not long after Penn's return to England when the people of Pennsylvania began to focus on their blessings and forgot to nurture the godly seed that had been planted in her. The very things Penn had warned them about were ignored.

Pennsylvania had been planted as an exception to a new colonial policy, and was forced to struggle to maintain her integrity. Economic pressures both within the colony and from the outside severely marred her tranquility. There were groups in Pennsylvania which attempted to secure political domination over the remaining freemen, and, on occasion, all the provincials joined to oppose the governor and proprietor. Fundamental differences of opinion existed in religion, and the main religious stream was divided by a schism which had political overtones. As an absentee Governor, William Penn could exert little control over the government or the citizens of his plantation. He was forced to sit helplessly by in England and watch the "holy experiment" slowly fade in the colony.[4]

THE CONTINUED PATH OF FREEDOM

Meanwhile, back in England, King Charles II died in February 1685, and James II succeeded him to the throne. King James, a loyal friend of Penn's, had become interested in Penn's ideas of religious freedom and made him one of his trusted advisers. Penn continued to see religious persecution of his native countrymen and through his friendship with King James II was able to applaud the passing of the *Declaration for Liberty of Conscience* in 1687 that set many religious prisoners free.

Shortly after this victory, Penn turned his efforts towards his colony to reinforce the message of freedom. He knew all too well that because the Quakers had been excluded from any judicial participation in England there was inexperience in the legal training of their own basic fundamental rights. In order to ensure that justice would always prevail within the civil and religious framework of the Holy Experiment, Penn arranged in 1687 for the printing of a small, legal reference book titled, *The Excellent Privilege of Liberty and Property*. Within the pages of this revolutionary book, printed for the first time in the western hemisphere, was the first American printing of the Magna Carta.* The rights provided by the Magna Carta were needed in the colony's courts of law. So, along with his constitution, Penn's publication further secured due process of law, clearly distinguishing his colony as a just and free society. This action brought greater distance between America and the political traditions of England.[5]

Then, in late 1688, England's *Glorious Revolution* drove King James II from the throne and William and Mary ascended to the royal power. Nevertheless, the principles of freedom Penn had so faithfully advocated were triumphant. In 1689, Parliament passed an *Act of Toleration* giving further substantial religious liberty for which he had so contended. However, believing that Penn was joining plots to restore the exiled James, William and Mary accused Penn of treason. Penn spent the next four years on the run and in hiding. His governmental powers over Pennsylvania were revoked on October 21, 1691.

---

* The Declaration of Independence, the United States Constitution and the Bill of Rights embodied the basic fundamental civil liberties of the Magna Carta, which is considered to be the foundation of modern democracy (see endnote #2, pg. 214).

During Penn's revocation of powers his beloved wife of twenty-two years, Gulielma, died on February 23, 1694. Six months later, on August 20, 1694, William Penn was finally cleared of all charges of treason and restored to the favor of William and Mary. After two years and four months, William and Mary gave Pennsylvania back to their "trusty and well beloved William Penn," as they then referred to him.

Penn's relationship with the Pennsylvania Indians continued to hold strong, even in his absence. On July 6, 1694, Tamanend, that great and wise Delaware sachem with whom Penn had entered into the *Great Treaty*, made his last public appearance before his death in 1701. He, along with a number of other Delaware chiefs, appeared before a council at Philadelphia and expressed to Lieutenant-Governor William Markham, his friendly feelings for the colonists:

> 'We and the Christians of this river (Delaware) have always had a free roadway to one another, and although sometimes a tree has fallen across the road, yet we have still removed it again, and kept the path clean; and we design to continue the old friendship that has been between us and you.'[6]

THE FIRST AMERICAN PLAN OF UNION

France, like England, was also contending for a claim in the New World. In 1603, the French explorer, Samuel de Champlain, sailing in the name of France, founded the colony of New France, in a land the Iroquois called *Cannata* (Canada). Over the next several years, New France pushed headlong up the St. Lawrence River, which connects the Great Lakes and the interior of America to the Atlantic Ocean, and established the settlements of Quebec in 1608, and Montreal in 1611. With the territories of France now being so close to the exposed northern boundaries of their American colonies, England feared of a possible French invasion of Pennsylvania and New York.

King William's War, as the American colonists called it, broke out in 1689, and was the first of four conflicts between England and France called the Colonial Wars[7] that spanned seventy-three years. Because of the war, England, to better govern their American colonies, had created the Board of Trade to oversee all colonial affairs. The Board was trying to negotiate a better colonial defense from a more unified American command.

Penn, still concerned over the lack of unity in America's colonies, recognized America's vulnerability and sought to bring greater security to the exposed northern boundaries of the province. He had foreseen the strategic importance of securing the northern borders of America for the English Empire. In 1696 Penn appeared before the Board and reasoned that if such a demand were to be put on the colonies that perhaps England's efforts would best be served if a continental congress were established among the colonies where each of their strengths could best be represented. In reality, Penn had grasped the nature of the problem and had formulated a solution—a blueprint for a more permanent union. The Board, however, took no action on Penn's plan and the war continued but with very few skirmishes in the American colonies.

The second of the Colonial Wars, Queen Anne's War, started in 1702, and once again threatened British interests in the north. On May 22, 1709, William Penn again sought the aid of Britain's Parliament. He sent a letter to the Duke of Marlborough, who was Britain's leader in the war. Speaking of the northern boundaries in America, he said:

> 'Without such a settlement of our American bounds, we shall be in hazard of being dangerously surprised at one time or other, by the French and their Indians...'[8]

Again, nothing was done.

PENN'S SECOND VOYAGE TO PENNSYLVANIA

When Penn was finally released from his trials in England, he returned to Pennsylvania on September 9, 1699. He was now fifty-four years old. His fifteen-year absence had pushed the seed further into dormancy but made him all the more purposeful about finally being able to establish a more permanent residence in the New World. Accompanied by his new (and almost three decades younger) pregnant wife, Hannah Callowhill, Penn and his grown daughter, Lititia, from his first marriage, landed in Philadelphia where Hannah would give birth to the couple's first child. Their home, Pennsbury Manor, on the Delaware River, north of Philadelphia, had been completed by now and Penn was filled with faith about tending the Holy Experiment. Before leaving England, he wrote a letter of farewell to his Quaker friends scattered throughout Europe, saying:

'…Let your eye be to the Lord, and wait upon Him; walk with Him; and He will walk and dwell with you; And then no weapon form'd against you, be it in particular, or in general, shall prosper…It may perhaps try you…But it shall never finally prevail against you, if you keep the eye of your minds to Him and have faith in Him…'

He continues thus:

'…Much I could say for my heart is open, and full, too, of Divine Love, but time fails me; therefore feel me, my dear friends, in that love of God, which is over sea and land; where distance cannot separate, or time decay, nor many waters quench.

'I send this parting salutation, of my most dear love in the truth, beseeching you all to have me and mine in your remembrance, not only upon the mighty waters, but when in the solitary deserts of America, if it please the Lord to bring us safe thither: For I am not above the love and prayers of my dear brethren, knowing I need them, and have often found, by good experience, that they avail much with the Lord…'[9]

When Penn arrived in Pennsylvania he found that his fears had become a reality. Men with alternative motives had begun to undermine his efforts. His colony had changed.

Nevertheless, the people in Pennsylvania felt that it was an exciting time in which to live. They believed that there were other things in the world besides "holy experiments," for the colony grew and prospered. During his second visit…Penn established a vigorous government, granted a liberal constitution, joined the Friends in worship, and realized…that he had planted a successful colony, though the "holy experiment" was nearly forgotten.[10]

THE CHARTER OF PRIVILEGES

Penn's fourth and final revision to Pennsylvania's Constitution, *The Charter of Privileges*, was adopted on October 28, 1701, and remained her Constitution until 1776. When Thomas Jefferson, writer of the *Declaration of Independence*, emerged onto the scene he referred to William Penn as, "The greatest lawgiver the world has produced."[11] It was the basic thought and philosophy of *The Charter of Privileges* that caused it to "stay the course" and resonate into America's future, serving as the outline and later adoption of our American liberties, the Constitution of the United States.

... Thomas Jefferson ...referred to William Penn as, "The greatest lawgiver the world has produced."

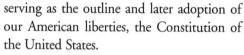

A little known fact about *The Charter of Privileges* is the relationship it has with one of the most celebrated and famous symbols of American independence, the Liberty Bell. In 1751, to celebrate the fiftieth anniversary of William Penn's *Charter of Privileges*, a bell was forged in England. To properly commemorate the purpose of the bell its creators appropriately inscribed the words from Leviticus 25:10 on its side, "Proclaim liberty throughout the land unto all the inhabitants thereof." The bell was hung in the State House at Philadelphia.

Today the Liberty Bell is fondly associated with the year 1776 when the Declaration of Independence was read in Philadelphia, although in actual fact it was created twenty-five years previous to the Revolution, in honor of William Penn and his great *Charter of Privileges* of 1701.

Here is the interesting story of the Liberty Bell as told by William Wistar Comfort in his book, *William Penn And Our Liberties*.

In 1753, when the Liberty Bell was finally received from the founders in England, twice recast, and placed in the tower of the State House, there was the French and Indian war still to be fought, and some years were to elapse before there was any question of severing the ties of the colonies with the mother-country. The connection of the Liberty Bell with political independence in 1776 is therefore entirely fortuitous: the big bell in the State House was simply the one nearest at hand when the hour of jubilation came.

What the Liberty Bell originally symbolized, then, was the freedom of spirit and liberty of conscience which Penn had bequeathed through a series of charters and privileges to his citizens in Pennsylvania. These privileges cherished in constitutional form in 1701 became the frame upon which the Articles of Confederation and the later Constitution of the

United States were built. These Articles and this Constitution were framed and subscribed in Philadelphia, in the very building over which the Liberty Bell swung. But it is only by chance that the Bell is associated with the declaration of independence from England. This fact, indeed, clinched its hold upon the imagination of posterity. But few people now need to be reminded of the Declaration of Independence. That page of history is closed.

What we need to recall now and to retain is the freedom of conscience and the civil rights which are our heritage, and which the Liberty Bell was first cast to commemorate. This national heritage comes to us Americans preeminently through William Penn, the Founder and Lawgiver of Pennsylvania, between 1681 and 1701.[12]

WILLIAM PENN'S LAST FAREWELL

In November 1701, only two years after he had returned to Pennsylvania, Penn again found it necessary to sail back to England. With another war threatening to erupt in Europe, the Crown was considering suspending all colonial proprietary governments, including Pennsylvania's. Protecting the rights of his colony demanded his presence back in London. Sadly, he never returned to Pennsylvania. Four intermittent years of overseeing his colony were all Penn had for giving his life, his strength and eventually, his entire fortune. Towards the end of Penn's life he would write:

'When it pleased God to open a way for me to settle that colony, I had reason to expect a solid comfort from the services done to many hundreds of people; and it is no small satisfaction to me that I have not been disappointed in seeing them prosper, and growing up to a flourishing country, blessed with liberty, ease, and plenty, beyond what many of themselves could expect; and wanting nothing to make them happy, but what, with a right temper of mind and prudent conduct, they might give themselves. But, alas! As to my part, instead of reaping the like advantages, **some of the greatest of my troubles have arisen from thence**; the many combats I have engaged in; the great pains and incredible expense, for your welfare and ease, to the decay of my former estate of which (however some there would represent it) I too sensibly feel the effects; **with the undeserved opposition I have met with from thence, sink me into sorrow; that, if not supported by a superior hand, might have overwhelmed me long ago**'[13] (emphasis mine).

AN ENDURING COVENANT OF THE HEART

Though Pennsylvania's original glory began to fade, its Indians continued to believe in what William Penn started and the message he brought to the New World.

The sachems (chiefs) assured him that they had never broken a covenant "made with their hearts and not with their heads."

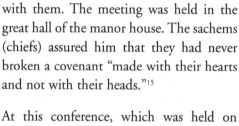

Shortly before embarking for England, in the autumn of 1701, William Penn assembled a large company of the Delawares at his manor house at Pennsbury[14] to review and confirm the covenants of peace and goodwill, which he had formerly made with them. The meeting was held in the great hall of the manor house. The sachems (chiefs) assured him that they had never broken a covenant "made with their hearts and not with their heads."[15]

At this conference, which was held on October 7th, 1701, Penn informed the chiefs that it was likely the last interview that he would ever have with them; that he had ever loved and been kind to them and ever would continue so to be, not through political designs or for selfish interest, but out of real affection. He desired them, in his absence to cultivate friendship with those whom he would leave in authority, so that the bond of friendship already formed might grow the stronger throughout the passing years.[16]

The affection of William Penn's enduring contribution to the Indians was returned by them many times and clearly illustrated in the following letter written in October 1701 by the Pennsylvania Indians to the King of England regarding their high esteem, devotion and respect of William Penn. The letter was closed with the signatures of six Indian chiefs.

'We the Kings and Sachems of the Ancient Nations of the Saswuehannah and Shavanah Indians, understanding that our loving and good friend and brother, William Penn, is to our great grief and the trouble of all the Indians of these parts, obliged to go back for England to speak with the great King and his Sachems about his government, can do no less than acknowledge that he has been not only always just but very kind to us as well as our ancient Kings and Sachems deceased, and careful to keep a good correspondence with us, not suffering us to receive any wrong from any of the people under his government giving us, as is well known, his house for our home at all times and freely entertaining us at his own cost and often filling us with many presents of necessary goods for our clothing and other accommodations, besides what he has paid us for our lands, which no Governor, ever did before him, and we hope and desire that the great King of the English will be good and kind to him and his children, and grant that they may always govern these parts, and then we shall have confidence, that we and our children and people will be well used and be encouraged to continue to live among the Christians according to the agreement that he and we have solemnly made for us and our posterity as long as the sun and moon shall endure, one head one mouth and one heart. We could say much more of his good council and instructions, which he has often given us and our people to live a sober and virtuous life as the best way to please the great God and be happy here and for ever. But let this suffice to the great King and his wise Sachems in love to our good friend and brother, William Penn.'[17]

THE LOSS OF A FRIEND

Upon his reluctant but compulsory return to England Penn was met with staggering news. Philip Ford, a fellow Quaker and steward of the Penn estate, had embezzled large sums of money from Penn. Adding to the insult, Ford had previously deceived Penn into unsuspectingly signing a deed transferring ownership of Pennsylvania to Ford: who now was demanding rent exceeding Penn's ability to pay. Philip died in 1702, but his wife, Bridget, sued Penn for payment of the fraudulent deed, also threatening to sell Pennsylvania. A long and expensive legal battle ensued. By 1703, greatly discouraged over mounting debt, a disillusioned Penn made an unsuccessful attempt to sell Pennsylvania's government to the Crown.

In 1708, still refusing to pay, Penn allowed himself to be thrown into debtors' prison. Nine months later he was released due to the mercy of the Lord Chancellor. Only after the financial help of family and friends and a decreased settlement was Penn finally able to put this tragedy behind him. But the years had taken their toll. In 1712, Penn suffered a debilitating stroke while writing a letter about the future of Pennsylvania. His mind broken at last, Penn was never again active in public life nor ever permitted his dream of settling on the banks of the Delaware River.

William Penn loved his province, travailing over it his entire life. James Logan, appointed by Penn as Secretary of Pennsylvania in 1699, was a trusted and loyal friend. Logan likened Penn to Job when he said, "One would think there was almost a commission granted, as against Job, for his trial; for such an accumulation of adversaries has seldom been known to attack a person that so little deserved them."[18]

Like Job, Penn's integrity never wavered through all he suffered. In response to those who hurled their barrage of discouraging and opposing words Job said,

"I will never admit you are in the right; till I die, I will not deny my integrity. I will maintain my righteousness and never let go of it; my conscience will not reproach me as long as I live."

Job 27:5,6

Grief stricken over sinking circumstances, Penn himself once wrote, "Oh, Pennsylvania, what hast thou not cost me!"[19] Nevertheless, William Penn's love for Pennsylvania exceeded the sacrifice he made. He continually longed to see her once again. Before his death he would write to the Friends, "I close when I tell you that I desire fervent prayers to the Lord for continuing my life, that I may see Pennsylvania once more before I die..."[20] But since his strength and health were failing, Penn's hope to see Pennsylvania again was never satisfied.

Well would it have been for the Colony of Pennsylvania, if Penn's successors had always emulated his example...in dealing with the Indians—if his successors had been imbued with his kindly spirit, and had treated the natives with justice. He died on the 30th of July, 1718, at Ruscombe, near Tywford, in Buckinghamshire, England, at the age of seventy-four;

and when his great heart was cold and still in death, the Red Man of the Pennsylvania forests lost his truest friend. During Penn's life there were no serious troubles between his colony and the Indian, and no actual warfare, as we shall see, for some years thereafter; but, less than a generation after this great apostle of the rights of man was gathered to his fathers, the Delawares, who had welcomed him so kindly, and the Shawnees, rose in revolt, after a long series of wrongs, and spread terror, devastation and death throughout the Pennsylvania settlements.[21]

Penn's Holy Experiment was fast becoming a vacuum many outside influences were eager to fill.

If his example had been followed, the Indians might possibly still be a flourishing race, instead of a miserable and decadent remnant allowed to live in preserves by the same courtesy accorded to bison. Because he never cheated them, never tried to outwit them, and, above all, because he went about among them as though he were one of themselves, they never betrayed his trust in them.[22]

Says Dr. George P. Donehoo, 'The memory of William Penn lingered in the wigwams of the Susquehanna and the Ohio until the last red man of this generation had passed away; and then the tradition of him was handed down to the generations which followed until today, when it still lingers, like a peaceful benediction, among the Delawares and Shawnee on the sweeping plains of Oklahoma.'[23]

Because of William Penn's genuine treatment of the Indians as equals, their treaty of love and friendship lasted for 73 years and was often referred to by both Indians and Englishmen in the handling of disputes for years to come. In no other colony along the Atlantic seaboard had any such policy been developed that would identify itself with such distinction with American Indians as did Pennsylvania. However, Penn's Holy Experiment was fast becoming a vacuum many outside influences were eager to fill.

CHRONOLOGICAL TABLE

1603	French explorer, Samuel de Champlain, names Canada New France.
1608	Quebec is founded by Champlain.
1611	Montreal is founded by Champlain.
1684	August 12. William Penn leaves aboard the ship *Endeavor* to return to England.
1685	February. King Charles II passes away and James II ascends as the king of England.
1687	(1) King James II passes the *Declaration for Liberty of Conscience* setting many religious prisoners free.
	(2) Penn had a legal book published for the courts of law in Pennsylvania titled, *The Excellent Priviledge of Liberty and Property*. In it is included for the first time in the western hemisphere the first American printing of the Magna Carta.
1688-1689	The *Glorious Revolution* deposes James II, and makes William and Mary rulers of England.
1689	Parliament passes the *Act of Toleration* substantially granting the religious liberty for which Penn had so contended.
1689-1697	King William's War, the first of four Colonial Wars between England and France.
1691	October 21. William Penn deprived of governmental powers by William and Mary.
1694	(1) February 23. William Penn's wife, Gulielma Maria Penn, passes away.

(2) August 20. William Penn's governmental powers restored.

1696   March 5. Penn marries Hannah Margaret Callowhill.

1699   (1) September 9. William Penn Leaves England for his second visit to Pennsylvania.
(2) November 30. William Penn arrives in Chester.

1701   (1) October. Farewell letter written to the King of England by the Indians in Pennsylvania.
(2) October 7. William Penn holds farewell assembly with the Delaware at his manor house.
(3) October 28. *The Charter of Privileges* is adopted, Pennsylvania's constitution until 1776.
(4) November. William Penn returns to England.

1702-1713   Queen Anne's War, second of the Colonial Wars.

1709   William Penn sends a letter to the Duke of Marlborough in an effort to secure the northern bounds of America for England.

1718   July 30. William Penn dies at age seventy-four.

1751   London casts a special bell to commemorate the fiftieth year of *The Charter of Privileges* now known as the Liberty Bell.

1945   Governor Edward Martin of Pennsylvania appoints a committee to compile and write a book called, *Remember William Penn 1644-1944*, celebrating the tercentenary (300th) anniversary of William Penn's birthday, October 24, 1644.

ENDNOTES

1. The beautiful estate of William Penn, Pennsbury Manor, has been fully restored to its original splendor. Pennsbury Manor is a popular tourist attraction and can be visited today in Philadelphia. It is located in lower Bucks County at 400 Pennsbury Memorial Road just east of Tullytown.

2. The acceptance of the border line between Pennsylvania and Maryland came in 1769 when surveyors Charles Mason and Jeremiah Dixon, ran the famous Mason-Dixon Line.

3. Soderlund, Jean R., *William Penn and the founding of Pennsylvania*, (University of Pennsylvania Press, Philadelphia, PA, 1983), pp. 395-396.

4. Bronner, Edwin B., *William Penn's "Holy Experiment," The Founding of Pennsylvania*, (Greenwood Press, Westport, Connecticut, 1978), p. 2.

5. Bronner, Edwin B., *The American Journal of Legal History*, Vol. 7, No. 3, (Temple University School of Law, Philadelphia, Jul., 1963), pp. 189-197.

6. Sipe, C. Hale, *The Indian Wars of Pennsylvania*, (originally published, Harrisburg, PA, 1931., reprinted, Gateway Press, Baltimore, MD, for Wennawoods Publishing, Lewisburg, PA, 1995), pp. 74-75.

7. The War of the Grand Alliance (King William's War, 1689-97); the War of the Spanish Succession (Queen Anne's War, 1702-13); the War of the Austrian Succession (King George's War, 1744-48); the French and Indian War (the Seven Years War, 1755-62).

8. William Penn Tercentenary Committee, The, *Remember William Penn 1644-1944*, (Harrisburg, PA, 1944), p. 105.

9. *Ibid*, pp. 27-28.

10. Bronner, Edwin B., *William Penn's "Holy Experiment," The Founding of Pennsylvania*, (Greenwood Press, Westport, Connecticut, 1978), p. 2.

11. Stefoff, Rebecca, *William Penn*, (Chelsea House Publishers, a division of Main Line Book Co., Philadelphia, 1998), p. 102.

12. Comfort, William Wistar, *William Penn And Our Liberties*, (The Penn Mutual Life Insurance Company, Philadelphia, Pennsylvania, 1947), pp. 3-5.

13. Cope, Thomas P., *Passages from the Life & Writings of William Penn*, (Friends' Book-Store, Philadelphia, PA, 1882), p. 500.

14. A total of nineteen treaties and conferences were held and concluded at Pennsbury.

15. Sipe, C. Hale, *The Indian Wars of Pennsylvania*, (originally published, Harrisburg, PA, 1931., reprinted, Gateway Press, Baltimore, MD, for Wennawoods Publishing, Lewisburg, PA, 1995), p. 79.

16. *Ibid.*, p. 80.

17. William Penn Tercentenary Committee, The, *Remember William Penn 1644-1944*, (Harrisburg, PA, 1944), pp. 119-120.

18. Cope, Thomas P., *Passages from the Life & Writings of William Penn*, (Friends' Book-Store, Philadelphia, PA, 1882), p. 500.

19. *Ibid.*, p. 490.

20. *Ibid.*, p. 509.

21. Sipe, C. Hale, *The Indian Wars of Pennsylvania*, (originally published, Harrisburg, PA, 1931., reprinted, Gateway Press, Baltimore, MD, for Wennawoods Publishing, Lewisburg, PA, 1995), pp. 80, 81.

22. Dobree, Bonamy, *William Penn Quaker and Pioneer*, (Riverside Press, Cambridge, Mass. 1932), p. 146.

23. Sipe, C. Hale, *The Indian Wars of Pennsylvania*, (originally published, Harrisburg, PA, 1931., reprinted, Gateway Press, Baltimore, MD, for Wennawoods Publishing, Lewisburg, PA, 1995), p. 81.

Part Two

BROKEN TRUST

6

THE GATHERING STORM

Pennsylvania started that series of events with the Delawares which cost her one of the most remarkable Indian invasions in colonial history.

—Joseph Walton

Following Penn's death his wife Hannah assumed proprietary rights over Pennsylvania. Hannah was a good administrator but was unable to ensure the values of Penn's Holy Experiment. Hannah died on December 20, 1726 and her three sons, John, Richard and Thomas, inherited the Proprietorship. John, the oldest of the three, was only twelve years old when Penn had his first stroke. Now, these young men were faced with the overwhelming responsibility of governing Pennsylvania without their dad's guidance and, more importantly, without their dad's faith.

As the Euro-population increased along the Delaware River the Indians began to detect serious differences regarding each other's relationship to the land. The Indians viewed the land the same way they viewed the sky, as sacred, not something that you could purchase an exclusive right to but as something to be mutually shared and enjoyed. The Europeans were territorial and expropriated whatever land they desired.

By 1717, William Penn's city of brotherly love, Philadelphia, exceeded a population of 10,000, and was fast becoming the largest city in the Thirteen Colonies. Many German, Swiss and Scotch-Irish immigrants, not content with city life, began to press beyond the limits of purchased land, and began settling in the homeland of the Delaware, regardless of standing treaties.

About 1718, as such encroachments continued unchecked, the Delaware clans of the Unalachtigo and the Unami accommodated the intrusions by embarking on a westward trek across the colony. They settled among their allies, another Indian tribe called the Susquehannocks (also called the Conestogas),[1] in the lower regions of the Susquehanna River.

It was here, on the forks of the Susquehanna River, that the Delaware moved their capitol city of Shackamaxon from the Delaware River and established a new capitol called Shamokin.[2] From 1724 through 1727, as the irrepressible tide of European squatters pushed into the valleys of the Susquehanna River, these two Delaware clans continued to migrate further west and north of the lower Susquehanna, and settled in the valleys of the North Branch of the Susquehanna, Allegheny and Ohio Rivers.

When the Delaware moved into the valleys of the Susquehanna and Ohio Rivers, they found themselves in the middle of a great power struggle surfacing in Pennsylvania. Different nations were rising and making earnest attempts to possess it.

To better understand this great conflict, let's go back to pre-colonial and subsequent pertinent history along the Ohio and Susquehanna River's before the arrival of the Delaware.

THE CONFEDERATION OF THE IROQUOIS

The powerful confederation of the Five Nations, or The League of the Iroquois, lived in New York. Their Great Council convened at Onondaga,[3] and was formed by the leadership and guidance of the great Mohawk chief, Hiawatha, at about the year 1570. This great Confederation was an alliance of their five kindred tribes.

Paul A. W. Wallace, author of *Indians in Pennsylvania*, tells us that the five kindred tribes of the Iroquois consisted of three Elder Brothers. They were the *Mohawks,* Keepers of the Eastern Door, the *Senecas,* Keepers of the Western Door and the *Onondagas,* who tended the council fire in the middle, the Fire That Never Dies. The two Younger Brothers were the *Oneidas* and the *Cayugas.*

> The Iroquois...had in their confederacy a political organization of the highest maturity. It was a federal union of five distinct Indian nations, each of which retained its sovereignty almost intact, without, however, weakening the integrity of the whole. In spite of individual differences in outlook and interest, and frequent disagreements in policy, the five nations as a whole possessed a strong sense of national identity.[4]

Later, in 1722, with the inclusion of the Tuscaroras, this Iroquois confederation became known as the Six Nations.

THE SUSQUEHANNOCKS

For generations the powerful Susquehannocks (or Conestogas) were the original occupants of the lower reaches of the Susquehanna River. However, the Susquehannocks had suffered greatly, almost to the point of annihilation, in a war with the Five Nations. Their defeat at the hands of the Five Nations ended at the Treaty of Shackamaxon on March 13, 1677. The subjugation of the Susquehannocks, by the Iroquois, brought claim to all the lands the Susquehannocks had occupied. It also meant the same for all those who dwelt on those lands thereafter. Consequently, when the Delaware moved into the region, the Iroquois claimed to have conquered them by "Right of Conquest" even though there had never been any recorded wars between the Iroquois and the Delaware. The Delaware, known for being peacemakers, willingly submitted to the Iroquois as their Uncles.

THE SUSQUEHANNA LANDS

Although, after the defeat of the Susquehannocks, the Iroquois claimed the lands of the Susquehanna River, the question of an official legal deed to these lands remained unsettled. The following is the interesting and confusing history of these Susquehanna lands.

In 1683, when William Penn was purchasing land from the Delaware, he also desired to purchase land along the Susquehanna River for settlement. In a deed dated September 10, 1683, the Susquehannocks conveyed to William Penn his right to these lands between the Susquehanna and Delaware Rivers. Penn thought it advisable to get the consent of the Five Nations, knowing that the Five Nations held the right to the land in question when they had conquered the Susquehannocks. Penn also contacted the Governor of New York, Thomas Dongan, who had already convinced the Iroquois to release the deed to these lands to him in 1679, two years after the defeat of the Susquehannocks. Wanting to deal with William Penn directly, Governor Dongan wrote Penn in the late fall of 1683 advising him of the purchase.

However, what Dongan didn't tell Penn was that the Iroquois had only given the deed to Dongan in trust and had in no way given up their right to the land in question.

On January 13, 1696, the Governor of New York went to England and sold the lands to Penn for a large sum of money. This gave William Penn a second deed of lease and release to the lands on the Susquehanna.

On September 13, 1700, William Penn concluded a treaty with the chiefs of the Susquehannocks confirming and ratifying his title to these lands. Only then did William Penn discover how the Governor of New York had deceived the Iroquois. William Penn then commenced to pay the Iroquois for these lands after already having purchased them twice, once from the Susquehannocks and secondly from Governor Dongan.

THE SHAWNEE

The Shawnee (meaning "Southerners," also called the Savannahs by the early settlers) migrated into Pennsylvania in 1698. The Shawnee came by invitation of the Delaware after being driven from South Carolina by the English. William Penn and the Five Nations entered into a firm treaty of peace and friendship with them in 1701, giving them permission to settle among the Susquehannocks on the Susquehanna River.[5]

The Shawnee were one of the last tribes to take up residence in the province, becoming a major factor with the Delaware Indians in Pennsylvania's later turbulent years. Then, starting in 1724, to escape the ruinous effects of the constant rum traffic brought in by English traders, the Shawnee joined the Delaware in their westward migration to the Ohio Valley.

THE FRENCH

The French explorer, Samuel de Champlain befriended the "Northern Indians" he had come in contact with in the upper reaches of the St. Lawrence River: the Ottawa and Huron, who were sworn enemies of the Iroquois. However, the fierce reputation of the Iroquois prevented Champlain from moving any further west up the St. Lawrence River, or south into the present state of New York.

Champlain and his men were the first white men many of these Indians had ever seen. The Indians had never seen a musket before, let alone the impression the French made when one of them was fired, which so frightened the Indians that they ran in terror, holding their ears. Once their fears were calmed, and were introduced to what Champlain called "thunder horns," Champlain quickly won their loyalty when he shared his intentions of joining them against the Iroquois.

In July of 1609, two years after the English had settled the town of Jamestown, Virginia, Champlain and a Huron war party, led by Ottawa scouts, pushed southward against the Iroquois. They descended in canoes down the watershed corridor known for centuries between these rival tribes as The Warpath of the Nations. In early America such river systems were the fastest and most effective means of travel, for trade, and for advancing war parties to strike against their enemies. The Warpath of the Nations is a lake-and-river chain that stretches southward from the St. Lawrence River, through the Richelieu River, through Lake Champlain, Lake George,[6] and the Hudson River to the sea at New York. This same watery corridor would be used a century and a half later between the warring French and English.

Paddling their canoes across Lake Champlain, a name Champlain had given in his own honor, Champlain and his Huron sighted an already advancing war party of Mohawk at Ticonderoga. Champlain landed and opened fire on them, killing two of their chiefs. Like the Huron, the Mohawk had never seen or heard such weapons of destruction—they turned and ran away. The Huron then attacked the already fleeing Mohawk, killing many, and then plundered their camp. The Mohawk never forgot what the French had done, and for the next century and a half thousands of Frenchmen would fall victim to Mohawk revenge. The Mohawk remained true to the English until the American Revolution.

81

THE MONTREAL TREATY

The colonies of New France, Quebec and Montreal, had been settled in Iroquois territory. Conflict was inevitable. Violent hostilities between the French and the Iroquois persisted over several years. The French found the Iroquois to be a formidable force and were unable to overthrow them. Recognizing the great power of this Confederacy, the French made an alliance of peace with them at the Montreal Treaty of 1701. In this treaty, the Iroquois gave their word to the French that if hostility ever were to break out between the French and the British, they would remain neutral ("sit on their mats") so long as the French never crossed Iroquois borders. Iroquois borders included all of New York and had reached as far south as Pennsylvania's Susquehanna Valley and west to the "Forks of the Ohio," where the Allegheny and Monongahela Rivers meet.

Peaceful Indian relations were vital to Pennsylvania's Holy Experiment.

Much to the relief of the British, the Montreal Treaty created a buffer against the French. Iroquois borders lay between French occupied Canada and British occupied Pennsylvania. The Iroquois, by armed neutrality, had become the balance of power between the British and the French. The power of the Iroquois came not so much by numbers or by brute force as by their skillful art of diplomacy and by their ability to play the French and English against each other. When the French and Indian War did break out, though France violated the treaty by trespassing into Iroquois territory, true to their end of the agreement, the Iroquois remained neutral.

The French continued to build an ever-bigger presence in the Great Lakes region and longed to fortify and control its position. Slowly, through good trade relations, their standing with the Iroquois began to improve. In 1725, the Iroquois permitted the French to build a trading post on the Niagara River, between Lakes Erie and Ontario. The Iroquois specified, however, that under no uncertain terms was it to be a fortification. The French agreed to the terms but only in pretense. They built a fort anyway while successfully masquerading it as a trading post. Its construction was completed in 1726 and the French referred to it as the "House of Peace." The French now had a fixed position at Niagara, and controlled the gateway to the west. The following year, the

British countered this measure with the building of Fort Oswego on the shore of Lake Ontario, 150 miles to the east. The Iroquois began to sense a threat to their dominion. The tide for conflict was rising.

A NEW "GO-BETWEEN" FOR PENNSYLVANIA

Peaceful Indian relations were vital to Pennsylvania's Holy Experiment. Nonetheless, those relations took a disastrous turn. Now that William Penn was gone, the Delaware and Shawnee lay at the mercy of a new administration. It was a critical juncture for the English and Indian alike. The Delaware needed the English to remember and honor the covenants they had made together. Likewise, Pennsylvania was also recognizing the need for better communications, and needed someone to act as a "go-between," or mediator. This, unfortunately, forever changed the way Pennsylvanians would relate to their Native brothers.

Conrad Weiser, a German immigrant in the New World, was chosen. Weiser had lived with the Mohawks for eight months in 1712 and had become "an adopted son of the Mohawk Nation." He had learned the Iroquois language and happened to be at the right place at the right time to become the official colonial ambassador and interpreter between the Indian Nations of Pennsylvania and the Pennsylvania government. He was in attendance as an interpreter at all the significant treaties between Pennsylvania and the Indians from 1731 until his death in 1760.[7]

Conrad Weiser was significantly used in setting the tone of Indian policy in Colonial Pennsylvania. Being an adoptive son of the Mohawk people, Weiser was a supporter of the Confederation of the Iroquois. Weiser cared little for the Delaware and Shawnee, favoring rather a future league of prominence between the Iroquois and Pennsylvania.

THE BREAK IN PEACE FOR THE DELAWARE

In 1727, the Great Council of the Six Nations appointed Shikellamy, an Oneida chief of the Iroquois, as the vicegerent (deputy) over the Forks of the Susquehanna. From his residence at Shamokin, Shikellamy was to conserve Iroquois interests and to keep a watchful eye on the remaining Delaware and Shawnee in that region. When the Shawnee moved west into the far reaches of the province, Pennsylvania became fearful they might yield to the influence of the French Canadian traders, and made attempts in the autumn of 1731 to persuade them to come back and live once again among the Conestoga. Pennsylvania had set aside a tract of land for them called the Conodoguinet Manor on the west side of the Susquehanna River between the Conodoguinet and Yellow Breeches Creeks. But the Shawnee refused to come back.

Pennsylvania refused to recognize the Delaware's right to sell or keep any of their own lands, making them merely tenants on land that was once theirs.

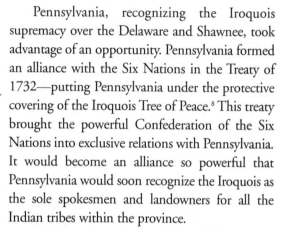

Pennsylvania, recognizing the Iroquois supremacy over the Delaware and Shawnee, took advantage of an opportunity. Pennsylvania formed an alliance with the Six Nations in the Treaty of 1732—putting Pennsylvania under the protective covering of the Iroquois Tree of Peace.[8] This treaty brought the powerful Confederation of the Six Nations into exclusive relations with Pennsylvania. It would become an alliance so powerful that Pennsylvania would soon recognize the Iroquois as the sole spokesmen and landowners for all the Indian tribes within the province.

Coming under the Iroquois Tree of Peace put Pennsylvania in a special relationship with the Iroquois. Along with New York, and other tribes who had come within Iroquois jurisdiction, Pennsylvania became the newest member of the Covenant Chain.[9]

Pennsylvania's treaty of friendship with the Iroquois prevented an all out war between them (the British) and this powerful and advancing confederation. Pennsylvania was very careful not to offend the Iroquois. The balance of power between Great Britain and France in the New World still remained in question. If the Iroquois were to join forces with France, British possession in the New World, as we know it, could have been suddenly limited or even become nonexistent.

THE SUBJUGATION OF THE DELAWARE

Knowing the Iroquois supremacy over the Delaware and Shawnee, Pennsylvania desired the Six Nations to do what Pennsylvania couldn't—persuade the Delaware and Shawnee to move back east among English settlements once again and away from the French. The Iroquois pressed the Shawnee just short of a confrontation, but were unable to bring them back under the watchful eye of the British.

The Six Nations would later discover and use their new alliance with Pennsylvania to their advantage. They demanded that the Penn brothers deal directly with them regarding the purchase of lands in Pennsylvania. Consequently, the Iroquois alienated the Delaware and Shawnee, as did the English. From this point forward the Iroquois, with the help of Pennsylvania, refused to recognize the Delaware's right to sell or keep any of their own lands, making them merely tenants on land that was once theirs.

The allied relationship of the Iroquois with Pennsylvania brought the just dealings between the Delaware and the Proprietary Government of William Penn to an abrupt and tragic halt. Though the Iroquois held supremacy over the territory by claiming "Right of Conquest" over the Delaware, they were not the primary inhabitants or landholders of Pennsylvania. William Penn never recognized, on the part of the Six Nations, any of their claims, which they were now making, to the original homeland of the Delaware east of the Susquehanna River.

From the first treaty with William Penn, the Delaware had always dealt directly with the Proprietary government regarding the selling of their own lands. From the landing of William Penn, there had never been a single break in the peace between the Delaware and the English in the province. Now, to the humiliation of the Delaware, the Iroquois, instead of the Delaware, occupied the seat of honor at all the Councils with the province. Because of this condition and neglect from the provincial authorities, which placed them further into the shadows, the Delaware and Shawnee became more ready to listen to the French traders who were coming among them in ever increasing numbers.

THE TREATY OF 1736

The Colonial Authorities of Pennsylvania were anxious to confirm the alliance of 1732 between them and the Great Council of the Six Nations. In October 1736, a conference was organized in Philadelphia under the instigation of Shikellamy and Conrad Weiser. This treaty, attended by one hundred chiefs of the Iroquois Confederation, was the largest delegation ever to appear in Philadelphia at any one-treaty conference. Together, Weiser and Shikellamy were able to secure the signing of two deeds between the Six Nations and Pennsylvania; the first on October 11, and the second on October 25, 1736.

After the signing of these two treaties, the Delaware would never again be treated with honor and dignity as they had been by their friend William Penn. Until the Proprietors of the province broke the terms of the *Great Treaty* at Shackamaxon between William Penn and the Delaware, the Delaware had kept the treaty to the letter. Now their entire world would be turned upside down as Pennsylvania began to disinherit its brothers, the Delaware.

THE FIRST DEED

The first was a deed (dated October 11, 1736), to all the lands on both sides of the Susquehanna, extending as far east as the heads of the streams running into the Susquehanna, as far west "as the setting sun" (afterwards interpreted by the Indians to mean as far as the crest of the Allegheny Mountains), as far south as the mouth of the Susquehanna, and as far north as the Blue, Kittatinny, or Endless Mountains.[10]

At this treaty in Philadelphia, the Iroquois reminded the Colonial Authorities of Pennsylvania that they had only deeded the lands along the Susquehanna River to Governor Dongan in trust and did not release any control or right to the land. Recognizing their rightful title to these lands and wanting to keep peace, Pennsylvania gave the deed for these lands back to the Iroquois. The Iroquois then turned and sold the deed to Pennsylvania. It was a diplomatic show of power for the Iroquois, but for the Delaware and Shawnee—this action brought about their immediate and final dispossession in the Susquehanna River Valley.

Ironically, Pennsylvania ended up paying for the Susquehanna lands four times: first, when William Penn purchased them from the Susquehannocks, secondly, from Governor Dongan of New York, thirdly, from the Iroquois, and now a fourth time when Pennsylvania paid the Iroquois again at this treaty in Philadelphia on October 11, 1736.

The sale of the Susquehanna lands greatly offended the Shawnees. When this tribe came to Pennsylvania, they were given permission by the Iroquois to live on these lands. Therefore, when the Shawnees learned of the treaty of 1736, they sent one hundred and thirty of their leaders with a belt to the French, saying; 'Our lands have been sold from under our feet; may we come and live with you?' The French readily consented, and offered to come and meet them with provisions.[11]

THE SECOND DEED

On October 25th, just two weeks after the signing of the deed of the Susquehanna lands, when most of the influential deputies of the Iroquois had left Philadelphia, and after those who remained, with the help of English Whiskey, had been drinking heavily, another deed was drawn up embracing all the Six Nations' claim to lands within Pennsylvania "beginning eastward on the River Delaware, as far northward as the ridge or chain of Endless Mountains as they cross ye country of Pennsylvania, from eastward to the West." This deed established a precedent for an Iroquois claim to all the lands owned by the Delaware Indians, and was the cause, as we shall see, of greatly embittering the Delawares.[12]

Walton[13] very truly says of this treaty and of the second deed: 'Weiser helped Shikellamy sow the seed which drenched Pennsylvania in blood from 1755 to 1764. In permitting this second deed Pennsylvania started that series of events with the Delawares which cost her one of the most remarkable Indian invasions in colonial history. And at the same time by securing this and thus conciliating the Iroquois and holding the key to their future attitude, Weiser and the proprietary made a future nation possible. Pennsylvania suffered that a nation might live. She brought upon herself after many years a Delaware war, but escaped a Six Nations war, a French alliance with the Iroquois, and the threatening possibility of the destruction of all the English colonies on the coast.'[14]

The purchase of these Delaware lands[15] from the Iroquois marked the beginning of a great and tragic change in the Indian policy of Pennsylvania.

Now they (the Delaware) were put in the background and could not sell a foot of their own land without the permission of the Iroquois. We can possibly realize what this meant to the proud chiefs, who remembered the days when the Penns treated them with respect, as the rightful owners of the lands upon which their ancestors had lived for countless generations, to suddenly discover that they did not have a right to a foot of the ground upon which they lived, and that without any warning whatever, the Iroquois could sell the lands to which they had moved when they left their villages on the Delaware River.[16]

CHRONOLOGICAL TABLE

1570	The Five Nations or The League of the Iroquois formed by the Mohawk chief, Hiawatha.
1609	July 29. The Huron and Ottawa, led by Champlain, attack the Mohawk at Ticonderoga, killing two of their chiefs.
1677	March 13. Treaty of Shackamaxon where the Susquehannocks suffer great defeat at the hands of the Five Nations who in turn claim all the Susquehanna lands.
1679	Governor of New York, Thomas Dongan, convinces the Iroquois to release the Susquehanna lands into his trust.
1683	September 10. William Penn purchases the Susquehanna lands from the Susquehannock or, Conestoga Indians.
1696	January 13. William Penn purchases the Susquehanna lands from Governor Thomas Dongan.
1698	The Shawnee arrive in Pennsylvania by invitation of the Delaware.
1700	September 13. Treaty between William Penn and the Susquehannock who ratify the title of Dongan's deed to Penn.
1701	(1) William Penn makes a treaty with Shawnees, Conoy, Susquehannock and the Five Nations welcoming the Shawnee to friendly relations with Pennsylvania.

(2) The French make a treaty with the Five Nations called the Montreal Treaty of 1701.

1712   Conrad Weiser lives with the Mohawk, learns their language and becomes an adopted son of the tribe.

1718   (1) July 30. William Penn dies at seventy-four. His wife Hannah assumes proprietary rights over Pennsylvania.

(2) The Delaware begin their westward migration to the Susquehanna River.

1722   Tuscarora admitted as the sixth member of the Iroquois Confederation.

1724-1727   The Delaware and Shawnee begin westward migration into the upper Susquehanna, Allegheny and Ohio Rivers.

1726   (1) The French build Fort Niagara on the Niagara River.

(2) December 20. Hannah dies and her and Penn's three sons, John, Richard and Thomas inherit the Proprietorship.

1727   (1) The British build Fort Oswego on the shore of Lake Ontario.

(2) Shikellamy, the Oneida chief, is sent as the vicegerent of the Six Nations to the Forks of the Susquehanna.

(3) Autumn - A tract of land on the west side of the Susquehanna River between the Conodoguinet and Yellow Breeches Creeks, called the Manor of Conodoguinet, was offered to the Shawnee to entice them to move away from the French back to the Susquehanna.

1731   December 10. Conrad Weiser comes into relations with the Colonial authorities of Pennsylvania as their interpreter between them and the Indian nations.

1732   August 23-September 2. Treaty at Philadelphia where the Iroquois enter into an alliance with Pennsylvania.

1734   Iroquois send message to the Delaware and Shawnee on the Ohio to return to the Susquehanna.

1736   (1) October 11. Treaty in which Pennsylvania purchases Susquehanna and Delaware lands from the Iroquois, greatly offending the Shawnee.

(2) October 25. A treaty signed in Philadelphia by the Iroquois and Pennsylvania recognizing the Iroquois claim to all the Delaware lands in Pennsylvania, greatly offending the Delaware.

ENDNOTES

1. Conestoga, the Indian town visited by William Penn in 1701, was the central seat of the Susquehannocks for generations. The town was located about four miles southwest of Millersville, Lancaster County, on State Route 3017 (Safe Harbor Road) at Indian Marker Road. A monument erected by the Pennsylvania Historical and Museum Commission and the Lancaster County Historical Society now stands marking the site of this historic Indian town.

2. Shamokin was located at the present site of Sunbury, Pennsylvania. Shamokin would remain as the Delaware's principle capitol until 1755 just before the outbreak of The French and Indian War.

3. Present Syracuse, New York.

4. Wallace, Paul A. W., *Indians in Pennsylvania*, (Commonwealth of Pennsylvania, The Pennsylvania Historical and Museum Commission, Harrisburg, PA, 1993), pp. 88-89.

5. This site has been historically established in or near present New Cumberland.

6. A French Roman-Catholic missionary, Isaac Jocques, who died a martyr's death at the hands of the Mohawk in 1646, had previously named Lake George, Lac St. Sacrement,. William Johnson, an Irish trader and interpreter amongst the Iroquois, and friend of the Mohawk, upon arriving on the lake in 1755, renamed the body of water Lake George, in the name of England.

7. The home of Conrad Weiser, built about 1732, is still standing and can be found in "Conrad Weiser Memorial Park" one mile east of Womelsdorf, PA.

8. Iroquois Legend tells that "The Tree of Peace was seen as a great white pine 'rising to meet the sun' (the Eye of the Creator), with branches representing the law and white (i. e., living) roots extending to the Four Quarters of the earth so that men everywhere might be able to trace peace to its source. Above the tree was the Eagle That Sees Afar, symbol of 'preparedness,' watching the horizon to warn peace-loving people of approaching danger." Wallace, Paul A. W., *Indians in Pennsylvania*, (Commonwealth of Pennsylvania, The Pennsylvania Historical and Museum Commission, Harrisburg, PA, 1993), pp. 94-95.

9. The Covenant Chain was "an interlinked set of alliances of British colonies and Indian tribes. In this confederation, New York and the Iroquois League acted as a sort of steering committee with New York supervising colonial negotiators while the Iroquois spoke in behalf of most of the tribes." Jennings, Francis, *Empire Of Fortune: Crowns, colonies, and Tribes in the Seven Years War in America*, (W. W. Norton & Company, New York, N. Y., London, 1988), p. 28.

10. Sipe, C. Hale, *The Indian Wars of Pennsylvania*, (originally published, Harrisburg, PA, 1931., reprinted, Gateway Press, Baltimore, MD, for Wennawoods Publishing, Lewisburg, PA, 1995), p. 106.

11. *Ibid.*, pp. 107-108.

12. *Ibid.*, p. 108.

13. Walton, Joseph S., author of, *Conrad Weiser and the Indian Policy of Colonial Pennsylvania*, (Philadelphia, George W. Jacob and Company, 1900).

14. Donehoo, Dr. George P., *Pennsylvania: A History, Five Vols.*, (Lewis Historical Publishing Company, Inc., New York, Chicago, 1926), p. 341.

15. "The two deeds gotten from the Iroquois at the treaty of 1736 embraced the counties of York, Adams, and Cumberland, that part of Franklin, Dauphin, and Lebanon southeast of the Blue or Kittatinny Mountains, and that part of Berks, Lehigh, and Northampton not already possessed." Sipe, C. Hale, *The Indian Wars of Pennsylvania*, (originally published, Harrisburg, PA, 1931., reprinted, Gateway Press, Baltimore, MD, for Wennawoods Publishing, Lewisburg, PA, 1995), pp. 109-110.

16. Donehoo, Dr. George P., *Indian Villages and Place Names in Pennsylvania*, (Gateway Press, Baltimore, MD, 1995), p. 58.

7

THE DISGRACE OF THE COLONIES

Cursed is the man who moves his neighbor's boundary stone.

Deuteronomy 27:17

The event you are about to read is one of the most disgraceful legacies of broken trust the Penn brothers left to the memory of their father, William Penn, and deserves its own chapter. It has special meaning to me because of what I believe the Lord allowed Lorrie and me to glean from His heart unexpectedly in the winter of 1997. It began with Lorrie's last minute searching for a breeder for our pet dog. Finding the right male to father our puppies led Lorrie to eastern Pennsylvania. The breeder was located in the Pocono Mountains. Little did either of us know how this unrelated event would lead us further into our conviction that God wants to do something here in Pennsylvania.

93

After the initial formalities and arrangements were established on the phone, we were on our way to increasing the number in our family. As we neared our destination and started our ascent of the Poconos, both Lorrie and I fell quiet. Simultaneously and without each other's knowledge, we began to experience a sense of brokenness. Lorrie finally broke the stillness with, *"We need to pray,"* neither of us knowing how to pray through the mysterious heaviness we were encountering.

Arriving at the breeders, we shrugged off whatever "that" was and made our acquaintances. We knew that effective intercession begins by receiving God's heart and praying his prayers, even when details are unclear at the moment one is burdened to pray. This was one of those times. We had no clue until later that day what it all might mean.

Why am I here and they are not?

After a brief visit, and leaving our dog, we were directed by the breeder to the nearby town of Jim Thorpe for a bite to eat in a quaint atmosphere. Surprisingly, the brokenness we experienced driving up returned while at one of Jim Thorpe's historic hotels.

Over lunch we discussed the history of Pennsylvania and the development of this book. We learned through our waitress that Jim Thorpe was formerly an area called Mauch (mock) Chunk by the Delaware. Neither of us could shake the grief we felt. With tears streaming down our faces, we considered the tragic loss to the Native Americans. Lorrie tried to put words on the intercession she made while driving up the mountain. She related a sense of grave conviction over the advantage we had in enjoying the beauty that surrounded us, somehow feeling that we didn't belong, like we were trespassing. She asked, *"Why am I here and they* (the Indians) *are not?"* She said it felt like being on a honeymoon *without* your spouse.

By now, we were inclined to believe the Lord was revealing His heart. I suggested that perhaps what we were experiencing could possibly have something to do with our geographic location, as extraordinary as it sounded. I seemed to recall that a treaty called "The Walking Purchase" took place somewhere around Jim Thorpe but wasn't really sure. We were baffled but not surprised. We finished our lunch, explored the town a bit and were soon on our way home. One more thing that puzzled us was how peculiar it was that as soon as we left the area we returned to our simple, unhampered selves not able to work up a single tear if we tried. We were curious. We were glad to be together. Who would believe such a story? I had to learn more!

As we arrived home I began to research the history of the area and to look at some maps. I learned that our intercessory perceptions had not betrayed us. I was glad not to have known more before we traveled to the Pocono's. To us, it was another confirmation helping us in learning to trust the Holy Spirit as He leads. We discovered that the town of Jim Thorpe was the end of a deceitful "walk" for the acquisition of the last of the ancestral lands of the Delaware. It is notoriously called The Walking Purchase. This chapter is that story.

THE WALKING PURCHASE

After 1735 the proprietary Penn family began to sell off unceded Indian lands (land where title had not been transferred) in the upper Delaware Valley, and to make these transactions seem legal they contrived the notorious Walking Purchase. The Penn brothers needed to sell much land in order to escape their creditors, but they lacked assets with which to purchase Delaware land for resale. They falsely represented to the Delawares that an old, incomplete, unsigned draft of a deed was a legally binding contract. They exhibited to the unlettered Indians a falsely labeled representation of the lands supposed to be conveyed by the spurious deed dated August 30, 1686. Vaguely, the deed stipulated that the ceded lands were to be bounded by a walk of a day and a half from the stipulated starting point, but did not specify the direction of the walk. After considerable argument, innumerable threats and strong pressures, the chiefs of the Delawares finally agreed to confirm the 1686 deed. On August 25, 1737, they signed what later became known as the fraudulent Walking Purchase Deed.[1]

This agreement was virtually a deed of release of the lands claimed to have been granted by the deed of August 30, 1686. We shall now see how well Thomas Penn and his associates were prepared for the "walk" and how it was accomplished:

The 19th day of September, 1737, was the day appointed for the "walk." It was agreed that the starting point should be a chestnut tree standing a little above the present site of Wrightstown,[2] Bucks County. The persons employed by the Colonial Authorities to perform the walk, after the Proprietaries had advertised for the most expert walkers in the Province, were athletes famous for their abilities as fast walkers; and, as an inducement for their making this walk a supreme test of their abilities, a compensation of five pounds in money and 500 acres of land was offered the one who could go the longest distance in the allotted time. Their names were Edward Marshall, a native of Bucks County, a noted chain carrier, hunter and backwoodsman; James Yates, a native of the same county, a tall and agile man, with much speed of foot; and Solomon Jennings also a man of remarkable physique. These men had been hunted out by the Proprietaries' agents as the fastest backwoodsmen in the Province, and as a preliminary measure, they had been taken over the ground before, spending some nine days, during which their route was marked off by blazing the trees and clearing away the brush.[3]

'YOU WAS TO WALK'

Two of the white walkers (Yates and Jennings) became so exhausted that they were forced to give up after the first day, (Yates died and Jennings became blind.) but the third walker (Edward Marshall)[4] endured the complete walk which took in about sixty miles. The Indian signatories intended the bound to be an ordinary walk, which would have taken a man about twenty-five or thirty miles in a day and a half, not a pace that caused the Indian observers to quit, one saying in disgust, 'You Run, that's not fair, you was to Walk.'[5]

In the agreement with Thomas Penn to have the bounds of the alleged deed made by a walk, the Delawares believed that as far as a man could go in a day and a half would not extend beyond the Lehigh Hills, or about thirty miles from the place of beginning; but the crafty and unprincipled Colonial Authorities had laid their plans to extend the walk to such a point as to include the land in the Forks of the Delaware and also farther up that river, it being their desire to obtain, if possible, the possession of that desirable tract of land along the Delaware River above the blue Mountains, called the "Minisink Lands." Having…reached a point more than thirty miles farther to the northwestward than the Delawares had anticipated, the Colonial Authorities now proceeded to draw a line from the end of the walk to the Delaware River. The alleged deed did not describe the course that the line should take from the end of the walk to the river; but any fair-minded person would assume that it should follow the shortest distance between these two places. However, the agent of the Proprietaries, instead of running the line by the nearest course to the Delaware, ran it northeastward across the country so as to strike the river near the mouth of the Lackawaxen, which flows into the Delaware River in the northern part of Pike county. The extent of this line was sixty-six miles. The territory as thus measured was in the shape of a great triangle whose base was the Delaware River and whose apex[6] was the end of the walk, and included the northern part of Bucks, almost all of Northampton, and a portion of Pike, Carbon, and Monroe Counties. This fraudulent measurement thus took in all the Minisink Lands and many thousand acres more than if the line had been run by the nearest course from the end of the walk to the Delaware.[7]

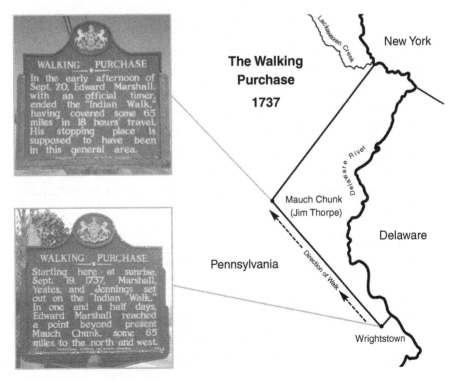

Promptly thereafter the so-called deed disappeared, leaving in its wake what the Penns called a copy.

This 1737 deed completed the acquisition of all the Delaware's ancestral lands in Pennsylvania and has been called "the disgrace of the Colonies." This treaty was one of the chief causes of the alienation of the Delaware and of their taking up arms, seventeen years later, against the colony during the French and Indian War. During The French and Indian War many German settlers, who had settled within the bounds of The Walking Purchase, lost their lives as a consequence of this fraudulent and deceptive act.

> Feeling frustrated and tricked, the Delawares refused to move and threatened to meet any intruders on their lands with force. Meanwhile, Thomas Penn (Proprietor) released a flood of patents to new buyers, and by 1740 more than a hundred white families were settled in the territory included in the walk.[8]

THE GREAT AWAKENING

As the Walking Purchase began scouring an indelible mark on the hearts of the Delaware, something else developed in the colonies of America—a spiritual renewal. We call it The Great Awakening and for the next two decades, starting in 1739, The Great Awakening took the colonies by storm. Through the preaching of George Whitefield and Jonathan Edwards hundreds of thousands were coming to the Lord in this great revival that swept up and down the East Coast from Georgia to Massachusetts. The affects of George Whitefield's preaching in Philadelphia were so irrefutable that even Benjamin Franklin[9] gave it legitimacy when he said,

> 'It seem'd as if all the world were growing religious, so that one could not walk thro' the town in an evening without hearing psalms sung.'[10]

It was the Moravians, riding on the wave of this Great Awakening, who ventured off the beaten path and into the backwoods to minister to the Indians. But the question remained, *"Could the Great Awakening or the Moravians curb the continual tide of injustices that roared against the Indians?"*

BETHLEHEM AND "TENTS OF GRACE"

In 1740, the Moravians, German forerunners of the United Brethren, had established a mission to the Mohican Indians at Shekomeko in the province of New York. The Moravians had come to the Mohicans in the same spirit as William Penn had to the Delaware: not to drive away their culture but to evangelize within it. The Moravians, like William Penn, had an honest faith in God's ability, and a desire to shine light into the heart of the Indians. The Moravians understood the Indians' point of view and worked with them, not through colonialism, absorption, condescension or by trying to make white men of them but through acceptance and love. This acceptance caused the Indians to listen to their message.

In December 1741, the Moravians settled in Pennsylvania and established the town of Bethlehem on the banks of the Lehigh River. At a conference in August 1742, the Moravian founder, German Count Nikolaus Ludwig von Zinzendorf, sought and was given permission from the great Iroquois chief, Canassatego, to build their missions among the Indians in Pennsylvania.

> *The Moravians, like William Penn, had an honest faith in God's ability and desire to shine light into the heart of the Indian.*

Throughout the 1740's the success of the Moravians among the Pennsylvania Indians began to spread. The Moravians began to build their missions amongst the ever-increasing population of Indian converts. In 1746, not far from Bethlehem, where Mahoning Creek empties into the Lehigh River, the Moravians established the town of Gnadenhutten,[11] meaning "Tents of Grace." Built for Mohican and Delaware converts, the town was complete with log houses, streets, gardens, farms and orchards. There was also a church and a school, where reading, writing, music, certain trades, and the latest farming methods were taught. A solution to the race problem and the best hope for peace was beginning to shed light.

The Moravians' success in establishing their missions throughout Pennsylvania and introducing the Christian faith to many of the Delaware and other Indians of Pennsylvania became one of the better chapters in the history of the Commonwealth.

THE TREATY OF 1742

Meanwhile, the Walking Purchase still lingered as a threat to the peace being established by the Moravian missionaries. The Colonial Authorities sent a message to the Six Nations asking them to force the Delaware to relinquish the lands acquired within the "Walk." The Six Nations agreed, and sent their deputies to Philadelphia. This and other matters were taken up in the Treaty of July 1742.

Once in Philadelphia, what Thomas Penn failed to tell the delegation of the Six Nations, whether intentional or by accident we do not know, was that during the deliberations of the Walking Purchase the Delaware had requested to remain on the land that had just been sold. In persuading the Delaware to confirm the deeds covered by the Walking Purchase, Thomas Penn promised the Delaware that they would not have to leave the lands acquired within the "Walk." However, upon the arrival of the Six Nations, Canassatego severely chastised the Delaware with a stinging speech ordering them to remove themselves off the land, hurling insults that were undeserved and unexpected.

'But how came you to take upon you to sell land at all? We conquered you; we made women of you; you know you are women and can no more sell land than women.'[12]

The Iroquois delegate then walked over, grabbed "King Nutimus," the Delaware chief of the Munsee Clan, by the hair, led him to the door and forcefully sent him out of the room only to proceed with the meeting as if nothing had happened.

Canassatego also took the opportunity during this treaty to complain about the whites that were daily settling on Indian lands north of the Kittochtinny Hills (Kittatinny, or Blue Mountains). In particular, German squatters were settling along the banks of the Juniata River and Scotch-Irish were settling in the valley's of what is now Juniata, Perry and Fulton Counties. Governor Thomas had the Germans removed the following year but the Scotch-Irish were not removed until 1750. Their cabins were then burned to the ground to prevent future settlements.[13]

However, as the Treaty of 1742 was made, even Canassatego began to sense the discrepancy regarding the value of the land and what the white man gave them in exchange. Though he had just been instrumental in ousting the Delaware, his misgivings about his part in the process were mounting. Canassatego addressed the Colonial Authorities with many words but none so powerful as these:

> 'We know our lands are now become more Valuable. The white People think we don't know their Value but we are sensible that the Land is Everlasting and the few Goods we receive for it are soon Worn out and gone.'[14]

THE DELAWARE STAND ALONE

Regardless of Canassatego's concerns, the Delaware now stood alone with no one on their side.

> The poor fellows (Nutimus and his company), in great and silent grief, went directly home, collected their families and goods, and, burning their cabins to signify they were to never to return, marched reluctantly to their new homes.
>
> Shortly after the treaty of 1742, the Delawares of the Munsee Clan left the bounds of the "Walking Purchase" and the beautiful river bearing their name, and began their march toward the setting sun.[15]

In hopes of removing themselves from the ever pressing white settlers and the power and control of the Iroquois, Nutimus and his people began their westward migration into the regions of the Ohio Valley. The Delaware realized that the good old days of William Penn, whom they called, "that great and good man," were over. But, as we shall soon see, the troubles for the Delaware had only just begun.

> The dispossessed Indians moved west to the Allegheny, Monongahela, and upper Ohio river watersheds—collectively known as "the Ohio country"—nursing deep resentments against Euro-Americans in general and the Pennsylvania government in particular.[16]

THE LANCASTER TREATY OF 1748

The Pennsylvania Provincial Council realized that something had to be done to win back the alienated tribes of the Delaware and Shawnee, else they would have a larger problem with France. The Councils feared the relentless influence the French traders on the Ohio were imposing upon these tribes. The English held a council to form another treaty, in Lancaster, Pennsylvania, from July 19 through the 25, 1748. Present were delegates from the Six Nations, Shawnee, Delaware, Miami, and Nanticoke tribes.

Scarouady, a friendly and wise Oneida chief favored among the English, who was also the Iroquois appointee given charge of all matters on the Ohio relating to the Shawnee, rebuked the Shawnee for removing themselves to the Ohio. Hearing Scarouady's emotional words caused many of the Shawnee to return from the Ohio, seeking forgiveness for leaving.

The Pennsylvania Provincial Council realized that something had to be done to win back the alienated tribes of the Delaware and Shawnee.

Taming Buck, a Shawnee chief, confessed:

'We have been a foolish people, and have acted wrong, altho the sun shone bright and showed us very clearly what was our duty. We are sorry for what we have done, and promise better behaviour in the future.'[17]

Taming Buck then presented to the commissioners a copy of the treaty that had been made between them (the Shawnee) and William Penn in 1701, which friendship had also been renewed in 1739. As he presented the paper, he said,

'We produce to you a Certificate of the renewal of our Friendship in 1739, by the Proprietor and Governor. Be pleased to sign it afresh, that it may appear to the world we are now admitted to your Friendship, & all former Crimes are buried & entirely forgot.'[18]

But the English did not reaffirm the friendship. Regarding this incident Donehoo relates:

Then was the time to have forgiven and won back the friendship of the Shawnee and that of the Delaware. But this plea for forgiveness was refused and the treaty was not signed.[19]

If this had been done, it is doubtful if France could ever have gained a foothold on the Ohio.[20] It certainly would have prevented the fearful defeat of General Braddock in 1755 (see chapter ten), and the darkest period in Pennsylvania's history which followed this disaster. The effect of this treatment of the Shawnee at Lancaster, in 1748, was felt in many a white settlement along the frontiers in the years that followed. Many a Shawnee warrior yelled his wild "death-hallo" on the hills of Pennsylvania, and many a log cabin was left a smouldering ruin because of the blunders which were made at Lancaster in 1748. Walton has well said (in his *Conrad Weiser and the Indian Policy of Colonial Pennsylvania*, page 127). 'In this affair Conrad Weiser again permitted seed to be sown which in a few years led the Shawnee into a French alliance and steeped Western Pennsylvania in blood.'[21]

CHRONOLOGICAL TABLE

1737	(1) August 25. The Delaware are manipulated to sign the Walking Purchase deed.
	(2) September 19. The fraudulent Walking Purchase removes the Munsee Clan of the Delaware from the last of their ancestral lands.
1740	More than one hundred settlers receive patents from Thomas Penn to settle within the bounds of the Walking Purchase.
1741	December. Moravians establish town of Bethlehem along the Lehigh River.
1742	(1) July. Treaty in Philadelphia where the Iroquois chief, Canassatego, orders the Delaware of the Munsee Clan to remove themselves from the bounds of the Walking Purchase.
	(2) August. Count Zinzendorf gains permission from Iroquois chief Cannasatego to build Moravian missions in Pennsylvania.
1748	July 19-25. Treaty at Lancaster where Scarouady, the Oneida chief, rebukes the Shawnee for removing to the Ohio. The Shawnee seek forgiveness from Pennsylvania, but none was given.

ENDNOTES

1. Jennings, Francis, *Empire Of Fortune: Crowns, colonies, and Tribes in the Seven Years War in America*, (W. W. Norton & Company, New York, N. Y., London, 1988), p. 25.

2. The Pennsylvania Historical and Museum Commission have placed a Historical Marker at the beginning and ending of the Walking Purchase. The first marker can be found at the beginning of the walk on State Highway 413 in Wrightstown, northeast of Philadelphia.

3. Sipe, C. Hale, *The Indian Wars of Pennsylvania*, (originally published, Harrisburg, PA, 1931., reprinted, Gateway Press, Baltimore, MD, for Wennawoods Publishing, Lewisburg, PA, 1995), pp. 111-112.

4. "The Munsee Clan of Delaware never forgave Edward Marshall for his part in the 'Walking Purchase.' " Sipe, C. Hale, *The Indian Wars of Pennsylvania*, (originally published, Harrisburg, PA, 1931., reprinted, Gateway Press, Baltimore, MD, for Wennawoods Publishing, Lewisburg, PA, 1995), p. 113.

5. Weslager, C. A., *The Delaware Indians A History*, (Rutgers University Press, New Brunswick, New Jersey, 1972), p. 189.

6. The apex, or end of the walk, was at or about the present town of Jim Thorpe. The second Historical Marker, noting the end of the walk, can be found two miles northeast of Jim Thorpe on State Highway 903.

7. Sipe, C. Hale, *The Indian Wars of Pennsylvania*, (originally published, Harrisburg, PA, 1931., reprinted, Gateway Press, Baltimore, MD, for Wennawoods Publishing, Lewisburg, PA, 1995), pp. 112-113.

8. Weslager, C. A., *The Delaware Indians A History*, (Rutgers University Press, New Brunswick, New Jersey, 1972), p. 190.

9. Benjamin Franklin arrived in Pennsylvania at the age of seventeen in 1723 and settled in Philadelphia.

10. Packer, J. I., "The Startling Puritan," p. 40, *Christian History* magazine, Issue 38 (vol. XII, No. 2), Des Moines, IA, 1993.

11. The Pennsylvania Historical and Museum Commission has erected a marker for Gnadenhutten on Pennsylvania State Highway 443 on the South end of Lehighton, PA.

12. Sipe, C. Hale, *The Indian Wars of Pennsylvania*, (originally published, Harrisburg, PA, 1931., reprinted, Gateway Press, Baltimore, MD, for Wennawoods Publishing, Lewisburg, PA, 1995), p. 115.

13. In the north east corner of Fulton County this area is called Burnt Cabins.

14. Wallace, Paul A. W., *Conrad Weiser: Friend of Colonist and Mohawk*, (originally published, Philadelphia, PA, 1945., reprinted, Gateway Press, Inc., Baltimore, MD, for Wennawoods Publishing, Lewisburg, PA, 1945), p. 128.

15. Sipe, C. Hale, *The Indian Wars of Pennsylvania*, (originally published, Harrisburg, PA, 1931., reprinted, Gateway Press, Baltimore, MD, for Wennawoods Publishing, Lewisburg, PA, 1995), p. 116.

16. Downey, Dennis B., and Francis J. Bremer, *A Guide to the History of Pennsylvania*, (Greenwood Press, Westport, Connecticut, London, 1993), p. 38.

17. Donehoo, Dr. George P., *Pennsylvania: A History, Five Vols.*, (Lewis Historical Publishing Company, Inc., New York, Chicago, 1926), p. 627.

18. *Ibid.*, p. 639.

19. *Ibid.*, p. 627.

20. The reason France would never have gained a foothold on the Ohio was that if Pennsylvania had forgiven the Shawnee when they had been given the opportunity, the Shawnee would have stayed faithful and loyal to the English, and may have assisted the English in resisting the French Invasion.

21. Donehoo, Dr. George P., *Pennsylvania: A History, Five Vols.*, (Lewis Historical Publishing Company, Inc., New York, Chicago, 1926), p. 628.

8

THE FRENCH MAKE
THEIR MOVE

I tell you, in plain words, you must go off this land. You say you have strong body, a strong neck, and a strong voice, that when you speak all the Indians must hear you. It is true, you are a strong body, and ours is but weak, yet we are not afraid of you. We forbid you to come any further; turn back to the place from whence you came.

—Tanacharison

In the summer of 1753, Great Britain was greatly alarmed when France trespassed into Iroquois territory (they had promised not to). Eager to secure a foothold in the "Ohio Country," two thousand French regulars had crossed over from Lake Ontario onto Lake Erie via the Niagara River and into Pennsylvania, the very same land the Delaware had just been forced to settle. They proceeded to build two forts in the northwest corner of the colony; Presque' Isle, located on the shore of Lake Erie, and Fort LeBoeuf,[1] fifteen miles south on French Creek. A third post, Fort Machault, was built in the autumn at the Delaware village of Venango, where French Creek empties into the Allegheny River.[2]

Ignoring the agreement of peace attained by the Treaty of Aix-la-Chappelle, which ended King George's War in 1748, the French provoked the British by this insolent show for dominance. The result of this bold move into Pennsylvania would soon result in France and Britain's fourth and bloodiest war of all, The French and Indian War.

THE PLEA AT CARLISLE

Upon hearing of the French advancement, James Hamilton, Pennsylvania's Lieutenant Governor from 1748-1754, through the consent of the Pennsylvania Assembly, appropriated eight hundred pounds for guns and ammunition to be given to the friendly Indians on the Ohio for their defense against the French invasion. The Indians, to ascertain whether the appropriation was true, sent a delegation of deputies consisting of a number of important chiefs from the Six Nations, Delaware, Shawnee, Twightwees (Miamis, as the French called them) and Owendaets to meet with Governor Hamilton's commissioners (one of whom was Benjamin Franklin). The conference was held in Carlisle,[3] Pennsylvania, from October 1 to 4, 1753.

> A large part of the Assemblies appropriation was to be a present of condolence to the Twightwees on account of the murder of their king, "Old Britain," at his village on the Miami, on June 21, 1752, by a band of Ottawas and Chippewas, led by Charles Langlade, a Frenchman, of Detroit.[4]
>
> The chief (Scarouady) replied that his people could and would not do any public business while the blood of their tribe remained upon their garments, and that 'nothing would wash it unless the presents intended to cover the graves of the departed were actually spread upon the ground before them.'[5]

The presents were soon given and the Twightwees responded with these words:

'The Ottawas, Chippewas, and the French, have struck us. The stroke was heavy, and hard to be borne, for thereby we lost our King, and several of our warriors; but the loss our brethren, the English, suffered, we grieve for most. The love we have had for the English, from our first knowing of them, still continues in our breasts; and we shall ever retain the same ardent affection for them. We cover the graves of the English with this beaver blanket. We mourn for them more than for our own people.'[6]

Many grievances the Indians had were satisfied, including the settling of land beyond the Alleghenies.

During these negotiations it became evident that the French were determined to draw the Indians from all friendship with the English, and that they were entering upon a grand scheme for the possession of a great empire in the North and West.[7]

Most of the Indians, up to that time, had declined the proposals of the French. However, the Indians were still confused.

'If the French own west of the Ohio and the English own east, where do the Indians live?' they asked.[8]

While the rival nations were beginning to quarrel for a prize which belonged to neither of them, the unhappy Indians saw, with alarm and amazement, their lands becoming a bone of contention between rapacious strangers. The first appearance of the French on the Ohio excited the wildest fears in the tribes of that quarter, among whom were those who, disgusted by the encroachments of the Pennsylvanians, had fled to these remote retreats to escape the intrusions of the white men. Scarcely was their fancied asylum gained, when they saw themselves invaded by a host of armed men from Canada. Thus placed between two fires, they knew not which way to turn. There was no union in their councils, and they seemed like a mob of bewildered children. Their native jealousy was roused to its utmost pitch. Many of them thought that the two white nations had conspired to destroy them, and then divide their lands. 'You and the French,' said one of them, a few years afterwards, to an English emissary, 'are like two edges of a pair of shears, and we are the cloth which is cut to pieces between them.'[9]

"THE RUM RUINS US"

During the negotiations at Carlisle, and many times before and after, the Indians requested the Colonial authorities to put an end to the constant traffic of rum and whiskey being brought into their country by the traders. For, said one chief, "The rum ruins us."

As eighteenth-century Indians, the Ohio Delaware, displaced as they were, had become dependent upon white traders for guns, ammunition, cloth, kettles, hoes, knives and other tools that had become essential for living. The English capitalized on this new dependency. The exploitation of the Indians by the English outraged many tribes. Often the only trade good brought to the Indians was rum. The intrusion of this English vice was already beginning to demoralize and corrupt the very fabric of Indian society with starvation, disease and sickness. The traders would intoxicate the Indians in order to deceive them in dishonest trade, whether it were for goods or for land.

Benjamin Franklin regarded the traders as, "the most vicious and abandoned wretches of our nation."[10]

William Penn saw the effects of alcohol on Indians, and as early as 1682 wrote laws prohibiting its trade.[11] Laws were enacted, but the ruthless, unprincipled traders continued unabated, exploiting the weaknesses of Indians, until today, generations later, alcoholism perpetuates itself among Indian Nations in America.

C. Hale Sipe in his book, *The Indian Chiefs of Pennsylvania*, says this about the English traders:

> In a word, the English traders, with few exceptions, were a vile and infamous horde, who, instead of contributing to the betterment of the Indian, corrupted and debauched him.[12]

> Said Governor Dinwiddie of Virginia, in a letter to Governor Hamilton of Pennsylvania, May 21st, 1753: 'The Indian traders, in general, appear to me to be a set of abandoned wretches.'[13]

The Pennsylvania Assembly, in a message to Governor Hamilton, February 27th, 1754, characterized the traders as 'the vilest of our own inhabitants and convicts imported from Great Britain and Ireland.'[14]

THE IROQUOIS RESIST THE FRENCH

During the Carlisle conference, it was learned by the commissioners that the Ohio Indians had received word of the threatened French invasion as early as May of that same year. On September 3, 1753, the Ohio Indians, represented by an Iroquois deputy, gave the French, who were then at Niagara, the first formal objection to their invasion, forbidding them to proceed any further toward the Ohio Valley. It stood within reason that the French should be called on to remember the commitment they had made to the Iroquois at the Montreal Treaty in 1701. When the French did not yield to this first notice, the Indians sent a second to the French that read as follows:

'Father Onontio,

Your children on Ohio are alarmed to hear of your coming so far this way. We at first heard that you came to destroy us. Our women left off planting, and our warriors prepared for war. We have since heard that you came to visit us as friends without design to hurt us, but then we wondered why you came with so strong a body. If you had any cause of complaint, you might have spoke to Onas, or Corlear (meaning the governors of Pennsylvania, and New York) and not come to disturb us here. We have a Fire at Logs-Town, where are the Delawares, and the Shawonese, and Brother Onas; you might have sent deputies there; and said openly what you came about, if you had thought amiss of the English being there; and we invite you to do it now, before you proceed any further.'[15]

The French officer's answer,

'Children,

I find you come to give me an invitation to your Council Fire, with a design, as I suppose, to call me to account for coming, here. I must let you know that my heart is good to you; I mean no hurt to you; I am come by the great King's command, to do you, my children, good.

You seem to think I carry my hatchet under my coat; I always carry it openly, not to strike, you, but those that shall oppose me. I cannot come to your Council Fire, nor can I return, or stay here; I am so heavy a body that the stream will carry me down, and down I shall go, unless you pull off my arm. But this I will tell you, I am commanded to build four strong houses (forts), vix. at Weningo, Mohongialo Forks, Logs-Town, and Beaver Creek, and this I will do. As to what concerns Onas, and Affaragoa (meaning the Governors of Pennsylvania and Virginia) I have spoke to them, and let them know they must go off the land, and I shall speak to them again; if they will not hear me, it is their fault, I will take them by the arm, and throw them over the hills. All the land and waters on this side Allegheny Hills are mine, on the other side theirs; this is agreed on between the two Crowns over the great waters. I do not like your selling your lands to the English; they shall draw you into no more foolish bargains. I will take care of your lands for you, and of you. The English give you no goods but for land, we give you our goods for nothing.'[16]

A THIRD WARNING

A third notice was delivered to the Commander of the French Forts. The Iroquois believed and said to the Commander, "The great Being who lives above has Ordered Us to send Three Messages of Peace before We make War." The Oneida chief, Tanacharison, delivered this third and final message to the French. Tanacharison served alongside Scarouady as the Six Nations vicegerent over the Delaware and others of the Ohio Valley from about 1747. The notice to the French read as follows (This notice being a major topic at the Carlisle meeting):

'Father,

You say you cannot come to our Council Fire at Logs-Town, we therefore now come to you, to know what is in your heart. You remember when you were tired with the war (meaning Queen Anne's War) you of your own accord sent for us, desiring to make peace with us; when we came, you said to us, children, we make a Council Fire for you; we want to talk with you, but we must first eat all with one spoon out of this silver bowl, and all drink out of this silver cup; let us exchange hatchets; let us bury our hatchets in this bottomless hole; and now we will make a plain road to all you countries, so clear that Onontio may sit here and see you all eat and drink out of the bowl and cup, which he has provided for you. Upon this application of yours we consented to make peace; and when the peace was concluded on both sides, you made a solemn declaration, saying, whoever shall hereafter transgress this peace, let the transgressor be chastised with a rod even tho' it be I, your father.

'Now, father, notwithstanding this solemn declaration of yours, you have whipped several of your children; you know best why. Of late you have chastised the Twightwees very severely, without telling us the reason; and now you are come with a strong band on our land, and have, contrary to your engagement, taken up the hatchet without any previous parley. These things are a breach of the peace; they are contrary to your own declarations: Therefore, now I come to forbid you. I will strike over all this land with my rod, let it hurt who it will. I tell you, in plain words, you must go off this land. You say you have strong body, a strong neck, and a strong voice, that when you speak all the Indians must hear you. It is true, you are a strong body, and ours is but weak, yet we are not afraid of you. We forbid you to come any further; turn back to the place from whence you came.'[17]

A VIOLENT TUG-OF-WAR

Before the conference at Carlisle had ended, it was learned that the French had received this third notice, the equivalent of an Iroquois declaration of war, in a very contemptuous manner. The French were not about to back down from an Iroquois threat. More than that, they reasoned that the Indians could be manipulated to their own advantage. If the French could somehow win the favor of the Indians to their supreme cause, they would possess the balance of power in the New World and were pulling all the stops to gain this end.

The English, on the other hand, continued to vacillate on their obligation to the covenant that had brought theirs and the Indian nations together. Future actions of the English would continue to jeopardize and forfeit that relationship, actually helping the French to capitalize on theirs. If the English were to continue to remain in good favor with the Indians, then better measures to protect that relationship would need to be secured.

However, it was becoming evident to the Indians that neither France, nor England, for that matter, had any endearing or sincere compassion for them. The Indians were beginning to see how they were being used to gain what both England and France wanted—their land. The Indians had been reduced to nothing more than mere tokens of war for the land that both these nations desired to possess. Having already been forced from their homes on the Delaware River by the English and now having to prepare to defend their homes against the encroaching French, the Delaware were thrown into the middle of this violent tug-of-war.

Still honoring their covenant with William Penn, the Delaware continued to extend grace to the English, despite past injustices. However, this grace was not without limit. Only nine months after Carlisle, events would ensue that would forever alter the destiny of Pennsylvania and the nation.

CHRONOLOGICAL TABLE

1748-1754	James Hamilton, Lieutenant Governor of Pennsylvania.
1748	Treaty of Aix-la-Chappelle ends King George's War between Great Britain and France.
1753	(1) In the spring and summer the French build Fort Presque' Isle on Lake Erie, and then advance into the valley of the Allegheny and build Fort LeBoeuf. (2) May. Iroquois learn of the French advance. (3) Autumn. The French build Fort Machault, at the Delaware village of Venango, at the confluence of French Creek and the Allegheny. (4) September 3. Iroquois deputy, Tanacharison, forbids French to advance into the region of the Allegheny and Ohio as the territory of the Six Nations. (5) October 1-4. Treaty with the Indians at Carlisle.

ENDNOTES

1. Fort Le Boeuf was located where the present town of Waterford, Pennsylvania, just south of Erie, now stands. Though there remains no traces of the fort today, on the south edge of Waterford, at 123 High St., a visitor center with exhibits relative to the fort's history can be visited.

2. Fort Presque' Isle was located where present Erie, Pennsylvania now stands and Fort Machault is now present Franklin, Pennsylvania.

3. Carlisle had just been established as the Cumberland County Seat, April 1, 1751.

4. Sipe, C. Hale, *The Indian Wars of Pennsylvania*, (originally published, Harrisburg, PA, 1931., reprinted, Gateway Press, Baltimore, MD, for Wennawoods Publishing, Lewisburg, PA, 1995), p. 142.

5. *Ibid.*, p. 143.

6. Boyd, Julian P. ed., *Indian Treaties Printed by Benjamin Franklin*, 1736-1762, (Philadelphia: Historical Society of Pennsylvania, 1938), p. 129.

7. Wing, Rev. Conway P., D. D., *History of Cumberland County*, (James D. Scott, Philadelphia, PA 1879), pp. 39-40.

8. Cornell, William A. & Altland, Millard, *Our Pennsylvania Heritage*, (Penns Valley Publishing, State College, PA, 1956), p. 66.

9. Parkman, Francis, *The Conspiracy of Pontiac*, (Collier Books, New York, Collier - Macmillian LTD., London, 1962), pp. 73-74.

10. Sipe, C. Hale, *The Indian Wars of Pennsylvania*, (originally published, Harrisburg, PA, 1931., reprinted, Gateway Press, Baltimore, MD, for Wennawoods Publishing, Lewisburg, PA, 1995), p. 779.

11. One of the articles written within William Penn's Great Law was the prohibitive sale of any alcohol to Indians, "That no person within this Province doe from hence forth presume to Sell or exchange any Rhum or brandy or any Strong Liquors at any time to any Indian within this Province & if any one shall offend therein ye person convicted Shall for every Such offence pay five pounds." Weslager, C. A., *The Delaware Indians A History*, (Rutgers University Press, New Brunswick, New Jersey, 1972), p. 159.

12. Sipe, C. Hale, *The Indian Chiefs of Pennsylvania*, (originally published, Butler, PA, 1927., reprinted, Gateway Press, Baltimore, MD, for Wennawoods Publishing, Lewisburg, PA, 1995), p. 550.

13. *Ibid.*

14. *Ibid.*

15. Boyd, Julian P. ed., *Indian Treaties Printed by Benjamin Franklin*, 1736-1762, (Philadelphia: Historical Society of Pennsylvania, 1938), p. 126.

16. *Ibid.*

17. *Ibid.*

9

DISTANT THUNDER

A shot fired in the woods of North America drenched all Europe in blood.
—Thomas Carlyle

Pennsylvania crossed the threshold into its most difficult and trying years in the fall of 1753. The atmosphere over Pennsylvania had become fully charged with an intense foreboding. The storm that had been brewing was about to break forth in all its fury. For over a decade, beginning in 1753, America trembled as nation rose against nation in an all-out effort to gain supremacy and control of this new land. It was a baptism of blood and fire. The precious lives of men, women and children hung in the balance as France and Great Britain, the Delaware and Shawnee being snared in the middle, collided in a great conquest for domination.

THE FORKS OF THE OHIO

The Forks of the Ohio (Pittsburgh's Golden Triangle) lay on the eastern rim of the "Ohio Country," Pennsylvania's western frontier, where the Allegheny and

Monongahela Rivers unite to form the headwaters of the Ohio River. The area surrounding the Forks had become the home of many dispossessed Indians who were still brooding over past offenses. This great waterway was the westward passage to the interior, connecting with the Mississippi and traveling all the way to the Gulf of Mexico. The English, French and Indians all knew the strategic location the Forks of the Ohio possessed. Commanding the vast expanse of America's interior hinged on its occupation.

England owned the small strip of land bordering the Atlantic and, as of yet, had shown no interest in anything further west of the Appalachians. France owned colonies in both Canada and Louisiana. To secure and sustain their colonies, France wanted to possess and fortify the Ohio, the one-and-only trade route to the interior. By moving south from Canada through the Great Lakes (which they had already begun to do), and into the interiors of the west through the Ohio and Mississippi Rivers, France would then have the upper hand over the vast majority of the rest of the continent. It was also within French interest to monopolize the Indian fur trade that was bringing England rich dividends back in Europe. To facilitate their desire, France continued its vigilant effort to win the Indians away from the English with persistent reminders that the only interest the English had in the Indians was in the taking of their lands.

Providing stimulus to the anguish already suffered, the French were stroking their way to controlling these great tribes and the great and mighty Ohio River they called *La Belle Riviere*, The Beautiful River.

VIRGINIA RALLIES AGAINST FRANCE

Pennsylvania's Ohio Country was all too quickly becoming a volatile piece of real estate. When France advanced into Pennsylvania in the spring and summer of 1753, with the building of forts, Virginia's Governor, Robert Dinwiddie, was the first to swiftly respond. Governor Dinwiddie had legitimate reason to be concerned. Virginia and London had collaborated a joint venture in 1748 called The Ohio Company for the purpose of colonizing the very same region that France had just settled. Virginia argued that Pennsylvania's Ohio Territory was part of their western frontier, granted by royal charter to the Jamestown settlers in 1607. Because of this, Virginia contended that the Ohio fur trade was also theirs, and theirs alone. Europe's high demand for furs was making everyone eager to trade with the Indians. It was a lucrative business, and needless to say, the Indians were already feeling the pressure.

The intrusion of the French did nothing but complicate Virginia's interests. Consequently, Virginia became very earnest about protecting their investments. After an unsuccessful attempt to arrange a joint protest through the governors of Pennsylvania and New York, Governor Dinwiddie drafted a letter to the French himself, protesting their encroachment into the Ohio Territory.

Three separate powers were about to fight for possession of the Forks: the French, the English and the Indians—all on Pennsylvania soil, each understanding the importance of this waterway for the people they represented.

ENTER GEORGE WASHINGTON

Someone, however, was needed to deliver the Governor's message to the French. Fort LeBoeuf lay deep inside Pennsylvania's trackless and unknown wilderness—nearly four-hundred miles to the northwest. Many declined the dangerous enterprise. But there was one: a young, twenty-one-year-old major in Virginia's militia named George Washington. As a young patriot eager to serve his country's bidding, Washington quickly volunteered and accepted Dinwiddie's commission to undertake the perilous journey to the French fort. Within the parameters of his mission he was also to take careful note of the fort's layout, its armament and the number of men garrisoned within.

And so it was, on October 31, 1753, that Washington set out from Williamsburg, Virginia to deliver the Governor's letter. Along the way he enlisted the help of a French interpreter, a surveyor, four servants, five Indian chiefs and an Indian interpreter.

> Here is the first official appearance of the young man who was destined to be the commander-in-chief of the armies of a people fighting against the very empire which he here represented, and destined to be the first president of the great Nation which should result from the series of events which he set into motion, when he, as the ambassador of Virginia's Governor threw down the gauntlet before the French Empire's representatives at Fort LeBoeuf.[1]

Travel in 1750's America was very difficult. Reaching Fort LeBoeuf was no easy task. Traversing the landscape was harsh, limited to the Indian trails that crisscrossed the wilderness. On December 12, 1753, Washington arrived at the French encampment and delivered the letter to the fort's commander, Captain Jacques Legardeur de St.-Pierre. Bits of Dinwiddie's letter read as follows:

> 'The lands upon the River Ohio, in the western parts of the Colony of Virginia, are so notoriously known to be the property of the Crown of Great Britain that it is a matter of equal concern and surprise to me, to hear that a body of French forces are erecting fortresses and making settlements upon that river, within His Majesty's dominions.
>
> '...It becomes my duty to require your peacable departure; and that you would forbear prosecuting a purpose so interruptive of the harmony and good understanding, which His Majesty is desirous to continue and cultivate with the most Christian King.'[2]

A CALL TO ARMS

Upon his safe arrival home, after nearly freezing to death in the harsh winter and getting shot at by hostile Indians, Washington delivered St. Pierre's response to the Governor at Williamsburg on January 16, 1754. The French responded to Dinwiddie's message with the following words:

> 'As to the summons you send me to retire, I do not think myself obliged to obey it. Whatever may be your instructions, I am here by virtue of the orders of my General, and I entreat you, Sir, not to doubt for a moment that I have a firm resolution to follow them with all the exactness and determination which can be expected of the best officer.'[3]

With these words, an imminent war with France on American soil was inevitable. Governor Dinwiddie had all the information he needed. It was time to resist their intrusion and "Knock the French on the head."[4]

Virginia urgently sent a company of men to erect a fort on the Forks of the Ohio. To be named Fort Prince George, work commenced on February 17, 1754, under the command of Captain William Trent. When word reached the French that the English were on the Ohio, the French marshaled a force of one thousand men and surrounded the half-finished fort. Greatly outnumbered, the English surrendered the fort without a fight. The French moved in and finished the fort in the spring of 1754, naming it Fort Duquesne.[5] Fort Duquesne became the furthermost French outpost in Pennsylvania.

Dinwiddie needed a larger army. However, the colonies ran so independent of one another that a united military force to contend with foreign intruders was non-existent, and not too many Virginians were all that anxious to throw themselves into harms way. Nevertheless, Virginia did succeed in mustering a small regiment of colonial militia. It would have to be enough. Leading this resolute army was George Washington, now a Lieutenant Colonel.

Starting from Alexandria, Virginia, Washington marched to the Ohio Country on April 2, 1754—the first military campaign of his illustrious career. Upon reaching the interior of Pennsylvania, at an opening in the mountains called Great Meadows, Washington made camp and referenced the spot as "a charming field for an encounter."

In Fort Duquesne, scouts brought back news of the approaching British force. A party of thirty Frenchmen, led by Ensign Joseph Coulon de Villiers, Sieur de Jumonville, was promptly sent out to investigate. Hampered by a steady downpour the French took shelter in a small clearing beneath an escarpment of large rocks.[6]

On the evening of May 27, Tanacharison, one of the chiefs who had accompanied Washington to Fort LeBoeuf, called Half King by the English, reported to Washington that the French had been spotted nearby, just six miles to the north. With forty of his men and a group of Indian allies, Washington set out. After an all night search Washington's patrol found the French encampment in the early morning hours of May 28. Under the cover of darkness and the dense forest Washington surrounded the camp as the French were just rising for breakfast. The sound of gunfire soon echoed throughout the serene landscape. After a battle that lasted only fifteen minutes, ten Frenchmen lay dead, Jumonville was wounded, and the rest of the French were taken captive. Washington confessed, "I heard the bullets whistle, and, believe me, there is something charming in the sound."

As Washington began interrogating Jumonville, Tanacharison, who had been taken captive by the French as a young boy and whose father had been murdered, approached Jumonville, and in French said, "Thou are not dead yet, my Father!" and sank his tomahawk into his skull. This event became known around the world as the "Jumonville Affair." Striking first blood,

Washington plunged France and England, who were not at war, into what was soon to become the French and Indian War.

'A shot fired in the woods of North America drenched all Europe in blood,' wrote the English author Carlyle.[7]

THE BATTLE AT GREAT MEADOWS

Knowing the French would retaliate, Washington returned to Great Meadows and constructed a bivouac he would appropriately call a "fort of necessity."[8] His Indian allies argued its poor defensibility, Tanacharison calling it, "that little thing upon the meadow," and abandoned the cause. Two weeks later, in the middle of June, two hundred Virginia reinforcements and one hundred British regulars from South Carolina arrived at Great Meadows augmenting Washington's ranks to four hundred men. Back in Fort Duquesne, on June 28, a French soldier who had escaped the ambush reported the news of the battle.

Silent and unseen, the Indians stood watching from within the shadows of the dense forest.

The French dispatched a far superior strength of five hundred troops and three hundred Indians commanded by Captain Louis Coulon de Villiers, Jumonville's older brother. On July 3, the French reached, surrounded, and opened fire on the small fort.

Washington was no coward, and had dug in behind the walls of Fort Necessity, determined to hold his ground. The two sides fought all through the night in a torrential rain. However, by morning, the 4th of July 1754, it soon became clear that the odds against Washington were far too great for him to continue. Not only was he outnumbered, but his troops had not had much time to rest, and provisions were slim. Washington was no longer able to hold the fort. Forced to capitulate, Washington surrendered Fort Necessity into the hands of the French. The tide for possession of western Pennsylvania thus remained in favor of France.

As the tranquil landscape was broken by the battle of these two nations, keen eyes kept an affected vigilance. Silent and unseen, the Indians stood watching from within the shadows of the dense forest, having withdrawn before the battle ever began. No one knew the backwoods like the Indians, nor the method of tactical fighting as they, but Washington, inexperienced with the Indians, had refused to listen to their advice. Instead, Washington desired to command them as his slaves. The Indians were a proud people and did not tolerate being disrespected or taken advantage of. The chiefs, who had accompanied Washington, could have changed the entire outcome at Fort Necessity by en-massing their braves, but as a result, by the time of the final engagement, had completely abandoned him.

The French allowed Washington to surrender Fort Necessity with the honors of war, taking with him his arms and the regimental colors he had hoped to display over the waters of the Ohio. The French flag was raised over the continent from the waters of the Potomac and Susquehanna to the Mississippi. Washington returned to Virginia and retired to Mount Vernon until he would be called upon again, to serve one year later under the command of General Edward Braddock in July 1755.

THE CONSEQUENCE OF WASHINGTON'S DEFEAT

Washington's defeat was a small enough matter if one considers only the number of troops engaged; actually it was a colossal disaster. It showed the Ohio Indians, as Thomas McKee said, that the English were a weak reed to hold to.[9] 'The Unlucky defeat of our Troops Commanded by Major Washington,' wrote William Johnson, July 29, 'gave me the utmost Concern… this will not only animate the French, & their Indians, but stagger the resolution of those inclined to Us, if not effectually draw them from our Interest… I wish Washington had acted with prudence & circumspection requisite in an officer of his Rank… he should rather have avoided an Engagement until our Troops were all Assembled.'[10]

Washington's defeat was considered serious largely due to the conflict he had created with the Indians. His defeat and surrender at Fort Necessity was a major loss for British interests in the West, for it not only left the entire Ohio Country wide open to French advancement but it left the Ohio Indians under their direct influence.

If Pennsylvania and Virginia had lost their protective screen of friendly Indians, anything might happen. 'You may expect to hear of nothing but continual Murders committed by the French Indians who may be immediately expected down upon the back inhabitants,' wrote William Trent, who had been at the Great Meadows with Washington; 'the French sent me word they intended to come & see me soon they make no doubt of being Masters of all America.'[11]

The defeat of Washington at Fort Necessity left the Ohio country vacant of British influence. Now, the only traders left in the Ohio country were French. The French readily received the Indians and gave them such as they had need. Leaving the Ohio Indians, who up to this point still remained British allies, in the hands of the French, was a lamentable development for English and Indian relations.

THE TREATY AT ALBANY

Meanwhile, as Fort Necessity fell to the French, leaving the Ohio Country in their hands, the British Ministry ordered a conference in Albany, New York, on July 6, 1754. The Treaty at Albany, also known as The Albany Purchase, would become another major blow to Indian-white relations in Pennsylvania.

> The treaty at Albany was for the purpose of forming a general alliance of the colonies and of the Indian nations for mutual defense, for settling the question of Indian lands and for fixing upon the best measures for future action.[12]

BENJAMIN FRANKLIN'S ALBANY PLAN OF UNION

Benjamin Franklin, during the Treaty at Carlisle in 1753, had proposed forming a union of the American Colonies as a means of better defense against the French: a plan that would ultimately, twenty years later, bring about the formulation of The United States. His plan was aborted in Carlisle, but now brought back to the forefront at the treaty in Albany, where he presented his newly formulated Albany Plan of Union.

With the pressure of the French mounting, the Colonies knew they needed to respond quickly. The best means of defense was for the Colonies to somehow become united. Thus, Franklin's Albany Plan of Union. However, the Colonies felt that such a proposal would threaten their autonomy and once again rejected Franklin's plan. England also rejected it for fear that it would give the Colonies too much power—England, like Franklin, knew the power of unity. For the colonies, though, a solution still needed to present itself.

Of all the colonies represented, Pennsylvania came to Albany for the purpose of purchasing all of the Ohio Country within the bounds of the Penn charter. The British, in order to form a greater defense against the French, reasoned that if a valid deed to the land within the charter limits of Pennsylvania could be shown to the world, then the intrusion of the French could be met legally. William Penn, however, had set a precedent; no British citizen could occupy land without the proper purchase from its legal owners, the Indians.

The Holy Experiment was failing. Pennsylvania was losing its ability to be an example.

However, when the English colonies convened and signed the Albany Treaty on July 6, 1754, with their Indian allies, the Six Nations, there was not sufficient representation from the tribes of Pennsylvania. Nevertheless, recognizing the title of the Iroquois claim to the Ohio Valley, a sale was effected for the whole province of Pennsylvania west of the Kittatinny Mountains and Susquehanna River. This treaty at Albany was not only a powerful factor in the final alienation of the Delaware and Shawnee but it also secured the neutrality of the Six Nations during the French and Indian War.

It was at the signing of this treaty at Albany that the Covenant Chain that had bound the English and the Indians together was further weakened, and showed signs of collapse. The purposes of the English were becoming increasingly more evident to the Indians. Until this time no other colony had coexisted with the Indians with respect and genuine love as did Pennsylvania. That had been a distinct accomplishment. But now, what had already happened in other colonies was happening in Pennsylvania. The Holy Experiment was failing. Pennsylvania was losing its ability to be an example. The English were losing their opportunity to fulfill Pennsylvania's calling.

CHRONOLOGICAL TABLE

1753	(1) October 31. Governor Robert Dinwiddie of Virginia becomes aware of the French advancement into Pennsylvania and issues a letter of protest.
	(2) December 12. George Washington delivers Governor Dinwiddie's letter to the French commander at Fort LeBoeuf.
1754	(1) January 16. George Washington returns to Williamsburg, Virginia, and delivers the French response to Governor Dinwiddie.
	(2) February 17. Under the command of Captain William Trent, the British begin building Fort Prince George on the Forks of the Ohio.
	(3) April-June. The French capture Fort Prince George and build Fort Duquesne on the Forks of the Ohio River.
	(4) May 28. The first skirmish of the French and Indian War where Washington defeats a small band of French soldiers.
	(5) June 28. The French march out against Washington.
	(6) July 3. The French attack Fort Necessity.
	(7) July 4. Washington surrenders at Fort Necessity.
	(8) July 6. The Albany Purchase greatly offends the Delaware and Shawnee.

ENDNOTES

1. Donehoo, Dr. George P., *Pennsylvania: A History, Five Vols.*, (Lewis Historical Publishing Company, Inc., New York, Chicago, 1926), p. 679.

2. Kent, Donald H., *The French Invasion of Western Pennsylvania*, 1753, (The Pennsylvania Historical and Museum Commission, Harrisburg, Pennsylvania, 1954), p. 74.

3. *Ibid*, p. 76.

4. Comment from Conrad Weiser to governor of Virginia, Robert Dinwiddie.

5. Fort Duquesne was named after the French governor at Quebec, the Marquis Duquesne, and would later become Fort Pitt after the defeat of the French - present Pittsburgh.

6 Jumonville Glen, as the site is now called, is located six miles southeast of present Uniontown, Pennsylvania, on a short, paved hike off U.S. route 40, near the summit of Laurel Mountain in present Fayette County. The site is much as it must have looked on May 28, 1754.

7. Cornell, William A. & Altland, Millard, *Our Pennsylvania Heritage*, (Penns Valley Publishing, State College, PA, 1956), p. 142.

8. Fort Necessity has been reconstructed with its stockade, storehouse and entrenchment's 11 miles southeast of present Uniontown, Pennsylvania, on U.S. Route 40, Fayette County. A visitor's center is at the location.

9. Aug. 14, 1754: Berks and Montgomery County Papers, 1693 1869, p. 181, Historical Society of Philadelphia.

10. Wallace, Paul A. W., *Conrad Weiser: Friend of Colonist and Mohawk*, (originally published, Philadelphia, PA, 1945., reprinted, Gateway Press, Inc., Baltimore, MD, for Wennawoods Publishing, Lewisburg, PA, 1945), p. 365. The Papers of Sir William Johnson (Albany, 1921), I, 409-410.

11. *Ibid.*, William Trent to James Burd, July 7, 1757: Papers of the Shippen Family, XV, 119, H.S.P.

12. Wing, Rev. Conway P., D. D., *History of Cumberland County*, (James D. Scott, Philadelphia, PA 1879), p. 14.

Part Three

A TIME FOR WAR

1 0

FORLORN HOPE

We, the Delawares of Ohio do proclaim War against the English. We have been Friends many years, but now we have taken up the Hatchet against them, and we will never make it up with them whilst there is an English man alive.

—Shingas

On September 4, 1754, two months after the Albany Treaty, two hundred Indians, representing the Six Nations, Delaware and Shawnee, came together at a conference with Pennsylvania at Aughwick.[1] Unaware of the land purchase in Albany, the Delaware were desperate to hold fast to the bond of unity that had originally brought them together with the English upon the arrival of William Penn. Attending the conference, representing Governor Hamilton, was Conrad Weiser.

King Beaver, chief of the Delaware, addressed the Six Nations as follows:

'Oncle I still remember the time when you first Conquered us, and made Women of us and told us that you took us under your Protection, and that we must not Mettle with Warrs, but stay in the House and mind Counsel affair, we have hitherto followed your directions, and Lived very easy under your Protection, and no high wind did Blow to make us uneasy. but now things seem to take another turn, and a high Wind is arising, we desire you therefore Uncle to have your Eyes open, and be Watchful over us your Cousins, as you have always been heretofore.'[2]

King Beaver bonded his word with the presentation of several strings of wampum.

Then the same Speaker (King Beaver) directed his Discourse to the Governor of Pensilvania and said.

'Brother. the Governor of Pensilvania I must now go into the Depth and put you in Mind of old Histories and our first Acquaintance with you, when William Penn first appeared in his Ship on our Lands we looked in his Face and judged him to be our Brother, and gave him a fast hold to tie his ship to. and we told him that a Powerful People called the 5 united nations had placed us here, and established a fire and lasting Friendship with us and that he the said William Penn and his People shall be welcome to be one of us. and in the same union, to which he and his People agreed, and we then erected an everlasting Friendship with William Penn and his People, which we on our side so well as you have observed as much as Possible to this day, we always looked upon you to be one Flesh and Blood with us, we desire you will look upon us in the same Light, and let that Treaty of Friendship made by our foreFathers on both sides subsist, and be in force from Generation to Generation. both our Lives, our wife and Childrens Life and those as yet unborn depends upon it. Pray Brother consider well what we say and let it be so.'[3]

King Beaver sealed his words with the presentation of a large belt.

Feeling that the Delaware's discourse was too substantial a matter for him alone to respond to, Weiser told the Indians that he would take up the matter with the governor himself once he returned to Philadelphia, to which the Indians agreed. Two months later, in November, Robert Hunter Morris succeeded James Hamilton as the Lieutenant Governor of Pennsylvania. After Weiser related the events of the council at Aughwick to Governor Morris, Governor Morris sent a message to the Delaware. It read as follows:

'We are very glad that you so well remember the arrival of that great Man William Penn and his People, the first settlers of Pennsylvania, and that you are desirous the Treaty of Friendship then made between our Forefathers on both sides should last from Generation to Generation as long as the World should stand. You judge right to say that we are one Flesh and Blood with you. We thank you for your Good Will and Kindness, and we do on our Side renew the Said Treaty made between our Forefathers.... Notwithstanding you now live at a great distance from us we look upon you to be one People with us, and that you sprung up out of the same Spot of Earth where some of us did, and now live upon it. We look upon the Place you now live on as a place of Sport and good Hunting; this never makes any Odds between Brethren. You are within Call, and we desire that a good correspondence may be kept between us and you from time to time, especially in time of Danger. Consider always that here is your Home, and here your Council Fire has been burning for many Years.'[4]

THE DEMORALIZING OF THE COVENANT CHAIN

In spite of the governor's message, the signs of relational strain between the English and the Delaware were evident. The scandalous ways of the white man were breaking through the cracks of a very weak facade. The Indians were a very forgiving people, but greater foresight about the repeated offenses against these powerful nations should have been considered. Because of this failure, the British would soon have more to deal with than the invasion of France. As the Indians were pushed further and further from their homes and hunting grounds, the injustices would turn them into a leading factor in the deterioration of Pennsylvania. The continuous warning signs went unheeded by the English.

After the close of the conference at Aughwick, the Delaware and Shawnee were made aware of the Albany Purchase.

The sale of their lands under the Treaty at Albany was looked upon by them as a high-handed and selfish act, the validity of which they could never acknowledge. They demanded that the lands, which had been repeatedly promised them by the provincial authorities as hunting grounds, should be preserved for their occupation or be adequately paid for into their hands. All attempts to mollify the wounded feelings of the great body, especially the Shawnee, were unsuccessful.[5]

Great consternation quickly enveloped the province. The councils of the Delaware and Shawnee were confused and divided. To whom should they turn? Their previous trusted relationship with the British had now become one of suspicion, contention and betrayal. The defeat of Washington, leaving the Ohio Country and its Indians in the hands of the French, combined with the constant selling of Pennsylvania, left the Delaware in a difficult and precarious position. They had no desire to go to war against the British, but the French continually reminded the Indians of their land grievances with the English and threatened to destroy them if they didn't side with France. The Indians also worried that if they made a stand against the French would Pennsylvania come to their aide. As the Indians weighed these decisions, Great Britain was making plans of their own for a counter strike against the French.

GENERAL EDWARD BRADDOCK

Washington's surrender at Fort Necessity not only produced a general alarm among the Delaware but also among the cabinet of King George II back in England. On December 21, 1754, Great Britain decided it was time to take action against the French. Major General Edward Braddock, appointed second-in-command of all British forces in America, was sent to America with two regiments of England's finest to resist their aggressions.

Under the command of Braddock, a fleet was sent to the Gulf of St. Lawrence to resist any reinforcements from reaching Canada, thus inhibiting the French from resisting any of their land campaigns. Braddock's land campaign to evict the French was fourfold. He was to personally oversee the march against Fort Duquesne. William Shirley, Governor of Massachusetts, was to march from Albany, New York, and seize Fort Niagara at the head of Lake Ontario. Braddock would then join forces with Shirley at Niagara. Sir William Johnson, trusted friend of the Mohawk, summoned from his home and trading post in New York's Mohawk Valley, was given two commissions. Braddock appointed him as superintendent of Indian Affairs and as Major General to lead a march to the southern end of Lake Champlain and seize Fort St. Frédérick at Crown Point.

Fort St. Frédérick was built on the southern tip of Lake Champlain, a location the English called Crown Point. The French had built the fort in 1737, whose constant presence served as a threat against Albany, New York.

And fourthly, an expedition was to be outfitted in Boston to eradicate two French forts on the Chignecto isthmus that linked Nova Scotia with present-day New Brunswick.

On February 20, 1755, General Braddock arrived in Virginia, where a detachment of Virginians joined him along with Colonel George Washington, who was commissioned to serve as one of his aides-de-camp. At a council of the Governors of Massachusetts, Virginia, New York, Pennsylvania, Maryland and North Carolina, it was decided that Braddock's force of one thousand four hundred and sixty men would march against Fort Duquesne in June, 1755.

Meanwhile, while the tension between France and Great Britain was mounting, the Delaware and Shawnee wavered about fully committing to one side or the other. They were waiting to see which side would win the impending contest, hoping that whomever it was would give them validity.

Braddock, unfamiliar with wilderness combat, was encouraged to enlist the support of those Indians still friendly to the English. Benjamin Franklin warned Braddock of the danger of being ambushed by the Indian allies of the French. An arrogant and overly confident officer, Braddock was certain that his forces would not be detained in taking Fort Duquesne.

'He smiled at my ignorance,' says Franklin in his autobiography, and replied: 'These savages may indeed be a formidable enemy to your raw American militia, but upon the King's regular and disciplined troops, sir, it is impossible that they should make any impression.'[6]

However, Braddock conceded to solicit some help from the Indians, but not without disdain. According to the Oneida chief, Scarouady, Braddock was a proud and ignorant man, and developed a very poor reputation with the Indians.

'He was a bad man when he was alive; he looked upon us as dogs, and would never hear anything what was said to him. We often endeavoured to advise him of the danger he was in with his Soldiers; but he never appeared pleased with us and that was the reason that a great many of our Warriors left him and would not be under his Command.'[7]

When a Delaware chief, Shingas, approached Braddock and asked what he intended to do with the land once he drove the French and their Indians away, Braddock responded, "The English Should Inhabit and Inherit the Land."[8] Shingas then asked if the Indians could live and trade among the English and have hunting grounds sufficient to support themselves and their families, to which Braddock responded, "No Savage Should Inherit the Land."[9]

Shingas then replied,

'That if they might not have the Liberty to Live on the Land they would not Fight for it To wch Genl Braddock answered that he did not need their Help and had no Doubt of driveing the French and their Indians away.'[10]

Painful and bitter rejection was felt by the Delaware when they were told, again, that they could no longer live on the land that had been repeatedly promised to remain as their own. When Shingas reported to his people all that had transpired between himself and Braddock, a party of them was so enraged that they immediately joined the French. The majority of the Delaware, however, stayed neutral, waiting rather to see the outcome of the coming engagement.

In June, the campaign against the French forts on the Chignecto isthmus in Nova Scotia turned out to be the most successful of Braddock's four campaigns. Fort Beauséjour was bombarded for four days until the French capitulated—a white flag of surrender was raised above the fort. Fort Gaspereau followed suit. The British took command of Fort Beauséjour, renaming it Fort Cumberland.

BRADDOCK'S MISERABLE DEFEAT AT THE BATTLE OF MONONGAHELA

The Monongahela River snakes its way through southwestern Pennsylvania until it joins with the Allegheny River to form the headwaters of the Ohio. At this confluence of waterways sat Fort Duquesne, the French stronghold of western Pennsylvania. The French had prepared for the British by rallying the support of the Potawatomis, Ojibwas, Ottawas, Chippewas, Hurons, Caughnawagas and Abenakis.

When waterways were not accessible, war campaigns would often take months to complete as roads had to be cut through heavy timber to provide passage for wagons and heavy artillery. Such was the case that labored and hampered Braddock's army as his axe men continued to cut their way toward Fort Duquesne. French scouts and Indian runners excitedly brought back word to the fort of the far superior numbers of the approaching army. The odds were nearly two to one. It seemed that the obvious outcome would be in Braddock's favor.

Soon the forest surrounding the British came alive with the roar of deadly gunfire.

The first thought of the French and their Indians was to abandon the fort and retreat. But then, the nearly two hundred and fifty French and Canadians, along with the six hundred Indians who had joined them, bolstered and ignited each other's courage. Instead of waiting for Braddock to come to them, they marched out to meet their foe for a possible surprise attack.

On July 9, 1755 ten miles east of Fort Duquesne, the British and the French were surprised by the sudden appearance of each other. The French had wanted to create an ambush to increase their chances of victory, but now it was too late. The British shouted, "French and Indians!" Immediately, from within the dense overgrowth, the French gave the orders to charge. Simultaneously, the well-disciplined British troops made formation and repulsed the charge with repeated bursts of musket-fire.

When the smoke cleared, it was discovered that the French commander, Captain Daniel Liénard de Beaujeu, had been shot and killed in the first volley, causing the French to immediately break and scatter. This action caused the courage of the Indians to waver also. Without a moment's hesitation, the French second in command, Captain Jean-Daniel Dumas, rallied the Indians and the French officers. Dumas commanded them to fan out to the wings of the British column and attack them at their flanks from the concealment of trees and rocks. The command was quickly obeyed. Soon the forest surrounding the British came alive with the roar of deadly gunfire. It was as though they were fighting an invisible foe. Never had the British encountered combat of this kind. Their well-ordered, shoulder-to-shoulder, platoon-style methods of fighting were incapable of repelling an enemy they couldn't see. Their courage began to fail. Francis Parkman, author of *The Conspiracy of Pontiac*, recounts the dreadful scene of this historic battle.

Illustration by Lorence Bjorklund

Wellman, Paul I., *Indian Wars and Warriors, East*
(Riverside Press, Cambridge, Massachusetts, 1959), p. 139.

In a few moments, all was confusion. The advanced guard fell back on the main body, and every trace of subordination vanished. The fire soon extended along the whole length of the army, from front to rear. Scarce an enemy could be seen, though the forest resounded with their yells; though every bush and tree was alive with incessant flashes; though the lead flew like a hailstorm, and with every moment the men went down by scores. The regular troops seemed bereft of their senses. They huddled together in the road like flocks of sheep; and happy did he think himself who could wedge his way into the midst of the crowd, and place a barrier of human flesh between his life and the shot of the ambushed marksmen. Many were seen eagerly loading their muskets, and then firing them into the air, or shooting their own comrades, in the insanity of their terror. The officers, for the most part, displayed a conspicuous gallantry; but threats and commands were wasted alike on the panic stricken multitude.[11]

WASHINGTON TAKES COMMAND OF THE FIELD

In the three hours of pitched battle, while carrying out his duties on the panic-stricken field, four horses were shot out from underneath Braddock, and yet, on he fought. After mounting a fifth horse, a well-aimed shot pierced his lungs, bringing Braddock's illustrious career to an end. All his aides had been wounded early in the ensuing battle leaving Washington as the only officer left on the field to carry out the general's orders and preserve what sanity was left.

Amid the noise and confusion, Washington, distinguished by his courage and calmness, tried to maintain order amid the frenzied multitude—men were screaming and falling on his every side. Contending from every part of the field, however, made Washington a conspicuous target—the Indians were shooting everyone on horseback or who appeared to have command. Singling him out, a chief and his warriors began repeatedly firing upon Washington. Two horses were shot out from underneath him, but the warriors were unable to put him down. Astonished, believing his life to be protected by the Great Spirit, the Indians ceased their fire upon him. The carnage, however, continued, totally demoralizing the British until a complete and abandoned withdrawal sent them retreating back to the safety of Philadelphia. In a single fell swoop, the French had totally, and surprisingly, routed the British.

'Take scalps. Kill the English, all of them. Kill them in any way you like...'

Later, four bullet holes were discovered in Washington's clothing though he escaped the bloody slaughter without a wound. Not all were so fortunate.

Braddock's presumption that the Indian was an unworthy opponent had proven to be a gross miscalculation. The toll had been far heavier than anyone could have imagined. After the battle, as an eerie silence fell upon the bloody scene, four hundred and fifty-six British and colonial soldiers lay dead on the forest floor. Of those who survived and made it back to Philadelphia, four hundred and twenty-one were wounded, many mortally. Sixty-three of the eighty-nine commissioned officers that went into battle that day were either killed or wounded. It was reported that the French suffered the loss of only seven Indians and four Frenchmen. In all of history, never were so many British officers killed in proportion to the number engaged. It would be the most crushing defeat ever executed against a British army on American soil.[12]

Arriving back at the fort, Captain Dumas, now the new commander of Fort Duquesne, capitalized on the British defeat and the weakness of the colonists. He held a war council with the Indians.

'Go out,' Dumas told them. 'Spread yourselves through the whole country as far as you can go. Take scalps. Kill the English, all of them. Kill them in any way you like—with club or gun, knife or tomahawk. Torture them with fire and coals. Burn their houses, destroy their livestock, destroy all they own. Drive them back to the sea-cities, and there our armies will come and finish the destruction. Kill them.'[13]

THE WARPATH OF THE NATIONS

Meanwhile, Governor Shirley had traveled up New York's Mohawk Valley to the shore of Lake Ontario, where he was staging his campaign against Fort Niagara. Shirley's base of operations, Fort Oswego, had become one of Britain's most important and strategic bases in America. From Oswego's port the British controlled Lake Ontario and its vital link between the St. Lawrence River and Lake Erie. Important trade relations between them and the Iroquois had also been established and maintained from its port.

While at Oswego, Shirley received the disheartening news of Braddock's defeat. It was already August, and Shirley's campaign against Fort Niagara had already been aggravated by enumerable delays, putting him weeks behind schedule. The British fleet sent to the Gulf of St. Lawrence to prevent French reinforcements from reaching Canada failed to complete its mission. This news, along with the discouraging news of Braddock's defeat, came as a stunning double-blow to Shirley. Shirley halted his campaign completely. He left two regular regiments to strengthen Oswego's garrison, and returned to Albany to lay plans for the following spring.

William Johnson's campaign against Fort St. Frédérick had also been plagued with setbacks. Johnson realized that in order to launch a successful assault against Fort St. Frédérick, a new fort of his own would have to be built for supplies and operations. So, in August, Johnson's 3,500 provincials, largely consisting of farmers, shopkeepers and craftsmen from New England and New York, along with about 500 Mohawks, proceeded to build a fort where the headwaters of the Hudson River make a sharp turn to the west. Johnson named it Fort Edward, in honor of the Duke of York. Fort St. Frédérick, Johnson's objective, lay approximately sixty miles to the north, beyond Lake George. For Johnson's army to reach Lake George from the Hudson, a sixteen-mile portage road had to be cut through the wilderness.

During the disaster and confusion at the Monongahela battlefield, all of Braddock's personal possessions, including his campaign papers, had been recklessly abandoned in the frenzied retreat. France had now become fully aware of the British objectives, including Johnson's. Under the command of Baron Ludwig August Dieskau, a German serving for the French, a powerful force of 3,200 French regulars, and Caughnawaga and Abenaki Indians, were presently gliding down the narrow channel that connects Lake Champlain with Lake George. Unknown to Johnson, Dieskau's army was advancing against Fort Edward.

THE BATTLE OF LAKE GEORGE

Leaving 500 men to guard the fort, Johnson took the rest of his men and made camp on the southern shore of Lake George. Johnson had no idea that Dieskau, through the eyes of his scouts, was watching Johnson's every move. Dieskau's men emerged from the forest onto Johnson's portage road just four miles south of Johnson's camp and quietly concealed themselves on both sides of the road and waited. That same evening, Mohawk scouts reported to Johnson of a substantial body of the enemy lurking about Fort Edward. Johnson sent a thousand men back to Fort Edward to reinforce it never knowing of the ambush that lay ahead.

On the morning of September 8, 1755, Johnson's detachment, led by Chief Hendrick and 200 of his Mohawk warriors, blundered into the trap. The woods exploded! From either side of the road a storm of bullets tore through their ranks. In the first few moments, Chief Hendrick and thirty Mohawks, along with fifty provincials, fell to the ground, dead. Thus began the Battle of Lake George, called by New Englanders as the "Bloody Morning Scout."

The surviving Mohawk and provincials caught in the crossfire, made a full-measured retreat back to Johnson's encampment, who, upon hearing the exchange of gunfire, quickly strengthened their defenses and prepared to meet the French.

The French came on like a raging bull. However, the entire charge was halted when, about 150 yards from the English, the Caughnawagas hesitated at the edge of the clearing. It seems that they took to arguing among themselves about their reluctance to march down the throat of an entrenched camp and against their own cousins, the Mohawk. This gave Captain William Eyre, Johnson's artillery commander and only redcoat to serve in the expedition, enough time to turn four of his fieldpieces to cover the road. As the Caughnawagas turned and left the field of battle, so did the Abenakis. The French, in an effort to shame the Indians for leaving them, formed their columns and rushed the British anyway. Captain Eyre's cannon thundered in response to their charge and ripped large, gaping holes in their ranks. His guns were loaded with canister, or grapeshot, not solid shot, which acted like giant shotguns. The French were annihilated and forced back. They broke and ran.

The surviving French and Indians returned to the sight of the original ambush and were surprised by a column of 200 New Hampshire provincials that had come up from Fort Edward when the sounds of battle had been heard. This was the moment of the greatest slaughter as the provincials attacked the disorganized survivors. It was over. The remaining French, totally demoralized, scrambled back to Fort St. Frédérick. The fall of night brought an end to the Battle of Lake George. Though it was counted as a British victory—the French had been driven from the field—both sides suffered even casualties.

It was getting late in the year and the bitter snows would soon require both armies to take up winter quarters. Besides that, both armies had had enough fighting for one season. In late September, Johnson, seeing that he was unable to proceed any further, built Fort William Henry on the southern tip of Lake George to keep a watchful eye on French activities and to keep them from progressing any further south.

Over the years, Fort St. Frédérick had fallen into such disrepair that it was determined that it would undoubtedly be unable to withstand a British assault. Instead of going through the lengthy repairs that were needed to strengthen its defenses, the French advanced ten miles south of Crown Point, to the north end of Lake George, and erected a new fort, Fort Carillon. The British had named this area Ticonderoga, which is actually a Mohawk word that means, "*Place Where Two Waters Meet.*" By the end of 1755, as both armies retired within the relative safety of their respective forts, their armies were now only separated by the thirty-two mile shimmering length of Lake George.

THE DELAWARE "TAKE UP THE HATCHET"

Back in Pennsylvania all hell was about to break loose. Braddock's miserable defeat at the hands of the French became the final turning point in the Delaware and Shawnee allegiance to the British. Twice now the Delaware had watched both Washington and Braddock defeated in trying to oppose the French, leaving the entire frontier completely defenseless. With the pressure of the French upon them, who now possessed the Ohio, the Delaware and Shawnee felt no recourse but to take up the cause of the French. The Delaware and Shawnee, having tried to remain neutral in the many years of conflict between Britain and France, finally, with nowhere else to turn, released their covenant with the English.

...the Delaware took on the role of the mighty warrior, exchanging their "petticoats" for the tomahawk.

This peace-loving people, not ashamed to have called the English their friends, were driven from one place to another without any consideration. Beginning with the Iroquois Alliance of 1732 their land was systematically "sold from under their feet." The Treaty of 1736, the Walking Purchase, and, adding insult to injury, the Albany Purchase, further alienated them from the English. What could they do? Inflamed by the French and manipulated by the English, the Indians had been pushed too far. The Covenant Chain had completely disintegrated. No longer the meek and mild people that William Penn had met, the Delaware took on the role of the mighty warrior, exchanging their "petticoats" for the tomahawk.

Nearly twenty years had passed since the Six Nations had referred to the Delaware as "women" and had thrown them off their ancestral lands. Now, when the Six Nations tried to prevent them from "taking up the hatchet" against the English, the Delaware responded with these words:

> 'We are men,' they declared, 'and are determined not to be ruled any longer by you as women; and we are determined to cut off all the English, except those that may make their escape from us in ships;...'[14]

Suddenly, the Delaware struck out against the Pennsylvania frontier with a vengeance. Terror reigned throughout the settlements. It had been thirty-seven years since the death of William Penn, and now the Indians, taking no more abuse, struck out against the province, shedding first blood known as The Penn's Creek Massacre.[15]

Seventy-three years of unbroken peace made between William Penn and the Delaware came to an abrupt end at Penn's Creek on October 16, 1755, when twenty-five German settlers were fallen upon by the Indians and either killed or carried away into captivity. Shingas, the mighty war captain who became known as Shingas the Terrible, proclaimed,

> 'We, the Delawares of Ohio do proclaim War against the English. We have been Friends many years, but now we have taken up the Hatchet against them, & we will never make it up with them whilst there is an English man alive.'[16]

The Pennsylvania Indians were now at war with the province whose founder, William Penn, they had so warmly trusted and welcomed with open arms.

THE FINAL APPEAL

On November 8, 1755, as the Delaware were wielding their tomahawks against the province, the Iroquois, in a desperate measure to prevent any more bloodshed and hostility, sent Scarouady to speak to Pennsylvania on behalf of the Delaware. Scarouady, accompanied by a delegation of Delaware, arrived in Philadelphia to learn of Pennsylvania's position with the Delaware and to "Brighten the Chain."[17]

In Philadelphia, Scarouady, with grief and concern,

> ...made a final appeal to the Pennsylvania government to support the western Indians against the French. He came not as a supplicant, but as a proud warrior, representing the Shawnee and the Delawares, and he demanded that the governor and the assembly hear him. His address was made in the State House, before the governor, the council, the assembly, and a large audience. His appearance was the most dramatic spectacle that the State House saw prior to the Revolution—indeed it was in a sense the Declaration of Independence of the Delawares. Through him the Indians he represented inquired whether 'This government...would give them the Hatchet and fight themselves.

If they would, he had something further to say. If not, they would soon know what to do.' To the assembly he said: 'We do, therefore, once more invite and request you to act like men, and be no longer women, pursuing weak measures, that render your names despicable.' To Governor Morris, he said: 'One word of yours will bring the Delawares to join you.'[18]

Scarouady, and the Delaware who accompanied him to Philadelphia, waited patiently for Pennsylvania to make a gesture of their commitment. After four days of waiting for a decision, the Assembly and Governor Morris, unable to come to an agreement as to who would finance the arming of the Ohio Indians, informed Scarouady of the impasse. Though an abundance of kind words and gifts were given, Pennsylvania gave no assurances. This silence and lack of promise was deafening to the

His appearance was the most dramatic spectacle that the State House saw prior to the Revolution...

chief. Scarouady, leaving in tears, guaranteed the Governor that this answer would mean the absolute defection of the Delaware.

The disillusioned Indians returned to the Ohio. Their repeated attempts to reach the heart of the English failed. They could not understand why the English would allow the bond of friendship they had once committed to extinguish. The English had made no attempt to embrace them. The Delaware had become outcasts in their own homes.

Soon the throb of the war drum could be heard throughout the Ohio and Pennsylvania forests. Though amply warned, Pennsylvania would not be ready for the tempest that was about to unleash the bloodiest Indian invasion in American history. The shedding of blood would now become the unfortunate medium of exchange as the Indians prepared to meet the English, their faces painted for war. It would be a dark hour for Pennsylvania.

CHRONOLOGICAL TABLE

1754	(1) September 4. After the Albany Purchase, a conference was held at Aughwick between the Delaware, Shawnee, the Six Nations and Pennsylvania. (2) November. Robert Hunter Morris succeeds James Hamilton as Pennsylvania's Lieutenant Governor and serves from 1754-1756.

1755

(1) July 9. General Braddock's defeat.

(2) August. Sir William Johnson builds Fort Edward at the headwaters of the Hudson River.

(3) September 8. The Battle of Lake George.

(4) Late September. Under the direction of William Johnson, the construction of a new fort, Fort William Henry, begins on the south end of Lake George.

(5) Late September. The French begin building Fort Carillon at the north end of Lake George.

(6) October 16. "The Penn's Creek Massacre."

(7) November 8. Iroquois vicegerent, Scarouady, chief of the Oneidas, goes to Philadelphia to try and gain Pennsylvania's support for the Delaware.

(8) November. The Delaware Indians proclaim war against the English.

ENDNOTES

1. Present Shirleysburg, Pennsylvania.

2. Wallace, Paul A. W., *Conrad Weiser: Friend of Colonist and Mohawk,* (originally published, Philadelphia, PA, 1945., reprinted, Gateway Press, Inc., Baltimore, MD, for Wennawoods Publishing, Lewisburg, PA, 1945), p. 369.

3. *Ibid.*

4. Donehoo, Dr. George P., *Pennsylvania: A History, Five Vols.,* (Lewis Historical Publishing Company, Inc., New York, Chicago, 1926), p. 710.

5. Wing, Rev. Conway P., D. D., *History of Cumberland County,* (James D. Scott, Philadelphia, PA 1879), p. 40.

6. Sipe, C. Hale, *The Indian Wars of Pennsylvania,* (originally published, Harrisburg, PA, 1931., reprinted, Gateway Press, Baltimore, MD, for Wennawoods Publishing, Lewisburg, PA, 1995), p. 178.

7. Jennings, Francis, *Empire Of Fortune: Crowns, Colonies, and Tribes in the Seven Years War in America,* (W. W. Norton & Company, New York, N. Y., London, 1988), p. 152. Pa. Council Minutes 6:589.

8. *Ibid.,* p. 154.

9. *Ibid.,* p. 154.

10. Weslager, C. A., *The Delaware Indians: A History,* (Rutgers University Press, New Brunswick, New Jersey, 1972), p. 225.

11. Parkman, Francis, *The Conspiracy of Pontiac,* (Collier Books, New York, Collier - Macmillian LTD., London, 1962), p. 82.

12. The French and Indian War Museum and Gallery can be visited at the First Carnegie Library at 419 Library St. in Braddock, PA. In the borough of North Braddock, two north of Braddock Ave., on Jones Ave., a statue of George Washington marks the spot of the battle.

13. Marrin, Albert, *Struggle for a Continent, The French and Indian Wars 1690-1760,* (Atheneum, Macmillan Publishing Company, 1987), p. 102.

14. Wallace, Anthony F. C., *King of the Delawares: Teedyuscung 1700-1763,* (Syracuse University Press, Syracuse, N. Y., 1949), p. 91.

15. The Pennsylvania Historical and Museum Commission have erected a Historical Marker just north of Selinsgrove, Pennsylvania, on State Route 2017 (old US 11 & 15), in commemoration of the Penns Creek Massacre.

16. Weslager, C. A., *The Delaware Indians: A History,* (Rutgers University Press, New Brunswick, New Jersey, 1972), p. 228.

17. *To Brighten the Chain* meant to forgive all offenses by "burying the hatchet" thus renewing and restoring friendship within the Covenant Chain.

18. Boyd, Julian P. ed., *Indian Treaties Printed by Benjamin Franklin, 1736-1762,* (Philadelphia: Historical Society of Pennsylvania, 1938), p. 1xix.

11

LIGHTNING STRIKES

A mighty shout arose which shook the very mountains, and all the Delawares and Shawnees, except a few old sachems, danced the war dance.

—C. Hale Sipe

When Pennsylvania failed to embrace the Delaware and arm them against the French, the deluge of blood did not stop at Penn's Creek. It was only the beginning. Unbridled revenge excited these people who had been denied their right to exist. Enraged warriors, incensed by broken English promises, struck out in all directions. Empowered by an irrepressible anger at the loss of their homes and the land they so dearly treasured, the alienated Lenape and Shawnee exacted repercussions that were so fierce and appalling that the entire countryside erupted in unrestrained violence. The wilderness settlements were sparse, scattered and unprotected, making them vulnerable to Indian attack. William Penn's covenant of peace had required no militia, making Pennsylvania's defenders few. The fortless province quickly became deplorable, as many unarmed and helpless settlers ran for protection from the rampaging Indians.

GREAT DARKNESS OVER THE LAND

Cries for help went unheard as the Indians attacked swiftly and fiercely, turning Pennsylvania into a bloody wasteland. Many suffered the ferocious raw steal of the Indian's tomahawk. Terror, fear and death became the constant companions of the unprotected settlements as the Indians ravaged the countryside. The back-woods suffered heavy casualties. Homes, farms and crops were burned to the ground while livestock were destroyed. The Indians, traveling light and unencumbered, spared nothing. Without mercy, entire families became the victims of the continual raids. Many were taken captive, never to be seen again, tortured to death at the hands of their ruthless captors. While others, allowed to live, were adopted into Indian families to replace those who had fallen in battle.

Terror, fear and death became the constant companions of the unprotected settlements...

The Moravian town of Gnadenhutten suffered a similar fate as that of the other frontier settlements. On November 24, 1755, nine years after the mission was established, a band of hostile Indians attacked it, killed the missionaries, and burned the buildings to the ground.

> Pennsylvania was literally saturated with blood along the Blue Mountains from the Delaware to the waters of the Potomac.[1]

Through November and December of 1755, the hardships suffered in the backwoods settlements were so unbearable that many of those mangled and murdered by the Indians were sent to Philadelphia in carts to protest the non-resistant Quaker policy. Mobs surrounded the house of Assembly and placed the dead bodies in the doorway, demanding immediate relief.

Provision was finally made, and under the supervision of former governor James Hamilton, and Benjamin Franklin, the settlements built a chain of forts and blockhouses, from December of 1755 through January of 1756, to serve as a protective wall to defend the settlements on the East Side of the Blue Mountains from Easton to Maryland.

Volunteering to enlist within the colonial militia and garrison a fort was a hazardous occupation. Death became a constant threat for those who were willing to protect the frontier and brave the elements. If the threat of Indian attack wasn't enough, there was always the threat of diseases like small pox and dysentery from poor sanitary conditions. Winters were harsh and cruel, while provisions could sometimes trickle in at a rate just sufficient to sustain the garrison.

As the savagery became more and more widespread, so did the fear that accompanied it. Fear of the marauding Indians would often lead to desertion, leaving the forts undermanned. Nevertheless, though the forts were built every ten to twelve miles apart and garrisoned within, nothing could stop the torrent of rage that consumed the frontier. Every fort was attacked.

Forts McCord, Bingham's and Granville were soon captured and burned to the ground. Not one county east of the Blue Mountains went untouched by the bloody incursions committed by the Indians, especially those of Juniata, Franklin, Perry, Cumberland, Dauphin, Lebanon, Schuylkill, Carbon, Berks, Lehigh, Northampton and Monroe. The country was ablaze.

Not one county east of the Blue Mountains went untouched by the bloody incursions committed by the Indians

The winter of 1755-56 was harsh. Dispatches from Canada boasted,

> The French and Indians have, since Admiral Braddock's defeat, disposed of more than 700 people in the Provinces of Pennsylvania, Virginia and Carolina, including those killed and those taken prisoners.[2]

Both the French and the British actively sought the support of the Southern Indians, namely, the Cherokee. Governor Dinwiddie's campaign against the cruelties of the Northern Indians succeeded with the Cherokee and convinced them to take up the hatchet against the French. The Cherokee also declared war against the Shawnees and sent one hundred and thirty warriors to protect the frontiers of Virginia.

The Quakers, on the other hand, felt that the Delaware had not been justly treated after the Iroquois had come into power in the Province, in any of the land sales of their own ancestral possessions, to which the Iroquois laid claim—and in this they were right. The Delaware had been driven from one place to another, by these land sales, and wherever they went the land was sold under their feet and they had no say whatever in the matter.[3]

PENNSYLVANIA DECLARES WAR AGAINST THE DELAWARE

On the advice and recommendations of the Six Nations and Conrad Weiser, the Governor of Pennsylvania, Robert Hunter Morris, declared war against the Delaware and Shawnee on April 14th, 1756. Governor Morris, who was not a Quaker but a member of the Church of England, made this declaration without the consent of the Assembly. With this declaration also came the unethical bounty he offered for their scalps, what he called the Scalp Act. Governor Morris addressed the Six Nations and Pennsylvania with these words:

'I therefore, by this Belt, declare War against the Delawares and all such as act in conjunction with them. I offer you the Hatchet, and expect your hearty Concurrence with us in this just and Necessary War. I not only invite you, but desire you will send this belt to all your friends everywhere, as well on the Susquehannah, as to the Six Nations and to their Allies, and engage them to join us heartily against these false and perfidious Enemies. I promise you and them Protection and Assistance, when you shall stand in need of it against your Enemies.

'For the Encouragement of you, and all who will join you in the Destruction of our Enemies, I propose to give the following Bounties or Rewards, Vist: for every Male Indian Prisoner above twelve Years Old that shall be delivered at any of the Government's Forts, or Towns, One Hundred and Fifty Dollars.

'For every Female Prisoner, or Male Prisoner of Twelve years old, one hundred and thirty Dollars.

'For the Scalp of every male Indian of above Twelve Years old, one hundred and thirty dollars.

'For the scalp of every Indian Woman, Fifty Dollars.'[4]

Pennsylvania had now declared war with those whose founder, William Penn, had once united within a covenant of peace and harmony. Peace, that had been so triumphant, and made so gloriously manifest, was now just a memory. The unity that had been so dearly purchased had prevailed, if only for a time. The Quakers, appalled at Pennsylvania's declaration of war against the Delaware, unable to help them, resigned their control of the Assembly in 1756.

When Pennsylvania declared war against the Delaware with the unscrupulous bounty for scalps,

A mighty shout arose which shook the very mountains, and all the Delawares and Shawnees, except a few old sachems, danced the war dance.[5]

Pennsylvania paid dearly for their shortsighted policy, which had alienated the friendly Delaware and the warlike Shawnee. If William Penn's successors had held true to his policies, Pennsylvania might have been spared the blackest pages of its history.

BRITAIN DECLARES WAR AGAINST FRANCE

The unrelenting pressure of the French, who now had the Delaware and Shawnee fighting at their side, caused Britain to declare war against France on May 17, 1756, thus officially beginning the French and Indian War. It was a conquest for Empire as the world's two superpowers, Britain and France, met face to face in a titanic clash of blood and fire for possession of the New World—America's first world war! The war was known in America as the French and Indian War but in Europe as the Seven Years War. It was the beginning of a war between Great Britain and France that would not limit itself to the North American continent but was to spread throughout Asia, Africa, India and the West Indies, and drug every major power in Europe into the battle.

The French and Indian War was the first major conflict between world powers on the soil of the New World. But, the title in itself can be a misnomer.

This war was not between the French and the Indians, but between France and England, with the possession of America and those trying to protect it lying in the balance. It was a war that found its beginnings within the borders of Pennsylvania—the very land the Indians were trying to protect—fighting for the soil they so dearly loved.

> In the Seven Years War for the first time the province of Pennsylvania and its Indian neighbors engaged in unrestrained violent conflict. Dispossessed Ohio country Delawares, Shawnees, and Senecas took advantage of French expansionism in the region to redress long-standing grievances with the Euro-Americans who had settled in the Susquehanna and upper Delaware watersheds.[6]

For the Delaware, the war for their own independence would continue well beyond the French surrender of 1763, raging on for a total of forty years. The Delaware would never recover.

THE FRENCH OFFENSIVE

While the Indians continued to pillage and wreak havoc on the frontier settlements of Pennsylvania, Maryland, Virginia and North Carolina, the new command of all French forces of His Majesty, King Louis XV, in the American wilderness was given to Louis-Joseph, Marquis de Montcalm. Montcalm's first order of business was to continue to concentrate the bulk of its military operations against the British forts in the province of New York, his first target—destroy Britain's military and commercial outpost on the shore of Lake Ontario, Fort Oswego.

Coming into the war the French knew nothing was more likely to retain the favor of the Indian nations fighting for France than to let them fight in their own ways, and under their own terms. However, the cultural dynamics of wilderness warfare horrified Montcalm. Montcalm was an officer, and a gentleman, and distrusted Indians for their departure from what he understood to be civilized standards of military conduct, and was reluctant to use them. But the severe shortage of French manpower left Montcalm little choice.[7]

Many of the Indian nations had originally refused to side with the French. To entice them, Montcalm promised them plunder. The Indians accepted.

154

Plunder, however, was a highly ambiguous word for the Indians. Plunder, to the Indians, was an opportunity to use the French proposal as license to take up their grievances against the British.

On August 14, 1756, Montcalm sacked and destroyed Fort Oswego. The defeat of Oswego was a stunning loss for the British. It not only gave the French control of Lake Ontario and its tributaries, but it also interrupted Britain's trade relations with the Iroquois.

Montcalm, a professional officer, exquisitely sensitive to the etiquette of surrender under civilized standards, had pledged safety for all prisoners of war taken at Fort Oswego. As the British surrendered to the French, the Indians saw their opportunity to take plunder, trophies and captives slipping away. Disregarding foreign military protocol, the Indians ferociously attacked, killed and scalped many of the sick, wounded and surrendering. Montcalm was unable to restore order and was intensely embarrassed by this "massacre" and felt dishonored as an officer.[8]

A similar, horrific fate awaited the provincials garrisoned within Fort William Henry.

"THE MASSACRE OF FORT WILLIAM HENRY"

The French continued to push forward. Montcalm's next strategic target was Fort William Henry on the shore of Lake George. Montcalm's fame at the destruction of Oswego had traveled throughout the countryside, causing many Indian nations to join his ranks. Through the watershed of the Warpath of the Nations marched Montcalm's army of 6,000 French regulars and nearly 2,000 Indian warriors, representing as many as forty-one different nations.

On August 9, 1757, after a six-day siege by Montcalm, Colonel George Monro capitulated his command to the French commander with the promise of safe passage, under French escort, to Fort Edward. In retrospect of Fort Oswego, Montcalm explained to the Indian chiefs the terms of the British surrender. The defeated soldiers were not to be harmed, and all provisions, food stocks, arms and personal effects, were to be respected as the property of "His Most Christian Majesty." It became clear to the Indians that their French "Father" had intended to deprive them of the reward they had so anticipated. The horrible fate suffered those at Fort Oswego was about to be repeated. As the British surrendered, the

Indians stormed the fort, attacked, killed and scalped the sick and wounded. The French were finally able to intervene, but for many it was too late.

The next day, as the British column made their way towards Fort Edward, the Indians waited along the road, jeering and menacing the procession with knives and tomahawks flashing. Then, with the signal of a bloodcurdling war cry, the Indians fell upon their helpless victims. Hundreds of warriors attacked the exposed rear of the column. All was confusion, as men ran screaming in every direction with Indians in pursuit. Before Montcalm and the French officers could bring order, as many as 185 British soldiers lay dead, while estimates of 300 to 500 were taken captive. Some found refuge among the French while others fled into the woods, eventually finding their way to Fort Edward. The Indians took what they came for and left. The French burned Fort William Henry to the ground.

Though a wave of French victories continued to discourage and overwhelm the British, never again did the French provoke such terror—never again would the Indians flock to the aide of the French. The Indians later discovered that before the attack on Fort William Henry, smallpox had broken out within the fort. Thus, all their plunder, captives, scalps and clothing, was poisoned with the deadly disease. A great epidemic, devastating their homelands, broke out soon after the Fort William Henry massacre.

The two armies, the British and the French, wouldn't fight again until the following year, and this time it would be the British who would be the aggressors, but at a terrible loss.

HUMILIATION AT FORT CARILLON

In the summer of 1758, the British, under the command of Major General James Abercromby, had amassed an army of sixteen thousand regulars and provincials to march against Fort Carillon on the Ticonderoga peninsula at the north end of Lake George. Without their Indian allies, Montcalm had only 3,526 men, hardly a force to withstand Abercromby's huge army. "Our situation is critical," wrote Montcalm's chief aide, Bouganville.[9]

However, Abercromby stalled in reaching Fort Carillon. Montcalm took advantage of the opportunity. The slow progress of the British afforded Montcalm the time to build an enormously long defensive breastwork three-quarters of a mile north of the fort called an "Abatis." An abatis is a network of fallen and tangled logs with sharpened branches built to impede the progress of the attackers, making them easy targets for musket fire.

At noon, on July 8, 1758, without so much as reconnoitering the French defenses or using any of his heavy artillery, Abercromby, with drums pounding and bagpipes wailing, ordered his men straight up the middle of the abatis. As the men encountered the mess of fallen trees, the French opened fire.

In attack after attack, the magnificently disciplined redcoats advanced into the barrier, only to be 'Cut . . . Down Like Grass,' according to a Massachusetts private, Joseph Nichols, who watched from the ranks of Colonel Jonathan Bagley's regiment, at the edge of the field. 'Our Forces Fell Exceeding Fast,' he wrote.[10]

As night settled and the smoke cleared, nearly two thousand of Abercromby's men lay either dead or wounded. Still retaining an army of fourteen thousand men, which was more than sufficient to destroy Fort Carillon, Abercromby ordered a retreat to Fort Edward. As the order was given, fear set into the ranks, and a general collapse of command resulted. A panic-stricken retreat ensued. The British abandoned the entire area leaving the French still in control of the fort. Second only to Braddock's defeat, the attack and retreat from Fort Carillon was the most humiliating defeat the British had suffered during the war.

PROPOSALS OF PEACE

Meanwhile, Pennsylvania continued to decay from a land of promise and influence to an upheaval of death, fear and misery. Fueled by revenge and supplied by the French, the Indians were well into the third year of the war with no sign of letting up.

From the onset of the struggle the English repeatedly tried to regain the trust of the Indians that had allied with the French, but to no avail. The brutal slaughtering had nearly demoralized the province and would have continued had it not been for two critical events.

First, on August 25-27, 1758, the British, under the command of Lieutenant Colonel John Bradstreet, captured and destroyed Fort Frontenac, the French outpost on the northeastern shore of Lake Ontario, thus cutting off all arms and supplies to Forts Niagara and Duquesne.[11] With the exception of Fort Niagara, the British now had control of Lake Ontario.

Second, and more crucial, the English held out a desperate hand to the Ohio Indians. One man, a Moravian missionary, bringing words of reconciliation and compassion to the Indians, gave the English the respite they needed, causing a pause to the disintegration of the colony. Bearing proposals of peace from the governor of Pennsylvania, this missionary ventured into the dangerous backwoods of Pennsylvania. Facing death on many occasions at the hands of the French and their Indians, he quenched the hostility and won the Ohio Indians, but only for a time.

> This stout-hearted emissary was Christian Frederick Post, a Moravian missionary, who had long lived with the Indians, had twice married among them, and, by his upright dealings and plain good sense, had gained their confidence and esteem. His devout and conscientious spirit, his fidelity to what he deemed his duty, his imperturbable courage, his prudence and his address, well fitted him for the critical mission.[12]

The Moravians made the greatest efforts to bring reconciliation between the two races during an epoch of gruesome bloodshed.

THE GRAND COUNCIL AT EASTON

Through the heroic negotiation efforts of Post beginning on October 8, 1758, more than five hundred Indians representing all the tribes involved in the war, met together in Easton, Pennsylvania. Represented were all the tribes of the Six Nations, plus the Delaware, Conoy, Tuteloes and Nanticokes. Also present were Pennsylvania Lieutenant Governor, William Denny,[13] members of the Provincial Council and Assembly of Pennsylvania, New Jersey Governor, Sir Francis Bernard, Commissioners for Indian Affairs in New Jersey and a number of Quakers from Philadelphia.

This Grand Council at Easton met not only for securing peace with the Pennsylvania Indians but also for the purpose of exposing the unjust land transactions that led to the dreadful consequences for the frontier of Pennsylvania.

The Albany Purchase of 1754, as we have already seen, caused the Delaware of the Susquehanna and the valleys of the Ohio and Allegheny to ally themselves with the French. The Walking Purchase was the other great land dispute brought before the council. The running of the lines of the fraudulent Walking Purchase was a great misrepresentation, deceiving the Indians of a just purchase, and in turn removed this tribe from their ancestral lands.

From the beginning of these meetings, Teedyuskung, a Delaware chief who had embraced Christianity, made several attempts to appeal to the humanity of the English authorities for their assistance of teachers and ministers to teach them reading and writing and of the Christian religion. *This was never done.* Speaking on behalf of his people, Teedyuskung shared,

'You must consider that I have a soul as well as another.'[14]

All in attendance at Easton saw the great improprieties of the land purchases and, along with the apologies of both Governors, these lands were deeded back to the Indians.

The success of the Grand Council at Easton was about much more than land, however. In reality it was a thread of hope for once again rekindling harmony between these two nations, the English and the Indian. Trust was severely damaged by now. A miracle of cooperation from the colonists and governing authorities was needed. Any chances of future reconciliations if these promises were unintended or insincere would be altogether difficult.

> *You must consider that I have a soul as well as another.*

The Grand Council ended on October 26, 1758, securing peace. Through the gallant efforts of Post, the Ohio Indians were drawn away from the French with the stipulation that once the French had been defeated, the English also would withdraw from the Ohio.

Unfortunately for all, the Grand Council would be remembered as the last calm before the grand storm of unbreachable fury. *None of the promises made to the Indians were kept.*

THE TIDE TURNS

One month after the events at Easton, on November 25, 1758, after four bloody years of possessing the valley of the Ohio, the French set fire to Fort

Duquesne and abandoned it to an advancing army of nearly nine-thousand British regulars and provincials from Pennsylvania, Virginia and North Carolina, commanded by Brigadier-General John Forbes. With the fall of Fort Duquesne the French recognized the vulnerability of their forts to the north, Machault, LeBoeuf and Presque' Isle. The French abandoned and torched these forts as well thus ending French dominion in the valley forever. Once again the British flag flew over the waters of the Ohio.

It had been three years since General Braddock had met his dreadful demise at Fort Duquesne. On November 28, three days after General Forbes had captured the fort, he sent a detachment to bury the bones of those soldiers that had fallen in that horrible defeat. When they arrived at the scene of the battle, their eyes were met with the grim remainder of that awful slaughter. Hundreds of skeletons littered the ground, still lying where they had fallen. Wolves, bears, and other wild creatures had torn many of the bodies asunder, scattering skulls and bones about the forest floor. Peacefully and quietly, the soldiers gathered the remains of their brave and fallen comrades, and interred them to their final place of rest.

The pressure on the French increased as the war began to turn in favor of the British. Though the past two years had carried the war into the Iroquois territory of New York, the Iroquois had remained true to their promise of neutrality. However, it had become obvious to the Iroquois that the French had done something that they had promised not to, fortify the trading post at Niagara. The French had deceived them. In a surprised turn of events, the Iroquois broke their neutrality and committed their warriors to the ranks of Sir William Johnson and brutally routed the French troops at Fort Niagara on July 25, 1759, giving the British full control of Lake Ontario. With Fort Niagara in British hands, the French retreated into Canada in August of 1759, but not before abandoning and destroying their Lake Champlain strongholds, Forts Carillon[15] at Ticonderoga and St. Frédérick at Crown Point.

The war would continue to be fought on the North American continent until the epic and decisive battle between the forces of British Major-General James Wolfe and Marquis de Montcalm on the Plains of Abraham which brought the fall of Quebec on September 13, 1759. Montreal was defeated on September 8, 1760. Thus would end 150 years of French possession on the North American continent. The war continued in Europe and ended with the surrender of the French at the signing of the Treaty of Paris in February, 1763.

No matter which side the Indians of Pennsylvania and elsewhere in the Northeast had chosen in the Seven Years War, the diplomatic and economic results were disastrous. Great Britain emerged from the conflict as the sole European imperial claimant to North America east of the Mississippi... As a result, the Seven Years War merged, almost without interruption, into a desperate forty-year struggle by Pennsylvania natives to maintain their independence from rule by Great Britain and—after the colonials' own successful war for independence—the United States.[16]

FRAUDULENT PROMISES

An offended brother is more unyielding than a fortified city, and disputes are like the barred gates of a citadel.

Proverbs 18:19

The British, however, did not abandon Fort Duquesne as had been promised to the Indians but reoccupied it and named it Fort Pitt[17] after England's prime minister, William Pitt.

The pressure to occupy these lands west of the Allegheny Mountains where the Delaware and Shawnee lived continued to mount. Little consideration was given the Indians for lands deeded back to them at the Grand Council at Easton. More councils were held at Fort Pitt, Philadelphia and Lancaster, and more treaties were made promising the Delaware and Shawnee the withdrawal of the English from the hunting grounds and homes of the Indians. *Again, these promises were never kept!*

By this point, too fragile was the hope the Indian had extended. Withdrawing his hand from years of forlorn compromise, with the aid of the great war-chief Pontiac, the Indians picked up their tomahawks and scalping knives once again. The Indians rose in even greater fury against the English in Pennsylvania, Maryland, Virginia and the region of the Great Lakes. Some of the bloodiest revenge on American soil happened after the French and Indian War had already concluded. No longer would the Indian be appeased.

CHRONOLOGICAL TABLE

1755	(1) November 24. The Indians attack the Moravian mission of Gnadenhutten, kill the missionaries and burn the town. (2) December 1755-January 1756. Pennsylvania begins building block houses and forts along the Blue Mountains to protect the settlements from the Indians.
1756	(1) April 14. Governor of Pennsylvania, Robert Hunter Morris, declares war against the Delaware and Shawnee and offers a bounty for their scalps. (2) Quakers resign their control of the Assembly when Pennsylvania declares war against the Delaware. (3) May 17. Britain declares war against France beginning the French and Indian War. (4) August 14. The French sack and destroy Oswego on the New York shore of Lake Ontario.
1757	August 9. After a six-day siege by the French, Colonel George Monro capitulates his command of Fort William Henry on the southern tip of Lake George.
1756-1759	William Denny, Lieutenant Governor of Pennsylvania.
1758	(1) Spring. Teedyuskung and his tribe move into the Wyoming Valley. (2) July 8. Under the command of Major General James Abercromby, the British suffer a humiliating defeat trying to capture Fort Carillon. (3) Summer and Autumn. Moravian missionary, Christian Frederick Post, begins peace mission to Ohio Indians.

(4) August 25-27. Under the command of Lieutenant Colonel John Bradstreet, the British capture and destroy Fort Frontenac along Lake Ontario, cutting off all arms and supplies to the French at Forts Niagara and Duquesne.

(5) October 8-October 26. "Grand Council" at Easton secures peace with western Indians and draws them away from the French.

(6) November 24. French abandon Fort Duquesne to the army of Brigadier-General John Forbes.

(7) November 25. British take possession of Fort Duquesne and name it Fort Pitt.

1759	(1) July 25. The British defeat the French at Fort Niagara. (2) September 13. The British defeat the French on The Plains of Abraham at Quebec.
1760	September 8. The French surrender to the British at Montreal.
1762	November. Preliminaries of peace are made between England and France.
1763	(1) February 10. Treaty of Paris where France formally surrenders to England all of its possessions in North America.

ENDNOTES

1. Donehoo, Dr. George P., *Pennsylvania: A History, Five Vols.*, (Lewis Historical Publishing Company, Inc., New York, Chicago, 1926), p. 774.

2. Jennings, Francis, *Empire Of Fortune: Crowns, colonies, and Tribes in the Seven Years War in America*, (W. W. Norton & Company, New York, N. Y., London, 1988), p. 193. N.Y. Col. Docs. 10:423.

3. Donehoo, Dr. George P., *Pennsylvania: A History, Five Vols.*, (Lewis Historical Publishing Company, Inc., New York, Chicago, 1926), p. 774.

4. Sipe, C. Hale, *The Indian Wars of Pennsylvania*, (originally published, Harrisburg, PA, 1931., reprinted, Gateway Press, Baltimore, MD, for Wennawoods Publishing, Lewisburg, PA, 1995), pp. 281-282.

5. *Ibid.*, p. 283.

6. Downey, Dennis B., and Francis J. Bremer, *A Guide to the History of Pennsylvania*, (Greenwood Press, Westport, Connecticut, London, 1993), p. 42.

7. Anderson, Fred, *Crucible of War*, (Alfred A. Knopf, New York, 2000), pp. 151-154

8. *Ibid.*, pp. 151-154

9. *Ibid.*, p. 242.

10. *Ibid.*, p. 244.

11. The attack on Fort Frontenac (Kingston, Ontario) was led by Lieutenant-Colonel John Bradstreet and 2,517 provincials (locals) and 135 regulars (British).

12. Parkman, Francis, *The Conspiracy of Pontiac*, (Collier Books, New York, Collier - Macmillian LTD., London, 1962), p. 106.

13. Lieutenant Governor William Denny served as Pennsylvania's governor from 1756-1759.

14. Donehoo, Dr. George P., *Indian Villages and Place Names in Pennsylvania*, (Gateway Press, Baltimore, MD, 1995), p. 261.

15. The British would rebuild Fort Carillon and rename it Fort Ticonderoga. On July 6, 1777, Fort Ticonderoga would be the scene of an American victory during the American Revolution.

16. Downey, Dennis B., and Francis J. Bremer, *A Guide to the History of Pennsylvania*, (Greenwood Press, Westport, Connecticut, London, 1993), p. 43.

17. Fort Pitt Museum can be visited today in Point State Park at the tip of Pittsburgh's Golden Triangle.

1 2

THE FURY OF THE STORM

We must exterminate from our land this nation whose only object is our death. We must destroy them without delay. There is nothing to prevent us... Why should we not attack them? What do we fear? The time has arrived... Let us strike. Strike! There is no longer any time to lose.

—Pontiac

With the defeat of the French, the English offered peace to the Indians but only as tainted water to a parched soul. The English began taking possession of all the lands the French had occupied without any consideration to former treaties that had promised these lands back to the Indians. Scenarios were beginning to repeat themselves that had launched the Indians into the French and Indian War. Historians Donehoo and Sipe both give the telling commentary of an all too familiar drama that was now inciting the Indians to go to war once again.

> Why should the Indians desire either the French or the English to remain on the Ohio? They realized fully that the fight was between France and Great Britain for the possession of the Ohio, and that all of the protestations of the benevolent schemes of the British were mere "hot air." The great trouble was that the Indians were not so foolish as the British authorities seemed to imagine. Their voice was the voice of Jacob, but their hand was the hand of Esau. They said that they did not want the lands on the Ohio, but in the meanwhile they went on building a fort, in order to hold it. The great trouble in the English, and American, method of dealing with the Indian was due to this constant misjudgment of the Indian's ability to see through flimsy excuses. The Indian was a diplomat by nature. All of his methods of hunting and fighting were based on his ability to deceive. Deception was an art, and yet the British officers and the Colonial authorities imagined that they could beat the Indian at a game, in which he was an expert, and they mere bunglers. The Indian was never deceived, in the sense in which an ignorant child is deceived. They saw through every scheme, but had to pretend they did not, in order that they might get what little they could get out of the wreck.[1]

The British forgot their promises and treaties as soon as they made them. But the Indian never forgot a promise, a treaty, a kindness or, an injury. The strongest love of his heart was the love for the lands he considered his own, as the gift of the Great Spirit. Now that the Indians' loved home and hunting grounds were invaded in violation of solemn promises and formal treaties, it is no wonder that the storm which had been brewing for ten years, broke with fury in the summer of 1763—it is no wonder that the warriors of Pontiac, Guyasuta and Custaloga rose in savage wrath in an effort to drive the English into the sea, and that the Pennsylvania valleys ran red with the blood of the pioneers.[2]

PONTIAC DECLARES WAR

Pontiac, a great Ottawa chief and masterful war tactician, had served alongside the French during the French and Indian War. Pontiac suspected that if he waited any longer for the English to stand by their promises, the Indian way of life would be completely exterminated.

Runners were sent in all directions to call together the councils of the Delaware, Shawnee, Seneca, Cayuga, Mingoe, Mohican, Miami, Ottawa and Huron (Wyandot) to declare war against the English. Never had so many tribes been united. From as far as a thousand miles apart the Cree and Nipissing from the north were joined together with the Chickesaw from the Mississippi Valley. Along came the Ojibwa, Chipewa, Potawatomies, Winnebagos, Sauk and Fox and the Kickapoo, all to take up their grievances against the English Empire.

When the councils of the Indian nations had gathered together, Pontiac spoke. A French trader recorded Pontiac's words.

'We must exterminate from our land this nation whose only object is our death. We must destroy them without delay. There is nothing to prevent us... Why should we not attack them? What do we fear? The time has arrived... Let us strike. Strike! There is no longer any time to lose.'[3]

In the summer of 1763, Pontiac's plan was executed. His confederation rose up in bitter revolt against the English to forcefully remove them from all the lands that had been repeatedly promised to the Indians and then reneged. Never was so great a gauntlet thrown down upon the English colonies. With an even greater ferocity than before, a state of siege was laid down before the colonies as the blood of both English and Indian began to flow, turning crimson the soil of the frontier. From north to south, for hundreds of miles, the country was wasted with fire and steel. The depredations the Indians inflicted upon the colonies

Illustration by Lorence Bjorklund

Wellman, Paul I., *Indian Wars and Warriors, East* (Riverside Press, Cambridge, Massachusetts, 1959), p. 150.

and its inhabitants far outweighed that of the previous war.

Along the Great Lakes and rivers to the west, Forts Quiatenon, St. Joseph, Edward Augustus, Sault Ste. Marie, Green Bay, Sandusky and Miami all fell as if by a single blow.[4] Fort Michilimackinac on the channel connecting Lakes Michigan and Huron met a horrible fate.[5] Fort Detroit was besieged for five-months. In Pennsylvania, Forts Venango, Le Boeuf and Presqu' Isle were captured and burned to the ground. The Juniata, Tuscarora, Sherman and Cumberland Valleys were invaded as Forts Ligonier,[6] Bedford[7] (General Forbes ordered the construction of these two forts during his 1758 campaign against Fort Duquesne) and Pitt were attacked. All the settlements between the Susquehanna and the Potomac Rivers were threatened by complete destruction as more than two thousand settlers were killed in the torrent.

No pen can describe nor tongue can tell of its horrors as the Indians swept from west to east. Like a great consuming flood churning with broken promises, the land was engulfed in a sea of anger.

THE DEVASTATION OF CUMBERLAND COUNTY

No other part of the region suffered more than that of the settlements along the entire frontier of Cumberland County,[8] Pennsylvania. Hundreds were killed or carried away into captivity. Losing both friends and family, with homes set ablaze, the settlers ran for the protective covering of the Colonial Authorities. Fort Lowther in Carlisle and Fort Morris in Shippensburg were filled with the terrified refugees of the settlements.

Listen, as Francis Parkman, from *The Conspiracy of Pontiac*, narrates two extracts from letters published in the Pennsylvania *Gazette* written from Carlisle during this time of upheaval in July of 1763.

> The surrounding country was by this time completely abandoned by the settlers, many of whom, not content with seeking refuge at Carlisle, continued their flight to the eastward, and, headed by the clergyman of that place, pushed on to Lancaster, and even to Philadelphia.
>
> Carlisle presented a most deplorable spectacle. A multitude of the refugees unable to find shelter in the town, had encamped in the woods or on the adjacent fields, erecting huts of branches and bark, and living on such charity as the slender means of the townspeople could supply. Passing among them, one would have witnessed every form of human misery. In these wretched encampments were men, women, and children, bereft at one stroke of friends, of home, and the means of supporting life. Some stood aghast and bewildered at the sudden

and fatal blow; others were sunk in the apathy of despair; others were weeping and moaning with irrepressible anguish. With not a few, the craven passion of fear drowned all other emotion, and day and night they were haunted with visions of the bloody knife and the reeking scalp; while in others, every faculty was absorbed by the burning thirst for vengeance, and mortal hatred against the whole Indian race.[9]

THE BATTLE OF BUSHY RUN

Under the leadership of Colonel Henry Bouquet, commander of the first battalion of Royal Americans, a military campaign against the Indians began in June of 1763. Bouquet's forces pressed west from Philadelphia enroute to Fort Pitt, sweeping through Carlisle and then Shippensburg, where nearly fourteen hundred terrified and starving refugees were huddled. Fifty miles from Fort Pitt, Bouquet's forces encountered Pontiac's confederation on August 5, 1763. There, at Bushy Run,[10] was fought the most bitterly contested battle between Indians and white men on the American continent. After two days of fighting, through the masterful strategy of Bouquet, the Indians were defeated on August 6, 1763.

> The Delawares and Shawnees, after this battle, smarting under their first real defeat, left their villages on the Allegheny, the Ohio and the Beaver, and retreated to the Muskingum and Tuscarawas[11]From these western villages, they continued to make raids into the Pennsylvania settlements, from time to time, until Colonel Bouquet led his expedition into their western stronghold in the autumn of 1764....[12]

MASSACRE IN THE WYOMING VALLEY

Ten years previous to Pontiac's war, during the negotiations at the Albany Treaty of 1754, an Indian trader named John Henry Lydius, thought by some to be a French agent, very irregularly convinced the Mohawks to sell a large tract of land on the North Branch of the Susquehanna River to Connecticut. Known for his reputation as a villain and a scoundrel, Lydius, through bribery and drunkenness, quietly convinced the Mohawks to sell the land to

Connecticut without the knowledge or consent of the Great Council of the Six Nations. This trickery would cause such an upheaval over the Wyoming Valley that many lives would soon be lost.

The Mohawks though, did not have the authority to act independently of the Great Council of the Six Nations to make such a purchase. This tract of land, known as the Wyoming Valley,[13] had been reserved at the Albany Treaty for the Delaware and Shawnee as a place of refuge from the French and as their own hunting grounds. The Six Nations had also promised at the treaty of 1736 not to sell any lands within the limits of Pennsylvania's royal grant except to "the said William Penn's Children." That meant that no one was allowed to purchase land within Pennsylvania outside the Penn family name.

Another perplexity for the Wyoming Valley was the error King Charles II made when he inadvertently overlapped the northern border of Pennsylvania with the southern border of Connecticut. When the King granted the Connecticut province in 1662, he had included within their northern and southern borders all the land from the Atlantic to the Pacific Ocean. In theory, at least, Connecticut's western boundary was the Pacific Ocean. At that time, the province of Pennsylvania did not exist and therefore was not under consideration.

CONNECTICUT ENTERS THE WYOMING VALLEY

Connecticut became interested in the Wyoming Valley as early as 1750. Unknown to Connecticut, the Wyoming Valley was the same valley that many of the Delaware had settled after their forced eviction from the Delaware Valley through the Walking Purchase dispute of 1737.

In 1753, Connecticut incorporated a land company called the Susquehannah Company, in which Lydius was the agent, and very readily bought the Wyoming Valley from the Mohawks at the Albany Treaty in 1754. Settlers from Connecticut began entering the Wyoming Valley in the spring of 1762.

In consideration of all the hostilities that had already been committed on the Pennsylvania frontier, for the Connecticut settler to take possession of the Wyoming Valley was, as Dr. Donehoo tells us, "the most foolhardy thing which was ever attempted in American history."[14] The crooked selling of this last great refuge for the Delaware and Shawnee led to the first of two terrible disasters in the Wyoming Valley, collectively known as the Wyoming Massacre.

Because Pennsylvania and the Indians repeatedly forbade the Connecticut settlers from settling in the valley, the impending result was a foregone conclusion.

> He (the Indian) did exactly what men have always done, and as they will always do, when their possessions are taken against their will, and after all appeals to law or equity have failed, then comes the inevitable appeal to the last Court of the Red Man and White Man, the bloody Court of Arms.[15]

On October 15, 1763, a band of one hundred and thirty-five Indians fell upon the unsuspecting Connecticut settlers. The results were devastating. Twenty Connecticut settlers were killed and the helpless survivors fled back over the mountains into Connecticut. King Charles II's error not only cost the lives of many a Connecticut settler, but consequently, removed the Delaware and Shawnee from their only remaining refuge in the east. Nonetheless, the Wyoming Valley dispute over settlement rights continued to brew between Connecticut and the Indians. Another horrible massacre would come later during the Revolution.

THE PAXTON BOYS

As Pontiac and his confederation of warriors were ransacking the countryside, the peaceful Susquehannocks remained at friendly terms with the English. After the Iroquois had defeated and dispersed this tribe in 1677, the Susquehannocks had slowly begun to recover at Conestoga along the Susquehanna River. For generations, long before the time that William Penn had visited this tribe in 1701, until Pontiac's war on the settlements in 1763, the Susquehannocks had always been able to remain and call Conestoga their home.[16] Never had they fought against the whites during the French and Indian War nor had they enlisted with Pontiac. However, because the Indian wars had turned Pennsylvania into a bloody battlefield, some groups of whites were developing an all-out hatred for the entire Indian population, regardless of tribe. Such was the case of a group of Presbyterian Scotch-Irish settlers from the area of Paxtang, near Harrisburg, called the "The Paxton Boys."

The Scotch-Irish were a pioneering people and often led the way into unsettled lands. This unquenchable spirit continually led them beyond the boundaries of purchased land into the homelands of the Indians, giving no heed to standing treaties. When the violent storm of Indian wrath erupted on the frontier in 1755, the Scotch-Irish found themselves in the wake of its path. The consequences were unavoidable. Many Scotch-Irish lost their lives.

As a result, when Pontiac's confederation began wreaking havoc on the colony, very bad feelings began to brood among the Scotch-Irish. They were saying that the only good Indian was a dead one, friendly or unfriendly, and that God had given them a mandate to rid the earth of these heathen, whom they called "red-vipers."

THE DREADFUL FATE OF THE CONESTOGAS

With Conestoga being so close to Harrisburg, the Susquehannocks were unaware of the impending danger. And even though the Susquehannocks were living under the protection of the Pennsylvania government, the insolence of the Paxton Boys brought about a terrible carnage for the meek tribe.

Led by Lazarus Stewart, an elder in the church, the Paxton Boys rode into Conestoga on December 14, 1763, and with a force of nearly fifty well-armed professing Christian men murdered and scalped six peaceful and defenseless members of their tribe: an elderly woman, another woman, three old men and a little boy.

Pennsylvania was appalled at the massacre and was unable to see any justification for the inhumane, senseless and brutal slaughter of these defenseless, unarmed Indians. A cry for justice went out against the perpetrators.

Afterward, the remaining Susquehannocks were removed to Lancaster and there put under protective custody in the local jail. However, thirteen days after the first murders, on Sunday morning December 27, when all the townspeople were in church, nearly one hundred Paxton Boys rode into Lancaster unopposed, broke into the jail and commenced to murder all the Indians who were being held there. Three old Indian men, three Indian women, five Indian boys and three little Indian girls lost their lives to the ruthless killers.

Sipe, in his book, *The Indian Wars of Pennsylvania*, gives us this historical narrative of the second massacre.

The details of the massacre of these unarmed and defenseless Conestogas are most shocking and revolting. Protesting their innocence and their love for the English, they, according to Benjamin Franklin, prostrated themselves with their children before their infuriated murderers, and pleaded for their lives; while the jailer says they died with the stoicism of their race. Their appeal was answered by the rifle, hatchet, and scalping knife. Some had their brains blown out, others their legs chopped off, and others their hands cut off.[17]

Thus, in 1763, came the tragic end of the Susquehannock Indians. The Paxton Boys then threatened to march on Philadelphia and kill the Moravian Delawares who had been taken there for protection. The soldiers who escorted these Christian Delawares to Philadelphia were very kind to them and said, "Would to God, all the white people were as good Christians as these Indians!"[18]

> *"Would to God, all the white people were as good Christians as these Indians!"*

The citizens of Philadelphia rallied together and took up arms against the Paxton Boys and prepared the city to protect the Christian Delawares. The Paxton Boys backed down and returned to their homes. Afterward, none of the Paxton Boys were ever brought to justice for their crimes against the friendly Conestogas.

THE END OF PONTIAC'S WAR

In the spring and summer of 1764, the Ohio Indians continued their raids into the frontiers of western Pennsylvania. Colonel Bouquet was summoned again and in the Fall of 1764 he led an army of fifteen hundred men beyond the Ohio, deep into the territory of "Indian Country." His efforts brought the submission of the Delaware, Shawnee and other western tribes and the release of the more than six hundred captives the Indians had taken in their many raids into the Pennsylvania frontier since 1755.

Governor Thomas Penn, on December 5, 1764, declared the end of the war, insomuch as Pennsylvania was concerned. However, the pressure on Indian land in the valleys of the Ohio and Allegheny would continue without end for another thirty-one years.

As Dr. Donehoo says, in his *Pennsylvania—A History*: 'The Indian has never fought for anything which did not belong to him, and he never fought for a principle unless that principle was upheld by a treaty or agreement with the white man. The Indian has been charged with being at peace today and on the warpath tomorrow. This is not true. The white man made promises with the Indian today and forgot them tomorrow, and then blamed the Indian because he also would not forget."[19]

The Indians were criticized for their lack of civilization; yet, who is the one less civilized—the one who keeps his word or the one who does not?

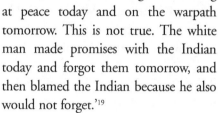

A PEOPLE OF COVENANT

The Indians honored declared covenants. Their society, with its history and culture, had always been passed from generation to generation by the oral traditions of the elders, believing that a man's integrity was found in the honor of his words. For them a covenant was an agreement—a promise made from the heart. Treaties were the same. When white men came making promises, Indians trusted them, welcomed them and invited them to live with them. For Indians, a man and his word were inseparable. This is why the treaty of peace underneath the great elm between William Penn and the Delaware was so unique and stood above the rest. It was the one treaty the Indians understood—the one treaty that spoke their language—one heart, one flesh.

White men's promises were put on paper; Indians' were memorialized on strings and belts of wampum, authenticating for generations promises fulfilled. To the Indians' utter bewilderment, white men's words were no better than the paper they were written on. It was the "pen and ink work," as the Indians called it, which was responsible for renouncing every vow ever made between the white man and every Indian nation.

The Indians were criticized for their lack of civilization; but who is the one less civilized—the one who keeps his word or the one who does not? God help us!

A good name is more desirable than great riches; to be esteemed is better than silver or gold.

Proverbs 22:1

CHRONOLOGICAL TABLE

1754   (1) July 6. At the Albany Treaty the Mohawks very irregularly sell the Wyoming Valley to the Susquehannah Company through the treacherous scheming of agent John Henry Lydius.

1762   Connecticut settlers begin entering the Wyoming Valley.

1763   (1) Spring. Pontiac, chief of the Ottawas, forms confederation of western tribes.

(2) Summer. Pontiac declares war on the colonies.

(3) June 17. Capture of Fort Venango.

(4) June 18. Capture of Fort Le Boeuf.

(5) June 22. Capture of Fort Presque' Isle.

(6) June and July. Siege of Fort Ligonier.

(7) June and July. Seige of Fort Bedford.

(8) July 26-August 1. Siege of Fort Pitt.

(9) July. Invasion of Juniata, Tuscarora, Sherman's and Cumberland Valley's.

(10) July and August. Colonel Henry Bouquet's march to relieve the western forts.

(11) August 5-6. Battle of Bushy Run.

(12) October 15. The first Wyoming Massacre.

(13) December 14 & 27. Murder of the last remnant of the Conestogas by the "Paxton Boys."

1764   (1) Autumn. Colonel Henry Bouquet's expedition into "Indian Country" of the Tuscarawas and Muskingum brings the submission of the western tribes.

(2) December 5. Governor John Penn issues proclamation of the submission of the Delaware and Shawnee and proclaims the end of the war.

ENDNOTES

1. Donehoo, Dr. George P., *Indian Villages and Place Names in Pennsylvania*, (Gateway Press, Baltimore, MD, 1995), pp. 204-205.

2. Sipe, C. Hale, *The Indian Wars of Pennsylvania*, (originally published, Harrisburg, PA, 1931., reprinted, Gateway Press, Baltimore, MD, for Wennawoods Publishing, Lewisburg, PA, 1995), p. 412.

3. Marrin, Albert, *Struggle for a Continent, The French and Indian Wars 1690-1760*, (Atheneum, Macmillan Publishing Company, 1987), p. 198.

4. All of these forts lie within the present states surrounding the Great Lakes region: Ohio, Michigan, Indiana, Wisconsin and Canada.

5. Many Indian tribes would compete against each other in traditional games of lacrosse. Before Fort Michilimackinac could be made aware of the possible danger of a threatened Indian attack the Chippewa staged a game with the Sauk in front of the fort and invited the garrison to come out and watch. When the fort opened its gates the Indians attacked and killed its defenders.

6. Fort Ligonier has been finely reconstructed to help the visitor feel what life must have been like in an eighteenth-century fort. The largest discovery of artifacts from The French and Indian War in the United States can be viewed here. Fort Ligonier is in the present city of Ligonier, PA, on U.S. Route 30 and PA Route 711.

7. Though the original fort no longer exists, the remake of the fort, the Fort Bedford Museum, helps the visitor reminisce of what it must have been like in colonial Pennsylvania. The Fort Bedford Museum is located in the town of Bedford, PA, on Juliana St.

8. To understand the scope of devastation committed by the Indians in Cumberland County, one must have an appreciation of the size of the county back in 1763. Cumberland County was the sixth county founded within the Province and included all of South Western Pennsylvania. The county didn't reach its present size until 1820.

9. Parkman, Francis, *The Conspiracy of Pontiac*, (Collier Books, New York, Collier - Macmillian LTD., London, 1962), pp. 305-306.

10. The Pennsylvania Historical and Museum Commission have erected a Historical Marker at the place of this battle, on State Highway 993, one mile east of Harrison City, Westmoreland County. There is also a visitor's center at the location.

11. The Muskingum and Tuscarawas Rivers lie within the present state of Ohio.

12. Sipe, C. Hale, *The Indian Wars of Pennsylvania*, (originally published, Harrisburg, PA, 1931., reprinted, Gateway Press, Baltimore, MD, for Wennawoods Publishing, Lewisburg, PA, 1995), p. 449.

13. The Wyoming Valley, located on the North Branch of the Susquehanna River, was referred to by the Indians as "large flats" or "great meadows." Today the Wyoming Valley is occupied by the city of Wilkes Barre, Pennsylvania.

14. Donehoo, Dr. George P., *Indian Villages and Place Names in Pennsylvania*, (Gateway Press, Baltimore, MD, 1995), p. 261.

15. *Ibid.*

16. Early American Explorer, John Smith (probably the first white man the Susquehannocks had ever seen), visited this tribe in 1608 when exploring the Susquehanna River.

17. Sipe, C. Hale, *The Indian Wars of Pennsylvania*, (originally published, Harrisburg, PA, 1931., reprinted, Gateway Press, Baltimore, MD, for Wennawoods Publishing, Lewisburg, PA, 1995), p. 465.

18. *Ibid.*, p. 468.

19. *Ibid.*, p. 828.

1 3

THE FINAL
DISPOSSESSION

*It grieves me to hear that our Frontier People are yet greater Barbarians
than the Indians, and continue to murder them in a time of peace.[1]*

— Benjamin Franklin

The year 1764 may have brought an end to Pontiac's confederation, but
it did not stop Indian hostilities on the frontier. Following the defeat
of Pontiac, the white population of the colonies continued to grow
and flourish. The colonists, anxious to settle new ground, continued to push
beyond the set limits. The governments of New York, Pennsylvania and
Virginia were unable to control their border populations as the colonists began
murdering the Indians with reckless abandon. The wholesale extermination of
Native Americans was considered a necessary evil in the name of progress.

Hostilities between the two nations continued until more treaties had to be signed to end the conflicts. The next treaty, called the Treaty at Fort Stanwix (Rome, New York), was signed on November 5, 1768, between the Six Nations (the Iroquois) and Pennsylvania to settle the issue of Indian lands. This deed released yet another very large portion of land into the hands of the English without any consideration or consent of the Indians actually living on those lands.

GNADENHUTTEN II

The Moravian missionaries and the Christian Indians continued to persevere during this time of great conflict. In 1765, after the French and Indian War and Pontiac's War, the Moravians moved their mission to Wyalusing on the North Branch of the Susquehanna, calling it Friedenshutten (Tents of Peace). So successful was this mission among the local Indians that both white men and Indians

The Power of the Gospel
Courtesy of The Moravian Archives, Bethlehem, PA

from far and wide came to see it. The colonies had never seen anything like it. In fact, so successful was this mission that the Great Council of the Delaware invited the mission into the Muskingum country of present Ohio so that all the Delaware, Shawnee, Wyandots and Iroquois could see how well this experiment in Christian brotherhood worked. The Moravians accepted the offer.

In 1772, two hundred Indian converts, along with all their possessions, moved to the Ohio and set up their missions. One of the missions, established along the Tuscarawas River, was called Gnadenhutten, named after the mission that was destroyed in 1755 along the Lehigh River. Great chiefs of the Delaware, impacted by the message of the Gospel, soon began joining the mission. The Indian nations were stirred. And yet, America, still in the throes of development, was about to enter the portal of yet another violent era.

AN AMERICAN REVOLUTION

At the close of the French and Indian War it became prudent of England to keep a peacekeeping force in America as a buffer against any further invasions from France, or Indians. However, there were nearly one hundred thousand British troops stationed in America,[2] and a way was needed to help pay and quarter (house) them all. The war had nearly depleted England's treasury resulting in a serious economic depression. England had become desperate to fund their troops and began looking to its newly formed and increasingly prosperous colonies in the New World for the investment needed. Besides, these colonies certainly could agree that their very existence was owed to the mother-country for her efforts in bringing an end to the war. And so England thought.

Parliament, now under King George III, had a plan to restore England's fallen revenue. Taxes! Slowly, over the next several years a long series of taxation was incorporated on all goods shipped to America. In April of 1764, the King approved the American Duties Act, known by Americans as the Sugar Act. There was the Stamp Act of March 1765, which taxed almost everything written or printed on paper or vellum. The Townshend Revenue Acts of June 1767, levied duties on glass, lead, painters' colors, paper, and tea. With each and every act that England passed the colonists objected. And though Parliament later repealed each of the acts, a fuse to a great powder keg of discontent had been lit.

The Pennsylvania Assembly petitioned the King in March 1771. The American colonists had no representation in Parliament and protested the continual levies put on them as taxation without consent. Though America was largely made up of British subjects, a self-sufficient independence had developed. The temperament of the American colonists began to change. Then came the Tea Act of 1773. Benjamin Franklin's plan of intercolonial union that he had proposed in Carlisle, 1753, and then again in Albany, 1754, was now needed more than ever before.

The climate began to heave with the sound of rebellion. The Americans insisted that it was to time to break from England and claim their own independence from the heavy hand of British law. The British Empire was about to lose their "Divine Right" on the North American continent.

A NEW CONSTITUTION

Philadelphia had risen to become the political nerve center of the Thirteen Colonies, and in 1776, Pennsylvania's Constitution was used as a blueprint to write a new Constitution to support and accommodate America's revolutionary and independent stand against England. In this revised Constitution, members of the Assembly still had to declare their faith in God and in the inspiration of the scriptures as set forth in William Penn's *First Frame of Government* in 1682. Penn had firmly stated in his Constitution that the true seeds of inspired government come from nowhere else. To create and run a government on these principles required a radical revolution upon the heart, not the law, indeed "A Holy Experiment." Governments rather depend upon men, than men upon governments, as Penn had alleged. However, it had been ninety-four long years since Penn had cast his original vision. The present Revolutionary government was about to prove again just how governments depend on men. While those who understood the brilliant truth Penn had bequeathed the new nation, those same men could not acknowledge its source. God would merely become one to whom men would casually 'tip their hats.'

By 1790, with the war for independence over, Philadelphia had advanced to become the nation's capitol, and the Constitution was once again revised, largely due to the improvement of the earlier revolutionary conditions of discontent. This time, however, the requirement of the Assembly to declare their faith in God and in the inspiration of the scriptures was omitted.

And then, in 1800, a dramatic decision was made to move the capitol from Philadelphia to Washington D.C. which marked the gradual decline of Philadelphia's influence in the political and economic affairs of the nation.

SECOND MASSACRE AT WYOMING

As the American colonists were revolting and severing their allegiance with England, their relationship with the Iroquois Confederacy quickly began to deteriorate as well. The Iroquois had always favored their long-standing relationship with the British and could not idly stand by and watch the land-hungry Americans devour their land before their very eyes. The British enticed the Iroquois to fight with them against the Americans. Danger loomed on the horizon as the Iroquois Confederacy began to break apart and take actions independently of one another. The Mohawks, Onondagas, Cayugas and

Senecas sided with the British while the Oneidas and Tuscaroras cast their allegiance with the "Thirteen Fires." The Americans made an attempt to woo back to their side those Iroquois who sided with the British, but this failed.

Originally, when the Revolution first broke out, the Americans and the British told the Iroquois to "sit still" and not get involved. However, an Iroquois saying that passed down from the French and Indian War was, "You can't live in the woods and stay neutral."[3]

In the midst of all this turmoil, the Wyoming Valley still lingered as a spur of contention in the heart of the Indians, especially since Connecticut settlers were once again on the increase in the valley. In view of all that had already transpired to offend the Pennsylvania Indians, the Connecticut settlers couldn't have chosen a worse time to be greedy for land that was not theirs.

You can't live in the woods and stay neutral.

On July 3, 1778, seven hundred Iroquois, mainly Seneca and Cayuga, led by four hundred Tories,[4] invaded the Wyoming Valley, killing the nearly four hundred gallant Continental and Colonial defenders on the field of battle. This slaughter was one of the most dreadful massacres in the annals of Pennsylvania's history.[5] The onslaught was so great and created such a panic that all of central Pennsylvania fled in great fear—called the "Great Runaway."

The decision of the Iroquois to join forces with the British in their fight against the Americans, however, proved too heavy a price for the Iroquois to bear. The Americans would later defeat the British and nearly completely destroy the Iroquois during the American Revolution.[6]

After a period of nearly twenty years of bloodshed and conflict in the Wyoming Valley (which included the Yankee, Pennamite Wars), on December 30, 1782, the Supreme Executive Council of Pennsylvania consented in favor of Pennsylvania. The order was called the Trenton Decree,[7] in which Connecticut yielded the area to Pennsylvania, resolving the border dispute of both states.

THE FIRST TREATY OF THE UNITED STATES

Now that the American Revolution was moving into the past, being written into the history books, the Americans, proud parents of their new Republic, conducted their very first treaty. On September 17, 1778, in an attempt to reconcile with the Indians, a treaty was held at Fort Pitt with the Delaware. With the extraordinary accomplishment of the Moravian missions and the Delaware on the Ohio the United States wanted to validate the "Original People's" sovereignty by promising to make them the fourteenth colony. The United States, willing to bring peace between theirs and the Delaware Nation, declared in article six this statement:

...the United States wanted to validate the "Original People's" sovereignty by promising to make them the fourteenth colony...

Whereas the enemies (the British) of the United States have endeavoured by every article in their power, to possess the Indians in general with an opinion, that it is the design of the States aforesaid, to extirpate the Indians and take possession of their country: to obviate such false suggestion, the United States do engage to guarantee to the aforesaid nation of the Delawares, and their heirs, all their territorial rights in the fullest and most ample manner, as it hath been bounded by former treaties, as long as they the said Delaware nation shall abide by, and hold fast the chain of friendship now entertained into.[8]

By the terms of the treaty as finally concluded, all offenses were mutually forgiven; a perpetual friendship was pledged; each party agreed to assist the other in any just war; the Delawares gave permission for an American army to pass through their territory, and agreed to furnish meat, corn, warriors and guides for the army. The United States agreed to erect and garrison a fort, within the Delaware country, for the protection of the old men, women, and children; and each party agreed to punish offenses committed by citizens of the other, according to a system to be arranged later. The United States promised the establishment of fair and honest trade relations; and lastly, the United States guaranteed the integrity of the Delaware nation, and promised to admit it as a state of the American Union, 'provided nothing contained in this article be considered as conclusive until it meets the approbation of congress.' With reference to the promise to admit the Delaware nation as a state of the union, the commissioners must have known that this was an impossibility.[9]

The Delawares' capacity to extend faith in the Americans was truly outstanding when they said,

'Brothers, we (the Delawares) are become one people. We are at a loss to express our thoughts, but we hope soon to convince you by our actions of the sincerety of our hearts. We now inform you that as many of our warriors as can possibly be spared will join you and go with you.'[10]

THE END OF A DREAM

In spite of this treaty, much blood was still being shed between both Indian and white. No one knew whom to trust, and hostile factions persisted. The frontiers of Western Pennsylvania, Virginia, West Virginia and Kentucky were in turmoil. In April 1781, a Delaware chief by the name of Buckongahelas came to the Moravian Indians at Gnadenhutten and tried to persuade them to remove themselves to a place of greater safety. He reviewed with them the history of Indian and white relations and warned them of their possible danger. The Rev. John Heckewelder recorded his words.

'I admit that there are good white men, but they bear no proportion to the bad; the bad must be strongest, for they rule. They do what they please. They enslave those who are not of their colour, although created by the same Great Spirit who created us. They would make slaves of us if they could, but as they cannot do it, they kill us. There is no faith to be placed in their words. They are not like the Indians, who are only enemies while at war, and are friends in peace. They will say to an Indian: "My friend, my brother." They will take him by the hand, and at the same moment destroy him. And so you (addressing himself to the Christian Indians) will also be treated by them before long. Remember that this day I have warned you to beware of such friends as these. I know the long knives;[11] they are not to be trusted.'[12]

Unrest persisted and the Indian raids continued. Eleven months later, as if Buckongahelas's warning was prophetic, a body of one hundred and sixty militia from Washington County, Pennsylvania, under the command of Colonel David Williamson, in pursuit of a band of hostile Indians, came upon the peaceful town of Gnadenhutten. Many of the Indian converts in the town were from the original mission in eastern Pennsylvania. When the militia came into the town, a vote was cast as to what should be done with the Moravian Indians. All but eighteen voted for their 'on the spot' execution. It was agreed upon that they were all to be slain the next morning.

Bishop Loskiel, in his *History of the Missions of the United Brethren*, says that the converts were informed that evening of the fate which awaited them, and that they spent the night in praying, singing hymns, and exhorting one another to die with the fortitude of Christians. Rev. Edward Christy, who accompanied the expedition, looked in at the windows of the cooper shop[13] and church on that night of anguish. Men were shaking one another by the hand and kissing one another. Tears were streaming down some faces, while others were full of lines of agony. Agonized mothers, with tears streaming down their swarthy faces, held their children in close embrace.

Accordingly, on the morning of Friday, March 8th, 1782, the terrible decree was carried into execution. The Indian men were led two by two to the cooper shop, where they were beaten to death with mallets and hatchets. The women and children were led into the church and there slaughtered. Many of them died with prayers on their lips, while others met their death chanting songs. Altogether forty men, twenty women, and thirty-four children were inhumanely butchered. Many of the children were brained in their wretched mothers' arms. One of the murderers after having broken the skulls of fourteen of the Christian Delawares, with a cooper's mallet, handed the blood-stained weapon to a companion with the remark: 'My arm fails me, go on with the work. I think I have done pretty well.'[14]

The non-Christian Indians who had been watching this experiment in Christian brotherhood turned away in complete revulsion and disgust, ready to take vengeance upon the ones who had taken the lives of their chiefs and loved ones. The Delawares were convinced that the Americans were evildoers and lost all respect for the white man's religion and his God.[15]

ONE HUNDRED YEARS OF BROKEN PROMISES

The ability of the Delaware to trust the Americans was continually short-lived. On October 23, 1784, again at Fort Stanwix (Rome, New York), a land treaty was signed between the Iroquois and the governing authorities of Pennsylvania. Only this time it was a treaty of farewell, as the Iroquois sold the last piece of free land to the government of Pennsylvania.

And so, in the matter of one hundred and two years, from 1682 through 1784, and thirty-three broken treaties later, the entire Indian right to the soil in Pennsylvania was forsaken.

Though the Delaware had lost Pennsylvania, their spirit remained strong. Ohio had become his new refuge. Many other tribes, along with the Delaware, continued to make their stand against the injustices—ever more determined to survive.

And so, in the matter of one hundred and two years...the whole Indian right to the soil in Pennsylvania was forsaken.

Dr. George P. Donehoo gives this fitting testament to the Indians of Pennsylvania and their relationship with the land they were forced to relinquish.

> The Pennsylvania Indians loved the hills, the mountains, the valleys, and the streams of this great state (Pennsylvania). They exulted in the fact that they were the first owners of this vast region, which they were fighting and dying to protect. They were proud spirits who were born free, and loved freedom more than life itself. They were a proud race that abhorred the thought of extinction. Now that they have yielded their pleasant land to the stronger hand of the white man, and live only in the songs and chronicles of the race that pressed them away from their loved hunting grounds, may these chronicles be faithful to their rude virtues as men. They were children of nature. They had no background of centuries of Christian civilization—no knowledge of the God of Revelation. Down the perspective of history comes the impartial verdict that the fate forced upon them by a more highly favored race was galling and unjust. And it shall be more tolerable for them, in the Judgment than their conquerors, the children of the God of Revelation.[16]

A PRESIDENT'S DISASTROUS DEFEAT

It was in the fall of 1791 when the worst and bloodiest disaster in the history of the Indian wars of America took place. The American Revolution was over, and on April 30, 1789, George Washington took the oath of office as the first president of The United States. Deep within the heart of the Northwest Territory of Ohio the western tribes of the Miamis, Shawnee, Delaware, and the Wyandots continued their alliance. They were still fervently clinging to the promise that Pennsylvania was theirs. Their unity and mutual bond had made them a strong and powerful adversary. President Washington was determined to stop the Indian raids by carrying the war into their own land.

Washington selected General Arthur St. Clair (Sinclair) to lead an army of twenty-three hundred regulars and militia into Indian Territory. St. Clair's troops came from Western Pennsylvania, Virginia and Kentucky and had assembled at Fort Washington (Cincinnati, Ohio). However, these were short-term soldiers, fulfilling an obligation, and were not fighting with the same passions as the Indians. Washington had first hand experience in dealing with the cunning and prowess of the Indians and offered some firm advice to St. Clair that should have been taken more seriously.

> 'Beware of surprise,' he warned. 'Trust not the Indian; leave not your arms for the moment; and when you halt for the night be sure to fortify your camp. Again and again, General: Beware of surprise.[17]

On September 17, 1791, St. Clair's army marched out of Ludlow Station, built and garrisoned Fort Jefferson (now Greenville, Ohio) on October 12, and on the evening of November 3, arrived on the banks of the Wabash River (near the present location of Fort Recovery, Ohio). Desertions and the garrison of Fort Jefferson had reduced St. Clair's numbers to no more than fourteen hundred soldiers. Not expecting to encounter any Indians in the vicinity, St Clair relaxed his guard that night and provided no defensive perimeter.

Little did St. Clair know that Indian scouts had been monitoring his every movement. At dawn the next morning, as many as two thousand Indians attacked the unsuspecting expedition and met the American challenge with fierce resistance. St. Clair's soldiers were unprepared for the surprise assault.

The Indians attacked like trained soldiers and surrounded the army. For three hours the battle raged. It was Braddock's defeat all over again. At last, the soldiers made a brave and daring maneuver that cut through the ring of Indians, providing the survivors an avenue of escape—twenty-nine miles back to Fort Jefferson. The damage, however, had been done. St. Clair's losses were thirty-seven officers and five hundred and ninety-three privates. The rest of those killed, two hundred in all, were camp followers (wives, children, mistresses, cooks and laundresses).

> The losses of this battle were greater than those incurred by Washington in any battle of the Revolution.[18]

Humiliated by this defeat, Washington then selected General Anthony Wayne, "Mad Anthony," to lead the next expedition. The strength and credibility of Washington's new nation was on the line. Washington's confidence in Wayne was demonstrated at Stony Point, New York, during the Revolutionary War, where on July 16, 1779, Wayne was responsible for leading a successful surprise night attack on the strongest British fort along the Hudson River.

In the summer of 1794, General Wayne and his army of three thousand men marched out and in July, erected Fort Defiance (now Defiance, Ohio). On August 20, approximately forty miles northeast of Fort Defiance, General Wayne engaged the Indians at the "Battle of the Fallen Timbers" where the power of the western tribes was broken forever.

DEFEAT AND SURRENDER

Finally, on August 3rd, 1795, the conquered tribes signed the Treaty of Greenville, Darke County, Ohio, by the terms of which they ceded to the United States 25,000 square miles of territory north of the Ohio River, about two-thirds of the present state of Ohio. That part of Pennsylvania west of the Allegheny River and hitherto known as 'the Indian country', henceforth was free from Indian raids. Settlers rapidly took up their abode in the fertile region, felling the forest, cultivating the virgin soil, and laying the foundation of the material prosperity, which there abounds today. Meanwhile the Indian continued his march toward the untrodden West before the great tide of white immigration that was pressing him away from the lands he and his forefathers considered their own, as the gift of the Great Spirit, Who had stocked the forests with game and the streams with fish for His Red Children.[19]

Countless times the Delaware fixed their names on treaties that promised them equality and freedoms. Throughout the entire process white men revolutionized the whole world to secure their own life. Simultaneously, Indians lost theirs. It may boldly be said that while America was celebrating the blessings of their new constitution and freedom to "Life, Liberty and the Pursuit of Happiness," Indians were excluded.

Unfortunately, many Americans in proclaiming their freedom maintained the idea carried over from their British "Right-to-Rule" heritage, that whatever method was necessary in promoting their pursuit of "happiness," was legitimate. The Americans justified their war against Great Britain to protect their freedoms from British tyranny. But the Delaware and Shawnee had already been fighting to protect their heritage and culture twenty-one years before the Americans conceived a Revolution.

Since the time of the Albany Treaty in 1755, the Delaware and Shawnee were forced into multiple wars they never wanted to fight, with and against the white man. Ironically, they were also forced to protect for themselves the very same lands and freedoms the Americans would fight to protect as their own.

> Unfortunately, many Americans in proclaiming their freedom maintained the idea carried over from their British "Right-to-Rule" heritage, that whatever method was necessary in promoting their pursuit of "happiness," was legitimate.

OVERVIEW

The migration of the Lenape, or Delaware, from the Atlantic to the Susquehanna and then to the Ohio, taking with it the warlike and powerful Shawnee, had a far-reaching influence in the development of civilization of the Continent. These two dominant tribes carried after them the great train of Indian traders from Pennsylvania, who roamed as far northward as Detroit and as far westward as the Mississippi. The presence of these traders in the territory claimed by France was the underlying cause of the French and Indian War, which was the first in the series of events resulting in the birth of the United States. With all of these events which were taking place, the migration of the Indians, the Indian trade, the rivalry between France

During this period of forty years,...the soil of the Province and then of State was literally drenched with blood.

and Great Britain, and then the long fight for possession of the continent, Pennsylvania was directly related.[20]

From the outbreak of the French and Indian War, in 1755, during the long years of Border Wars and the American Revolution, to the Treaty of Greenville, made by General Anthony Wayne, the "Indian problem" was practically in the hands of Pennsylvanians. The physical reason for this was because Pennsylvania was the Gateway to Ohio, Indiana and the West, as well as to Kentucky and the South. The Ohio River, having its headwaters in Pennsylvania, was the great trail to the Mississippi and to the French possessions in Louisiana. The vast territory through which this great stream flowed was more easily reached from Pennsylvania than from any other of the Colonies, and, notwithstanding the claims of New England historians, this great stream became the highway over which the Pennsylvania influence and not that of New England, reached to the uttermost limits of the Continent, founding new settlements and then moulding the institutions wherever it went.[21]

The period of Border Wars in Pennsylvania is one of the most thrilling and bloody chapters in American history. Pennsylvania suffered more than did any of the other Colonies during this long period stretching from 1755 to 1795. The massacre at Penn's Creek, 1755, marks its actual commencement and the Treaty at Greenville, in 1795, marks its ending. During this period of forty years, Pennsylvania was engaged in an unbroken war with the Indians, and during that time the soil of the Province and then of State was literally drenched with blood. Years after a new Nation had been born, and after peace had come to the settlements east of the Alleghenies, the settlers on the Ohio were still fighting to hold what they possessed, and it was not until General Anthony Wayne finally conquered the Indians, that peace came to the harried frontiers of Pennsylvania.[22]

THE END OF A LEGACY

By the end of the eighteenth century the epic for eastern Native Americans had come to an end. The ensuing demise of America's western tribes would mirror that of the Delaware, Shawnee, Iroquois and other native tribes along the Atlantic seaboard as Europeans swept across the rest of the continent.

After the death of William Penn, the future of the Delaware, as well as many other tribes, was very slim. Suffering broken treaty upon broken treaty, encroachment upon encroachment, they were thrown from their own lands into the hands of the English and then tossed back and forth between the English and the French. Eventually they fell to the mercy of the Americans, who with appalling casualness pushed them from Pennsylvania to Ohio to Indiana to Missouri to Kansas, until finally they were settled among the Cherokee in Oklahoma (Indian Territory) in 1869, where they remain today. The Oklahoma Delaware were not recognized as American citizens until 1907 when Oklahoma became a state. In 1996, after a long struggle with the Bureau of Indian Affairs (BIA), the Oklahoma Delaware were recognized by the federal government as a sovereign Native American nation. And even though a remnant of Delaware continue to reside in Pennsylvania to this day, they remain (as of this writing) unrecognized.

The Shawnee suffered a similar fate, until:

In 1869 the Shawnee became incorporated with the Cherokee, with whose history they have always been associated, in Oklahoma, where the great majority of them are now living. The Shawnee have produced some of the strongest characters in Indian history. Among these may be mentioned Cornstalk and Tecumseh.[23]

By the year 1965, due to the construction of the Kinzua Dam on the upper Allegheny River—lands guaranteed to the Seneca Indians by treaty since 1791—the last of a free Seneca community were completely removed from the state of Pennsylvania. Shamefully closing the door on a forgotten people, Pennsylvania now has no Indian reservations—if that were an answer at all.

The following poem written by an unknown author shines a light into the hearts of these who lost the most during this tragic period of history:

> 'Ye say they have all pass'd away,
> That noble race and brave,
> That their light canoes have vanish'd
> From off the crested wave;
> That 'mid the forest where they roam'd
> There rings no hunter's shout:
> But their name is on your waters;
> Ye may not wash it out.
> Ye say their cone-like cabins,
> That cluster'd o'er the vale,
> Have disappear'd as wither'd leaves
> Before the autumn gale;
> But their memory liveth on your hills,
> Their baptism on your shore,
> Your everlasting rivers speak
> Their dialect of yore.[24]

CHRONOLOGICAL TABLE

1760-1820 King George III rules England.

1764 April 5. England begins a series of taxation on all goods shipped to America when the King approves the American Duties Act, known by Americans as the Sugar Act, placing a tax on sugar and molasses.

1765 (1) March 22. The Stamp Act taxes almost everything written or printed on paper or vellum..
(2) The Moravians move their mission to Wyalusing on the North Branch of the Susquehanna, calling it Friedenshutten (Tents of Peace).

1767 June 29. The Townshend Revenue Acts levied duties on glass, lead, painters' colors, paper, and tea.

1768 November 5. Treaty at Fort Stanwix where Penns make purchase of lands from the Six Nations.

1772 The Moravians accept the invitation of the Great Council of the Delaware to set up their missions in the Ohio Country. Gnadenhutten II is established on the Tuscarawas River.

1773 May 10. The Tea Act.

1776 July 4. Signing of Declaration of Independence.

1778 (1) July 3. Second massacre at Wyoming.
(2) September 17. United States makes alliance with the Delaware.

1781	April. Delaware chief, Buckongahelas, warns the Moravian Delaware in Gnadenhutten to move out of harms way.
1782	(1) March 8. The massacre of ninety-four friendly Christian Delaware in the town of Gnadenhutten.
	(2) December 30. The Supreme Executive Council of Pennsylvania rules in favor of Pennsylvania, called the "Trenton Decree," in which Connecticut must yield the Wyoming Valley to Pennsylvania.
1784	October 23. Treaty at Fort Stanwix in which Pennsylvania makes final purchase of Indian lands in Pennsylvania, extinguishing all claims of the Indians.
1789	April 30. George Washington becomes the first president of The United States.
1790	Philadelphia becomes the nation's capitol.
1791	November 4. St. Clair's Defeat.
1794	August 20. The "Battle of the Fallen Timbers" where General Anthony Wayne defeats the western tribes.
1795	Western tribes sign Treaty of Greenville, Darke County, Ohio, ending forty years of war with Pennsylvania.
1800	The nation's capitol is moved from Philadelphia to Washington D. C.
1869	Delaware and Shawnee settle in Oklahoma "Indian Territory" with the Cherokee.

1907	Oklahoma becomes a state, and the Delaware are recognized as United States citizens.
1965	Kinzua Dam Project along the upper Allegheny River removes the last of a Seneca community, forever removing all Indians from Pennsylvania.
1996	The Oklahoma Delaware are federally recognized as a sovereign Native American nation.

ENDNOTES

1. Wallace, Paul A. W., *Indians in Pennsylvania*, (Commonwealth of Pennsylvania, The Pennsylvania Historical and Museum Commission, Harrisburg, PA, 1993), p. 159. Sullivan, Flick, and Hamilton (eds.) Papers of Sir William Johnson, XII, 425, 178.

2. Anderson, Fred, *Crucible of War*, (Alfred A. Knopf, New York, 2000), p. 560.

3. Wallace, Paul A. W., *Indians in Pennsylvania*, (Commonwealth of Pennsylvania, The Pennsylvania Historical and Museum Commission, Harrisburg, PA, 1993), p. 160.

4. Tories were Americans who upheld the cause of the British Crown against the supporters of colonial independence during the American Revolution.

5. "The 'massacre of Wyoming,' cruel and bloody as it was, has been repeated again and again, not by Indians, but by civilized men of every race. The 'Battle of Wounded Knee,' in which United States troops slaughtered harmless Indian women and children with the death-dealing machine guns, was without a shadow of the excuse which the Indians had for the 'Massacre of Wyoming.' The one was committed as an act of revenge, upon harmless women and children, by the army of a Christian nation; the other was an act of vengeance for broken promises, and committed only after every other appeal had failed. Both were brutal, but one can be justified-if any appeal to arms can be justified-while the other, in the light of calm reason, was without even the shadow of an excuse." Donehoo, Dr. George P., *Indian Villages and Place Names in Pennsylvania*, (Gateway Press, Baltimore, MD, 1995), p. 261.

6. As a result of the massacre at Wyoming, in the summer and fall of 1779, under the command of Major-General John Sullivan, five thousand soldiers set out from Easton, Pennsylvania, and marched two hundred and eighty miles into Iroquois territory. They destroyed over forty Iroquois towns, burning their homes, killing their livestock and setting ablaze their crops.

7. "The words of the decree were as follows: 'We are unanimously of opinion that the State of Connecticut has no right to the lands in controversy. We are also unanimously of opinion that the jurisdiction and pre-emption of all territory lying within the charter boundary of Pennsylvania, now claimed by the State of Connecticut, do of right belong to the State of Pennsylvania.' " Russ, William A. Jr., *Pennsylvania's Boundaries*, (Times and News Publishing Co., Gettysburg, PA, Pennsylvania History Studies: No. 8, The Pennsylvania Historical Association, The Pennsylvania State University, University Park, PA, 1966), p. 51.

8. Washburn, Wilcomb E., *The American Indian and the United States*, (Random House, New York, 1973), pp. 2263-2266.

9. Sipe, C. Hale, *The Indian Wars of Pennsylvania*, (originally published, Harrisburg, PA, 1931., reprinted, Gateway Press, Baltimore, MD, for Wennawoods Publishing, Lewisburg, PA, 1995), pp. 569-570.

10. *Ibid.*, p. 570.

11. The Indians attributed the term "Long Knives" to the officers of the Virginia militia who fought with swords.

12. Sipe, C. Hale, *The Indian Wars of Pennsylvania*, (originally published, Harrisburg, PA, 1931., reprinted, Gateway Press, Baltimore, MD, for Wennawoods Publishing, Lewisburg, PA, 1995), p. 651.

13. A coopers shop was a place where casks and tubs were made.

14. Sipe, C. Hale, *The Indian Wars of Pennsylvania*, (originally published, Harrisburg, PA, 1931., reprinted, Gateway Press, Baltimore, MD, for Wennawoods Publishing, Lewisburg, PA, 1995), pp. 649-650.

15. "In the modern city of Gnadenhutten, Ohio, there is a public park where you may see the mound that covers the remains of the Indian martyrs of 1782. Beside it stands a monument with this inscription: HERE TRIUMPHED IN DEATH NINETY CHRISTIAN INDI-ANS." Wallace, Paul A. W., *Pennsylvania, Seed of a Nation*, (Harper & Row Publishers, New York and Evanston, 1962), p. 153.

16. Sipe, C. Hale, *The Indian Wars of Pennsylvania*, (originally published, Harrisburg, PA, 1931., reprinted, Gateway Press, Baltimore, MD, for Wennawoods Publishing, Lewisburg, PA, 1995), p. 550.

17. Battin, Richard, *Early America's Bloodiest Battle*, (The News-Sentinel, Fort Wayne Indiana, 1994), http://earlyamerica.com/review/summer/battle.html p. 3.

18. Sipe, C. Hale, *The Indian Wars of Pennsylvania*, (originally published, Harrisburg, PA, 1931., reprinted, Gateway Press, Baltimore, MD, for Wennawoods Publishing, Lewisburg, PA, 1995), p. 700.

19. Sipe, C. Hale, *The Indian Chiefs of Pennsylvania*, (originally published, Butler, PA, 1927., reprinted, Gateway Press, Baltimore, MD, for Wennawoods Publishing, Lewisburg, PA, 1995), p. 548.

20. *Ibid.*, p. 8.

21. *Ibid.*, pp. 7-8.

22. *Ibid.*, pp. 8-9.

23. Donehoo, Dr. George P., *Indian Villages and Place Names in Pennsylvania*, (Gateway Press, Baltimore, MD, 1995), p. 197.

24. Sipe, C. Hale, *The Indian Chiefs of Pennsylvania*, (originally published, Butler, PA, 1927., reprinted, Gateway Press, Baltimore, MD, for Wennawoods Publishing, Lewisburg, PA, 1995), p. 13.

Part Four

RECONNECTING

1 4

REDISCOVERING AMERICA

A nation which does not remember what it was yesterday, does not know what it is today, nor what it is trying to do. We are trying to do a futile thing if we do not know where we came from or what we have been about.[1]

—President Woodrow Wilson

For as long as I can remember I've always been fascinated with thoughts of finding treasure. Mark Twain said, "There comes a time in every rightly constructed boy's life that he has a raging desire to go somewhere and dig for hidden treasure." For me, I think it all started in the fifth grade when I found a half cent coin between the floor boards of an old house. It was the coolest coin. I had never seen anything like it. Then, on a field trip with my Earth Science class, our teacher threw out a challenge. The first person to find a fossil would receive five extra-credit points on the next quiz. I was instantly captivated, not by the five extra-credit points, but by the possibility of finding a fossil. It didn't take long to uncover a beautiful impression of a leaf in the bedrock of an old railroad cut. I got the five extra-credit points and kept the fossil for many years. And it didn't stop there. Throughout my life, right up to the present, experiences like these continued to define my personality and confirm the motivations behind my thrill of discovery—the digging, the revealing, the telling. But treasure, as I learned, can sometimes come to us in ways we least expect it, and just might surprise us. My discovery of William Penn was one such find.

After my experience on the Washington Beltway and subsequent visit to the Capitol Rotunda in Harrisburg, my trips to the building increased. I couldn't seem to pull myself away. Penn's quote in the capitol's rotunda had gripped me and wouldn't let go. I eventually found my way into the Governor's Reception Room and was greeted by beautiful wall-to-wall paintings of Penn, giving me a glimpse into his extraordinary life. I was transfixed as I slowly walked through the room, absorbing each painting. In the Senate Chamber, the House Chamber and the Supreme Court there were even more paintings. A visual record of Penn's life had been captured for all to see. However, it was more than art to me and only created a greater desire to know more. I was directed to the Pennsylvania Capitol Preservation Committee, hoping to find the story behind the quote the builders chose to use in the rotunda. No one knew.

Not to be outdone, I left the capitol and continued my search in the area retail bookstores. Surprisingly, I found nothing. Even the "local interest" sections left me empty handed. What I did find was an abundant supply of material on the American Revolution and the Civil War, but wondered why there were no books about Pennsylvania's founder and his accomplishments. And if there were, why were they so hard to find? Even generalized American history books, when talking about Pennsylvania, only patronized Penn with maybe a paragraph or two. There I was standing in Pennsylvania, the birthplace of American democracy, and could find nothing about her conception—I was taken aback. What happened? Moreover, to my dismay, I soon discovered that any pertinent information on Penn was only to be found in dark, dusty corners of the local library and was now long out of print. Why has Penn been relegated to such obscurity? Was history being rewritten or just simply omitted?

I remained undaunted. Rummaging through old, used bookstores became my new favorite thing to do. A long but fun trek ensued as Pennsylvania's used bookstores became the primary focus of my search. I even expanded into historical sites, antique shops, libraries and museums. After all was said and done I finally secured good, solid reading material, a full library actually. Enough, anyway, that I could confirm everything I was learning with as many credible sources as possible.

AMERICA'S FIRST FOUNDING FATHER

As I became acquainted with the life of William Penn, his prophetic utterance that grace's the capitol's rotunda became very clear. Penn was an architect of freedom. His significance in the establishing of our American liberties, in which friendship with Pennsylvania's indigenous people set the precedent, was enormous. He had conceived a constitution so revolutionary that it became the foundation for the seed of freedom to grow. When he endorsed his constitution with the printing of the Magna Carta[2] in Philadelphia, the advancement of this freedom eventually gave way to Pennsylvania's nickname, The Keystone State. His further design for a Continental Congress through the unity of the colonies made him a forerunner of the inevitable—the evolution of a nation. Little could Penn have realized then how his efforts would continue, lighting the fires of revolution less than a century later.

Yet, the epochal events of the American Revolution seemed to have eclipsed the swell of his precursory accomplishments. Maybe this was why I knew so little about him. But, I felt as if the information was far too important not to be known. Why has he never been honored for this? Penn was a nation builder, a man seemingly born before his time. I was sure others would want to know. A rediscovery seemed necessary. It seemed to me a forgotten, even missing page of history: a page from which Penn could speak right now, particularly regarding the issues of civil equality and the largely misunderstood motivation behind the Separation of Church and State. And further yet, the more I learned, the more surprised I was at my own ignorance. Before me was an America of greater spiritual substance than I had ever known.

When Penn said, "my God will make it the seed of a nation," he knew the seed was not an evolution of political government, although it included it. The seed was the Holy Experiment—a divinely inspired covenantal government. Out of that seed was born Penn's constitution, the Charter of Privileges, for which the Liberty Bell was forged with Leviticus 25:10 inscribed on its side,

"Proclaim Liberty throughout all the land unto all the inhabitants thereof."
Out of that seed national figures like Jefferson acknowledged Penn's contributions and called him, "the greatest lawgiver the world has produced," and our inspired American liberties were born— the U. S. Constitution.

By this time I was fully embracing who Penn was becoming in my own mind: America's first Founding Father.

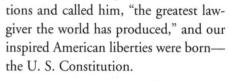

By this time I was fully embracing who Penn was becoming in my own mind: America's first Founding Father.

In his book, *Architect of a Nation*, John Trussell states,

...the fact remains that in the process of creating a colony where men enjoyed the broadest individual freedom yet known, he laid the foundations for what became some of the most fundamental guiding principles of an entire nation. Not only in Pennsylvania but America as a whole owes him a lasting debt.[2]

THE BIRTH OF A NATION

Can a country be born in a day or a nation be brought forth in a moment?

Isaiah 66:8

From 1750 to 1950 England colonized over one-quarter of the world. Yet, because of William Penn's position in history Pennsylvania was the first sanctioned English colony in which the king did not interfere with the establishing of the government. Pennsylvania was the first and only colony ever allowed such a radical departure from *Divine Rights*. From the time when King Charles II granted Penn the Charter for Pennsylvania until the end of the American Revolution,[3] Pennsylvania was a British Colony—but not in all instances governed like one. Furthermore, King Charles II had no idea that relinquishing power over this one colony would exempt England from power in the New World a century later. He merely thought he had done England a favor by ridding the mother-country of these religious radicals.

The magnitude of William Penn's position as sole proprietor proved to be enormous. Yet, as far as Penn was concerned, the most important consideration for his new colony was a government where God would hold preeminence.

In 1 Chronicles 22, we see how King David prepared a place for the Lord to dwell among His people, and the Lord came. Jesus tells us in Matthew 18:20 that He is in the midst of those who come together *in His name.*

Consistent with giving place to the Lord was William Penn's realization of the necessity of a clear conscience. To Penn, it would be impossible to expect God to bless a nation while at the same time offending Him through disobedience and misrepresentation. God had duly impressed upon Penn, before coming to America, that it was the existence of a good conscience (see 1 Peter 3:21) that enables people to hear from God, experience His presence, and thus be governed by His ways. Conversely, there could be no freedom if through selfish acts the conscience is damaged. Penn's thoughts were to honor God, knowing that His blessing was dependant upon the people of his province living in the freedom that God would provide.

> *...there could be no freedom if through the selfish acts of humanity the conscience is damaged.*

A BROKEN NATION

Woe to him who builds his realm by unjust gain to set his nest on high, to escape the clutches of ruin! You have plotted the ruin of many peoples, shaming your own house and forfeiting your life. The stones of the wall will cry out, and the beams of the woodwork will echo it. Woe to him who builds a city with bloodshed and establishes a town by crime!

Habakkuk 2:9-12

I knew that if I were to give any kind of accurate historical account of our American liberties, I would have to include those nations who should have participated in and been sustained by those liberties. If I were going to write about Penn I had to write about the Indians. How could I not? They were here first and were an integral part of everything Penn had accomplished. Their well-being and inclusion would be a witness proving the Holy Experiment.

The guiding principles created by William Penn were grand opportunities for this land's own indigenous people, and every other ethnic group that came to America, to know God, not through manipulation, but through a righteousness that firmly confessed the value of all men. And it worked. The Delaware and their offspring were as much a part of that covenant as were Penn and his sons. Only in Pennsylvania did these two nations, white and red, dwell together in a mutual bond of unity.

However, a righteous nation is limited and can only succeed to the degree that men allow it's continuance. William Penn so eloquently said this in the preface to his *First Frame of Government*: "Wherefore governments rather depend upon men, than men upon governments." God ordained government, but when men fail to live up to the standards set within that government it is time for brave men with brave hearts to make the necessary corrections.

Regretfully, after the death of William Penn, there came a death to his vision as well. It was then that the Indians tragically realized that the righteous government brought to the New World by Penn was characteristic to him alone. What God wanted to do through Penn for the Indians, and ultimately for every ethnic group in America, was fatefully forgotten as the Holy Experiment was abandoned and the Indian lost hope. The great tragedy was that Penn's vision for the nations could only succeed him if it were to be carried on through others with like passions. Penn's sons and successors did not carry the purposes of the Holy Experiment.

A GRIEF REMEMBERED

...no one can set aside or add to a human covenant that has been duly established...

Galations 3:15

It was then that the grief I had experienced on the road from Virginia Beach began to make sense to me. The seed of the Holy Experiment and the liberties that it birthed had become a sword that pierced and alienated the heart of America's First Nations, reversing the precedent Penn had established.

It didn't take long before I sensed a deep shame in the heart of our nation. The more history I uncovered the more I struggled. America's liberties had not been applied to Native America. I became sorely embarrassed as it became obvious that it had all gone terribly wrong. In fact, the closest I ever came to being aware of the plight of the American Indian was through the 1971 hit song, *Indian Reservation (The Lament Of The Cherokee Reservation Indian)* by Paul Revere and the Raiders, if this, indeed, could even be called awareness. I liked the song but it just goes to show you how ineffectively I had translated its lyrics into current affairs. I could hardly bear what I thought I now knew; these folks, growing up Native, suffer still.

I was now finding myself unable to escape the reality of America's past. Who will be responsible? I wanted to skirt the issue entirely, and not write about it. It was all much too painful. But, it was already written into the memory of the land. Besides, these people, the Native people, have not forgotten.

Native Americans were the host people of America—the original keepers of the land. They still are America's First Nations. They stood at the forefront of the American frontier and yet we came to them assuming we were the hosts, giving them "right of passage." How could this be freedom? Our example of liberty was grossly misrepresented. How completely illogical!

PREDETERMINED TIMES AND PLACES

From one man he made every nation of men, that they should inhabit the whole earth; and he determined the times set for them and the exact place where they should live.

Acts 17:26

When God refers to nations, He is speaking of the "*ethnos*" of the earth. Ethnos is where we get our English word "ethnic." In the Greek it literally means a "*people, race* or *tribe*." From God's perspective, nations are people-groups regardless of geographical borders.

The totality of God's expression on the earth, and in America, will be when all nations, of every ethnic and cultural expression, come and worship Him together. That's what America was to express: a place where all could have the opportunity to know Him, as He would draw them and as they would choose.

James W. Loewen, in his 1995 best selling book, *Lies My Teacher Told Me*, surveyed the top ten high school history books in America. He found that a large percentage of Native American history has been completely whitewashed and marred with "blind patriotism, mindless optimism, sheer misinformation, and outright lies." Why is this? He states the reasons below.

> It is understandable that textbook authors might write history in such a way that students can feel good about themselves by feeling good about the past. Feeling good is a human need, but it imposes a burden that history cannot bear without becoming simple-minded. Casting Indian history as a tragedy because Native Americans could not or would not acculturate is feel-good history for whites. By downplaying Indian wars, textbooks help us forget that we wrested the continent from Native Americans. Today's college students, when asked to compile a list of U.S. wars, never think to include Indian wars, individually or as a whole. The Indian-white wars that dominated our history from 1622 to 1815 and were of considerable importance until 1890 have disappeared from our national memory.[4]

A LAND OF CONFLICT

There was no greater struggle for possession of any other colony than that of Pennsylvania. Because of the seed of liberty planted during Pennsylvania's founding, she became a major focal point of conflict, challenges that prevented William Penn from ever taking up a permanent residency. As the Indian looked on, three different colonies, Connecticut, Maryland and Virginia, all laid claims in Pennsylvania before Penn received his charter from King Charles II. Penn's charter cancelled their claims, yet it took nearly a century of bloodshed for each of these disputes to be resolved.

The Indians watched in amazement as nation after nation grappled for their land. The Indians were constantly befriended only to be pulled into the fray of each and every one of these conflicts, used as leverage from every side. They turned, however, and used this leverage to their own advantage—their very survival depended upon it. They were successful for a time but were eventually overcome by overwhelming numbers and scandalous words.

The root sin of our land is not the spilling of blood that stained its soil but the severed trust that came through deceit. Bloodshed was the consequence.

The thousands of lives that were lost during The French and Indian War was the result of multiple broken covenants. Once this cycle started, the schemes of darkness (see Ephesians 6:11) to prevent our "freedom" were established. From then on, for one hundred and ten years, from the opening of the French and Indian War in 1755, through the American Revolution, to the closing of the Civil War in 1865, the cycle of judgment became all too familiar. And this doesn't even begin to include the numerous Indian wars that rolled from the East to the West. An unprecedented amount of blood was spilled on America's soil. From the first contact between Europeans and Native Americans until today, many of these wounds remain unhealed. The heart of Native America is on the ground.

In the mid-1840's, the philosophy of American expansionism resurfaced with new terminology. Actually, it was just a new face-lift on an old mindset, the *Right to Rule*. Democratic congressman John L. O'Sullivan coined the phrase, Manifest Destiny, believing that it was America's destiny to possess, dominate and absorb the whole of North America, *regardless of its present population*. And it was so! In the first half of the nineteenth century, millions of Americans traveled thousands of miles, pushing west, beyond the Appalachians and the Mississippi to the Pacific Coast, growing nearly three times as fast as the original thirteen states. Growth was so expediential that a new state was added to the Union on the average of one every three years.[5] The Indian didn't stand a chance as white America, like a great steamroller, rolled over the top of him.

> 'Yes, more, more, more!' echoed John L. O'Sullivan, inventor of the phrase Manifest Destiny. 'More…till our national destiny is fulfilled and…the whole boundless continent is ours.'[6]

I'm not saying that America's expansion was not to be; but it is quite possible that many of our Native brothers could have come with us. Penn proved it possible! Many Native people had opened their hearts and invited us in. But after Penn, there was no co-existing; every Indian tribe in America lost their original lands and their identity. Today, the cry of Native America continues largely unheard. They are rarely even included in the discussions about race.

IDENTITY CRISIS

We cannot fully comprehend who we are as a nation without Native Americans. They were the host and steward people of the land. When we removed them from their homelands, we also removed part of our own identity. We are incomplete, and do not represent the full diversity, character and nature of God, or the freedom we are to symbolize as the United States of America. One cannot subjugate a people and not expect to suffer the consequences, even to oneself, of that subjugation. Scripture irrefutably teaches, "Do not be deceived: God cannot be mocked. A man reaps what he sows." (Galations 6:7) The next verse tells us that the one who sows to please his sinful nature will reap destruction (see Galations 6:8).

Selfish pursuits can lead to the contamination and destruction of godly foundations. That same principle applies to any realm or sphere of influence, whether it is a family, business, church, region or nation. We cannot sweep our soiled conscience under the rug and expect it to stay there. It has an indelible way of working its way back to the surface and haunting us. It must be dealt with. Native Americans are fellow-heirs of the Kingdom of God; yet it has not been a clear road for the gospel.

THE WHITE MAN'S BOOK

They must keep hold of the deep truths of the faith with a clear conscience.

1 Timothy 3:9

It is inconceivable to think that all the broken promises made on this continent by European men and women who claimed to be ambassadors for Christ can happen without consequence for the land or us. Certainly they do not go unnoticed in the heavens, nor do our brothers and sisters, the Native Americans, forget them. By the time the missionaries came through Pennsylvania it was very difficult for the Indians to receive the message of the Gospel. After what they had experienced of the white-man's character, they could not reconcile him with "Good News."

Following are the testimonies from three great chiefs from three separate nations, the Huron, Shawnee and Delaware, who gave testimony of the white-man's efforts at presenting the Gospel to the Native Americans in the New World.

210

Adario, chief of the Huron, made the following statement:

When told that God had sent the Europeans to America to save the souls of the Indians, this great Huron replied that it was more likely that God had sent the Europeans to this continent to learn to be good; 'for', said he, 'the innocence of our lives, the love we tender to our brethren, and the tranquillity of mind which we enjoy in contemplating business to our interest, these, I say, are the three great things that the Great Spirit requires of all men in general.'[7]

In 1742, when Count Zinzendorf, founder of the Moravian church, was setting his missions in Pennsylvania, a very memorable conversation was had between him and the great chief of the Shawnee, Kakowatchiky.

The old chief thanked the count 'in the most courteous manner' for proposing his conversion to the Christian faith. He said that he, too, believed in God, who created both the Indian and the white man. But he went on to explain why, after what he had seen of white men on the frontier, he preferred Indian ways and beliefs; for, he said, the white man prayed with words while the Indian prayed in his heart.

He himself was an Indian of God's creation and he was satisfied with his condition had no wish to be a European, above all he was a subject of the Iroquois, it did not behoove him to take up new Things without their Advice or Example. If the Iroquois chose to become Europeans, and learned to pray like them: he would have nothing to say against it.... He liked the Indian Way of Life. God had been very kind to him even in his old Age and would continue to look well after him. God was better pleased with the Indians, than with the Europeans. It was wonderful how much he helped them.[8]

The following American Indian cry that C. Hale Sipe, author of *The Indian Wars of Pennsylvania*, illustrates best how sorely our opportunities were missed. In 1782, a Delaware chief spoke to Moravian missionary, David Heckewelder, after the ninety-four Christian Indians were slain in the Moravian town of Gnadenhutten.

It is true, they confess, that when they first saw the whites, they took them for beings of a superior kind. They did not know but that they had been sent to them from the abode of the Great Spirit for some great and important purpose. They therefore welcomed them, hoping to be made happier by their company. It was not long, however, before they discovered their mistake, having found them an ungrateful, insatiable people, who, though the Indians had given them as much land as was necessary to raise provisions for themselves and their families, and pasture for their cattle, wanted still to have more, and at last would not be contented with less than the whole country. 'And yet,' say those injured people, 'these white men would always be telling us of their great Book which God had given to them; they would persuade us that every man was good who believed in what the Book said, and every man was bad who did not believe in it. They told us a great many things, which, they said, were written in the good Book, and wanted us to believe it all. We would probably have done so, if we had seen them practice what they pretended to believe, and act according to the good words which they told us. But no! While they held their big Book in one hand, in the other, they had murderous weapons, guns and swords wherewith to kill us, poor Indians. Ah! and they did so, too; they killed those who believed in their Book, as well as those who did not. They made no distinction!'[9]

MISREPRESENTATION

These lost opportunities and gross misrepresentations of the Lord pierce the heart of America and testify against us. Because we've destroyed the freedom of our fellow citizens we cannot claim the freedom we do. It really happened; it really has compromised the message not to mention our national conscience. As the "Birthplace of Freedom" our nation becomes more accountable to that freedom than anyone else does. Other nations are still watching America; they still "want a precedent." The very freedom that birthed this nation obligates us to its debt. In Luke 12:48, Jesus said,

'From everyone who has been given much, much will be demanded; and from the one who has been entrusted with much, much more will be asked.'

That is a seriously provoking scripture. It speaks of great responsibility. Because the covenant between William Penn and the Delaware was established *within* that covenant of freedom, the division that followed the broken covenant between them remains as a primary stronghold across the entire nation. It affects all ethnic and cross-cultural relations. Whenever someone is devalued in *any way,* it sets the stage for all manner of abuse and evil schemes that keep people in bondage.

What happened in Pennsylvania and throughout the nation was the diametric opposite of William Penn's, or can we now say, God's desires. Instead of manifesting what could have been possible, had the example of genuine openness and love between ethnic groups been allowed to grow, our nation's cities are now riveted with racial tension. Our media still debates.

Our way of dealing with injustices through political and social agendas reflects more of our unwillingness to really see ourselves in light of God's truth than of our compassion for people. Placing Indians on reservations and giving them compensation does little to heal or even appease the brokenness they feel. Coming up with strategies speaks of our humanistic tendencies to protect ourselves from further hassle or discomfort. It takes courage and strong character to be willing to identify with one another, to do whatever is necessary to begin the hard work of building trust.

Our way of dealing with injustices through political and social agendas reflects more of our unwillingness to really see ourselves in light of God's truth than of our compassion for people.

The succession of broken promises to the Native Americans throughout this nation not only broke the spirit of a great people, but also wounded us in the process. We were never created to be exclusive or independent of one another. Nor were we intended to so grossly misrepresent the Gospel that we would make God an offense to the very nations with whom we were to partner and love. Since God created *all* in His image, for His glory, we cannot push His creation away without also diminishing His Kingdom in our own lives. His Kingdom is righteousness, peace and joy (see Romans 14:17). Do we have the right to claim these facets of His life? Absolutely! But know this: His Kingdom only exists where He is preeminently loved and obeyed. His love compels us to other-centeredness, to see reality as it really is. "Out of sight, out of mind" only works where love does not exist. When we love Him and people, we won't be able to forget. We won't settle for less. Love will be our standard, however tough it may be. We will contend to gain it. We will contend to keep it. It is ours.

ENDNOTES

1. DeMoss Foundation, Arthur S., *The Rebirth of America*, (printed in the United States, 1986), p. 12.

2. In the early part of the 13th Century, King John of England had engaged in a series of costly and disastrous military adventures against France that drained the royal treasury. These abuses of the king's power caused the English barons to turn against the king. On June 15, 1215, the barons met on the plains of Runnymede, on the Thames River near Windsor Castle, to present a list of sixty-three demands to their king. These demands—known as the Articles of the Barons—were intended as a restatement of ancient baronial liberties, a limitation on the king's power to raise funds, and a reassertion of the principle of due process under law, at that time referred to as the "law of the land." Under great pressure, King John accepted the barons' demands on June 15 and set his royal seal to their set of stipulations. Four days later, the king and barons agreed on a formal version of that document. It is that version that we know today as Magna Carta. Thirteen copies were made and distributed to every English county to be read to all freemen. (http://www.magnacharta.org/enews82000.htm)

3. Trussell, John B. B., *William Penn Architect of a Nation*, (Pennsylvania Historical And Museum Commission, Harrisburg, PA 1994), p. 72

4. The signing of the peace treaty between the United States and England was in September, 1783.

5. Loewen, James W., *Lies My Teacher Told Me*, (A Touchstone Book, Simon & Schuster, New York, N.Y., 1995), p. 133

6. McPherson, James M., *Battle Cry Of Freedom*, (Oxford University Press, New York, N.Y., 1988)

7. *Ibid.*, p. 48.

8. Sipe, C. Hale, *The Indian Wars of Pennsylvania*, (originally published, Harrisburg, PA, 1931., reprinted, Gateway Press, Baltimore, MD, for Wennawoods Publishing, Lewisburg, PA, 1995), p. 27.

9. Wallace, Paul A. W., *Indians in Pennsylvania*, (Commonwealth of Pennsylvania, The Pennsylvania Historical and Museum Commission, Harrisburg, PA, 1993), p. 127.

10. Sipe, C. Hale, *The Indian Wars of Pennsylvania*, (originally published, Harrisburg, PA, 1931., reprinted, Gateway Press, Baltimore, MD, for Wennawoods Publishing, Lewisburg, PA, 1995), pp. 21-22.

1 5

PUTTING AN END TO HOSTILITY

For the creation was subjected to frustration, not by its own choice, but by the will of the one who subjected it, in hope that the creation itself will be liberated from its bondage to decay and brought into the glorious freedom of the children of God.

Romans 8:20-21

On two levels, governmentally and relationally, William Penn dedicated in covenant both Pennsylvania, her government and her people—both white and red, to the Lord when she was founded. And yet, if we are to retain any redemptive quality in who we are and be healed of our wounds, then it becomes imperative for us to take a panoramic view of these relationships, know that they are non-disposable, and comprehend how we complement and complete one another. The consequences are far too great for us to turn our backs and forget any longer.

Our nation's history proves and reminds us how miserably people suffer when we fail to see through the eyes of a covenant-keeping God and act accordingly. In light of this it is prudent to take note of the forces that continue to separate us from each other, and from God. We cannot be sure that these wounds from deep within our nation's past, from many generations, do not haunt us, giving power to the divisions that we live with and sometimes talk about. But no one talks about the forces behind current issues. So much of the discussion on national television and talk radio could be settled if the elements that created the problems were known. Years ago noted sociologist, C. Wright Mills, discovered that Americans feel a need to locate themselves in social structure in order to understand the forces that shape their society and themselves.[1] That's what Americans are trying to do. But so many times I have joined the conversation from the edge of my seat knowing that the hope of bringing peace has a better chance when a bigger piece of history is in view.

James Loewen, author of *Lies My Teacher Told Me*, tells us,

Perhaps I do not need to convince you that American history is important. More than any other topic, it is about *us*. Whether one deems our present society wondrous or awful or both, history reveals how we arrived at this point. Understanding our past is central to our ability to understand ourselves and the world around us.[2]

Unless we gain the courage to free ourselves from these cultural curses that we have accepted as norm and lead one another to the Healer of wounds, there is little hope. If we are to assume any mandate this will be required. That's why repentance and reconciliation are musts and will be discussed. We will look at examples from scripture. Hopefully we will look at our own individual insecurities that prevent healing. And we will trust Him to bind us together with cords of love and hope.

Knowing where to begin is always intimidating. Taking on a cultural mandate in view of history even more. But it doesn't have to be. I'll never forget the day I was speaking at an event at the Pennsylvania Capitol when one of the state's senators approached me with tear-filled eyes and asked what he should do (regarding the issues presented in this book). His consciousness had been awakened and his heart compelled him to action. His question really was something many ask, "How do we redeem our culture?" The odd thing is, I didn't have an answer for him, at least not an answer I could prescribe in foolproof sequential steps. That never works. Compassion cannot be legislated. Yet, what was really great about this congressman was that he had allowed his own life to be challenged, had allowed his consciousness to be awakened, and had made room for vulnerability. As far as I was concerned he was closer to the answer than he knew, closer than he knew to taking the first step in being useful. The cultural mandate must always begin with the individual.

When confronted by the insecurity of not knowing what to do, all of us have choices to make. What we do about it affects everything else about us and can keep us from moving forward. Whenever a problem (which is most times relational in nature) presents itself, we either move towards God and other people or we become indifferent. If we ignore a difficult situation we soon forfeit our ability to relate interdependently with others. As this happens the dulling of the senses becomes evident. Connection is lost. Afterwards, many things substitute, distract, and basically cover up the vulnerability, making the focus inward and detached. The grimness of it is that relationships become shallow and reduced. Therefore, we can never really know freedom to give because our own emptiness creates need to get. This problem is illustrated in the Bible between earth's first two siblings, Cain and Able.

"YOUR BROTHER'S BLOOD CRIES OUT"

One day both Cain and his brother Abel presented their offerings to the Lord. God was pleased with Abel's but not with Cain's, which made Cain jealous and angry at his brother. God knew what was in Cain's heart and spoke to him,

> *'Why are you so angry? Why is your face downcast? If you do what is right, will you not be accepted? But if you do not do what is right, sin is crouching at your door;* **it desires to have you,** *but* **you must master it.** *' (emphasis mine)*

Genesis 4:6,7

Refusing to listen to the Lord's exhortation and warning, Cain plotted and killed his brother. Afterwards, in Genesis 4:9, an interesting conversation takes place between the Lord and Cain. God asked Cain,

I believe it was Cain's *'Where is your brother Abel?'*

conscience that God And Cain, refusing to answer honestly, said,

was appealing to; the *'I don't know, am I my brothers keeper?'*

Lord was giving Cain Listen to what the Bible says in James 4:1-3 about conflict, and what it reveals

an opportunity to make about us:

a right response.

What causes fights and quarrels among you? Don't they come from your desires that battle within you? You want something but don't get it. You kill and covet, but you cannot have what you want. You quarrel and fight. You do not have, because you do not ask God. When you ask, you do not receive, because you ask with wrong motives, that you may spend what you get on your pleasures.

It's simple. Abel's relationship with God revealed what was already in Cain's heart. Cain wanted to make life work *his way*, and when he couldn't get it *his way*, he became angry and allowed that anger to define who he was. In Genesis 4:10 God said to Cain:

'What have you done? Listen! Your brother's blood cries out to me from the ground.'

God said to Cain, "Listen!" Listen to what? Was there an audible cry of Abel's blood or was God trying to engage Cain's conscience? I believe it was to Cain's conscience that God was appealing to; the Lord was giving Cain an opportunity to make a right response. God had already seen the injustice, heard the cry of Abel's blood, but was still giving Cain a chance to answer. It stands to reason then that the question was not about Abel's whereabouts but about Cain's heart for his brother and equally the Lord.

Instead of using the opportunity to confess, the Lord's question to Cain became his indictment. Unavoidable judgment was the sentence for his indifference. He was cursed, and for millennia to follow, the heart and nature of mankind has been the same. We *are* our brother's keeper and when the shedding of innocent blood cries for justice, our response must be brokenness and repentance. To me, the healing we are asking for is tied to this principle.

The story of Cain, however, is far from completed. Like Cain, we still take matters into our own hands and try to make our own way, leaving God out.

THEIR BLOOD IS ON OUR HANDS

Do not pollute the land where you are. Bloodshed pollutes the land...

Numbers 35:33

We learn a powerful truth when Cain killed his brother. Not only was Cain unable to avoid the inescapable justice of Abel's shed blood but the land felt its impact.

Historians have shown us how the conflict between Native Americans and Europeans literally drenched the soil of Pennsylvania and her neighboring states with blood for forty years. Forty years of bloodshed. And it didn't stop there but continued until we had possessed the entire continent. It's overwhelming!

No other nation in the world boasts more proudly of her godly heritage than that of America. Yet, in attaining that heritage we broke so many promises—in blood—with the host people. What has the spilling of this blood produced? Does the earth not see? Does it go unnoticed in the heavens? Do the actions and decisions of our forefathers bear any consequence? Is our land barren of spiritual fruit? If so, has our barrenness, in turn, conceived a haven for all types of spiritual rebellion? Luke 11:24-26 tells us that evil spirits love arid and unoccupied places.

A NEW PARADIGM

So from now on we regard no one from a worldly point of view. Though we once regarded Christ in this way, we do so no longer.

2 Corinthians 5:16

219

When we look at people from "a worldly point of view," we see through our own prejudices and comparisons. We categorize people according to our personal judgments. God doesn't want that. Our job is to regard people as God does and see the potentiality in each. This does not mean we overlook where people are, who they are, or what they've done, but it does mean we refuse to look on those natural and obvious characteristics as the only truth. There is a truth that is more real than what the natural senses can perceive, that calls people from places of bondage into truth that is above every other truth—a truth that calls people into their destiny. It calls people into life and freedom. It lies in the reality of who God is for any individual, for the asking. It grabs hold of a faith that calls things that are not yet (the promises of God for an individual) as though they already were (see Romans 4:17).

PREJUDICES REVEALED

In Acts 10, the Apostle Peter came to see his own prejudices through a strange vision. In the vision, the Lord presented to Peter many forbidden animals as food for him to eat. Three times the Lord did this and three times Peter refused. What was Peter to do? But the vision wasn't really about food. It had everything to do with nations, in particular, a nation Peter had been plainly forbidden to associate with. God wanted the message of salvation to come to the home of a Roman centurion named Cornelius. However, for Peter, associating with a Gentile was totally outside his paradigm. The Lord was challenging him about his smug belief systems. Only after he obeyed did Peter come into a full understanding of the vision; the message of the Gospel was not for the Jew alone. In Acts 10:29 Peter said,

'God has shown me that I should not call any man impure or unclean.'

He continues in verses 34 and 35, saying,

'God does not show favoritism but accepts men from every nation who fear him and do what is right.'

Jesus was constantly demonstrating to His disciples the value of all men and women. As when He stopped by a well to speak a life-giving word to a Samaritan woman. It was taboo for a Jewish man to do such a thing, but Jesus was constantly showing His disciples how compassion "colors outside the lines."

Jesus' blood destroyed the dividing wall of hostility between Jew and Gentile, making them "one new man." Through His blood He has brought peace between the two (see Ephesians 2:13-18). This one act forever broke the power of the hostility that once separated us from God and each other. If Jesus' work on the cross, through the shedding of His own blood, destroyed the dividing wall of hostility, bringing peace, then what we have to do is appropriate what He has already done. The mystery, as Paul reveals in Colossians 1:27, is "Christ in us, the hope of glory." His life within the believer enables us to exchange hostility for His peace. A life of continual reconciliation is the result.

THE MESSAGE OF RECONCILIATION

Therefore, if anyone is in Christ, he is a new creation; the old has gone, the new has come! All this is from God, who reconciled us to himself through Christ and gave us the ministry of reconciliation: that God was reconciling the world to himself in Christ, not counting men's sins against them. And he has committed to us the message of reconciliation.

2 Corinthians 5:17-19

Webster's dictionary defines "reconcile" as: "To restore to friendship or harmony; to submit or accept something unpleasant." This definition closely parallels the Greek for "reconcile," which means: "to put an end to hostility."

God profusely demonstrates reconciliation from Genesis to Revelation. The reason; as long as men were covenant-breakers there would always be a need. God could only stay connected with His people if they chose to stay connected to Him. Reconciliation is the amazing operation He uses to end the hostility. This truth must find expression in our lives. Notice the dependency on being a new creation. Paul connects reconciliation with the regeneration of the believer. Without this message running through our lives, as evidence of "Christ in us," the good news is no good at all.

To be true reconcilers then is more than just knowing it's the right thing to do; true reconciliation can only be offered by a people who know that it's God's idea, who receive His heart about it and put themselves into His hands, trusting Him for the outcome. Restitution is a result of true repentance, but cannot be offered by a people who do not trust God. Without trust, the conscience is damaged and the Holy Experiment fails. Truth becomes evasive, every relationship becomes warped (including relationship with God), and purpose is narrowed to individual "pursuits of happiness." This is true for the individual as well as for the nations.

As we witness an increase in reconciliation events being demonstrated throughout the world, and begin participating in them, we could be tempted to think of it as something new to the Church, but it's not. It may be new to the Church as far as her participation but God has been asking us to demonstrate reconciliation all along. As we begin walking closer with God and having a more accountable relationship with Him, the Church is realizing that He is requiring a more accountable relationship *between* one another. He is requiring reconciliation from you and me.

THE TOLL OF RACISM

Shortly after beginning the research for this book, Lorrie and I attended an "Interceding For Your City" conference at one of the local churches in our area.

God has been asking us to demonstrate reconciliation all along.

In this conference phrases like "spiritual mapping" and "identificational repentance" were being spoken and defined by the keynote speakers. We had never heard such terms. But, as they were being explained, I immediately felt a witness. Especially after Lorrie nudged me in the ribs and said, *"They have words for what we've been doing."* We were astonished that others were communicating the very things that we had already been sensing. God was up to something, we were more certain. Likewise, we realized that the research of this book would unite these two phrases with its major themes, reconciliation and freedom.

At this conference, however, Dr. Peter Wagner made a statement that really opened my eyes. He said, *"America's number one sin is racism."* It was a shocking in-your-face truth. I felt greatly convicted! It's not that I hadn't known this before. I had, it's just that I had never heard anyone speak about it so boldly, from within the Church. In all my years of being a Christian I had never heard this verbalized so profoundly. From my limited world-view, which was being tremendously expanded, it hadn't been so obvious. Never had I faced this reality for all its ugliness. Not only did I recognize in a moment of stark reality America's racism, but I also felt equally guilty for failing to recognize the ministry of reconciliation with which we have all been entrusted.

GOD IS MAKING HIS APPEAL "THROUGH US"

We are therefore Christ's ambassadors, as though God were making his appeal through us.

2 Corinthians 5:20

It is absolutely amazing and humbling to me how God chooses to limit himself to His people to accomplish this great universal task of reconciliation. 2 Corinthians 5:20 is telling us that God is making His appeal "*through us.*" On His own, God could interrupt all of history and make everything right. But He doesn't. He wants to, and chooses to, partner with imperfect people. It shows us how His Kingdom simultaneous works to complete itself in us and for us, if we'll only grasp it. This is difficult for us because our nature is to be self-centered instead of other-centered. But I am convinced that God, as the Great Enabler, is able to make an appeal through us to the nations. Only as we are reconciled unto God can we receive the awesome responsibility of becoming His ambassadors, to reconcile all men to God, husband to wife, son to father, government to its people or nation to nation.

If we recognize reconciliation as a mandate from God, and desire to be the kind of reconcilers He's calling for, then we must begin at the level of personal responsibility. It begins in our hearts and works its way to the surface—it must find expression. There are prerequisites before reconciliation can take place.

1. We must be reconciled to God ourselves, making him Lord over every area of our lives—that means seeing an end to the hostilities of our lives. It begins as we see our need for Him. (Note: hostilities are those things in opposition, conflict and resistance to the ways of God.)

2. We must have faith in God's ability to do what He promises.

3. We must be convinced God wants to pour His love through us.

4. We must be convinced that God wants and waits to use us to participate with Him.

5. We must receive His heart for people.

6. We must identify with the people who need to be reconciled.

7. We must lay down our rights.

8. We must *"recognize"* the need for reconciliation for injustice, injury and wounding committed.

9. We must take *"personal responsibility"* for those hurts by assuming a posture of *"confession, repentance and brokenness."*

10. We must absolutely trust Him for the healing, restoration and restitution.

DAVID AND THE GIBEONITES

There's a perfect story to illustrate the heart of God on reconciliation in 2 Samuel 21. This story not only shows us how the breaking of covenants can release a curse upon the land but also how the sins of our forefathers carry over to future generations, creating the need for generational identification and reconciliation. In this particular story this need would be discovered in such a way: a three-year famine had fallen upon Israel during the reign of King David.

> *During the reign of David, there was a famine for three successive years; so David sought the face of the Lord.*

> 2 Samuel 21:1

God had given David no warning about the coming famine. In fact, the famine had already completed its third successive year before David finally asked the Lord about it. The land's barrenness caused David to turn and seek God and the Lord replied,

> *'It is on account of Saul and his blood-stained house; it is because he put the Gibeonites to death.'*

> 2 Samuel 21:1

Wow! The famine was the direct result of Saul's putting to death the Gibeonites. But why was the land affected and who were the Gibeonites?

To answer these questions and understand the principle behind what the Lord was saying to David, we need to look into Israel's past and ask, *"What is the connection between the famine and what Saul had done to the Gibeonites?"*

Four hundred years prior to David's inquiry of the famine, the Gibeonites were residents of the land that Israel, under the leadership of Joshua, was marching to possess—the Promised Land. In great fear of Israel, the Gibeonites feigned a long journey to meet with them and deceived Joshua, telling him that they were from a distant land. Joshua spared the Gibeonites and entered into a treaty with them, ratifying it with an oath[3] (see Joshua 9:15). Years later, after Saul had become king of Israel, in his zeal to lead the nation, he tried, though unsuccessfully, to annihilate the Gibeonites.[4] When David succeeded Saul as king over Israel, God remembered the covenant that Joshua had made with the Gibeonites, and what Saul had tried to do. The result of not honoring the four-hundred-year-old covenant was the famine, released because covenant blood had been shed.

David's inquiry of the Lord regarding the famine brought together Saul's injustice against the Gibeonites and the four-hundred-year-old promise that God had made with them through Joshua. But none of the answers would have come if David had not asked the question, "Why?" Let's take a moment to look at this a little further.

THE EARTH IN BONDAGE

'See, I am setting before you today a blessing and a curse—the blessing if you obey the commands of the Lord your God that I am giving you today; the curse if you disobey the commands of the Lord your God and turn from the way that I command you today...'

Deuteronomy 11:26-28

The wounding of the Gibeonites threw David into an interesting predicament. Why, or so it would seem, would God hold David responsible for a crime that Saul had committed—and why with a famine?

Some things in this life are as irrefutable as gravity itself. Breaking covenant and the ensuing curses that follow is one such thing. The people of Israel, as with any people, were dependent upon the land for their livelihood.

In the land was life. However, disobedience to God's commands abrogates this process and is the procurement for a curse. Curses bring an end to heaven's life-giving flow and start a cycle that is both rampant and destructive. Without the nourishing flow of water the earth becomes unfruitful—a desolate wasteland. The focus here, however, is not the natural elements of land and rain. God uses famines to mirror the condition of the human heart. As the land needs rain to bring forth life so God's people need His immutable grace, His life-giving rain, to be productive. The famines that result from our direct or indirect rebellion are usually indicative of a spiritual drought, a place stripped bare of God's presence. Whether natural or spiritual the consequences are the same—barrenness, hunger, and ultimately, death.

The answer to David's famine was not to be found within any fault God was putting on David, but within a principle of God's violated by his forefather, Saul. The curse, however, had still fallen and had become David's obligation to deal with. Was it fair? It didn't matter—the Gibeonites were still offended. After discovering that the famine was the result of a curse, David's first pursuit became the righteousness of God regarding the broken covenant.

BROKEN COVENANTS

Before we can continue with this story, I want to look with you at a few other examples where God disciplined His people in this way. There were actually many famines recorded throughout the scriptures that, as to their reasons, remain a mystery. Some, like the one David experienced, was the direct result of a broken covenant.

As far back as Eden we can find where God had cursed the land for disobedience to His covenants (see Genesis 2-3). When Adam was put in the Garden, God established a covenant between Adam and the Garden. Adam was to steward the land. As long as Adam was obedient to his part of the covenant—worked and cared for the Garden, and stayed away from the forbidden fruit—the Garden would continue to yield its rich harvest. It was a divine alliance, and God said it was good. However, when Adam failed to obey the Lord regarding the forbidden fruit, he lost his Garden inheritance, and God judged the relationship between Adam and the ground with a curse. Adam's disobedience had brought forfeiture to the covenant. He was now disqualified from reaping its fullest benefits.

Another example is found in Deuteronomy 30. When God established His Promised Land covenant with the nation of Israel for the second time, stern conditions had become part of the covenant. God warns.

'See, I set before you today life and prosperity, death and destruction. For I command you today to love the Lord your God, to walk in his ways, and to keep his commands, decrees and laws; then you will live and increase, and the Lord your God will bless you in the land you are entering to possess.

'But if your heart turns away and you are not obedient, and if you are drawn away to bow down to other gods and worship them, I declare to you this day that you will certainly be destroyed. You will not live long in the land you are crossing the Jordan to enter and possess.'

Deuteronomy 30:15-18

Then God said something both striking and extraordinary to Israel. He said,

'This day I call heaven and earth as witnesses against you that I have set before you life and death, blessings and curses. Now choose life, so that you and your children may live and that you may love the Lord your God, listen to his voice, and hold fast to him. For the Lord is your life, and he will give you many years in the land he swore to give to your fathers, Abraham, Isaac and Jacob.'

Deuteronomy 30:19-20

The Lord called upon heaven and earth to serve as third-party witnesses to the covenant He was re-establishing between Him and Israel. It's almost as if the Lord appoints the earth as chief executor of His covenants. God allowed the land to stand in the balance, as a type of overseer, of kept or un-kept covenants. Consequently, when covenants are broken, the earth suffers. The Bible tells us in Leviticus 18:28 that if the land is defiled it would vomit out its inhabitants. To say the least, life doesn't go well.

In 1 Kings 17-18, King Ahab had broken covenant with the God of Israel to worship his wife Jezebel's pagan god, Baal. As a result, God cursed Israel with a famine, and the rains only returned when, under the leadership of the prophet Elijah, the people repented of their wickedness, returned to the Lord, and the prophets of Baal destroyed.

In the very last verse of the Old Testament, Malachi 4:6, there is found a very similar passage. I have heard the first part of this quoted many times. It says that before the great and dreadful day of the Lord's return He is going to send the prophet Elijah to turn the hearts of the fathers to their children, and the hearts of the children to their fathers. All of this has always sounded so wonderful to me that I had never paid much attention to the second part of that verse, until only recently. He says that if there is not a turning of hearts He will come and *strike the land*, not the fathers or the children, with a curse.

In the New Testament, there is no scripture that more clearly defines the necessary, *and needed*, transformation than Romans 8:19-21.

> *The creation waits in eager expectation for the sons of God to be revealed. For the creation was subjected to frustration, not by its own choice, but by the will of the one who subjected it, in hope that the creation itself will be liberated from its bondage to decay and brought into the glorious freedom of the children of God.*

The earth will be free when we are free, and not until then. The liberation of creation (of which we are a part) is dependant upon the freedom of the children of God. The earth and the saints alike groan (see Romans 8:23) for their restoration. But it's not the saints that wait for the earth; the earth eagerly waits for the saints to turn their hearts toward heaven, and cry out.

"WHEN I SHUT UP THE HEAVENS"

In recent years 2 Chronicles 7:14 has become one of the most popular models for needed prayer.

> *...if my people, who are called by my name, will humble themselves and pray and seek my face and turn from their wicked ways, then will I hear from heaven and will forgive their sin and will heal their land.'*

But there was more behind this passage than just a great outline for prayer. We continue to quote this verse out of context of the complete statement that actually started in verse 13. It was a word for Solomon after God had chosen to dwell within the temple that Solomon had just built. The Lord appeared to Solomon and said,

> *When I shut up the heavens so that there is no rain, or command locusts to devour the land or send a plague among my people…*

Why would God forecast such curses upon His own people? If you read ahead to verses 19 through 22 of chapter 7, God warns Solomon what would cause the release of such curses.

> *But if you turn away and forsake the decrees and commands I have given you and go off to serve other gods and worship them, then I will uproot Israel from my land, which I have given them, and will reject this temple I have consecrated for my Name. I will make it a byword and an object of ridicule among all peoples. And though this temple is now so imposing, all who pass by will be appalled and say, 'Why has the Lord done such a thing to this land and to this temple?' People will answer, 'Because they have forsaken the Lord, the God of their fathers, who brought them out of Egypt, and have embraced other gods, worshiping and serving them—that is why he brought all this disaster on them.'*

It was in all fairness to Solomon that the Lord gave him this warning. Accepting the liabilities for inviting the presence of God to dwell with Israel came with enormous responsibilities. There were grave repercussions for disobedience, and breaking covenant with God is a serious offense. God is a very jealous God (see Exodus 34:14)! His name is Jealous!

It was the Lord's first choice, as it has always been, to dwell with His people. But at the same time, He also knows the failure men have in honoring *their* commitment to Him. The Lord wanted to protect Israel from what He Himself would have to release upon them if they disobeyed. Famines, locusts, and plagues are all indicative of the disobedience that damages that relationship. Verse 14 becomes the outline for healing—a repentant heart that pursues God. The healing of the land comes through a people who identify with the Lord through a posture of humility and brokenness, who know how to pray, seek His face, and turn from wickedness.

HEALING THE CURSE

Now let's return to our story of David and the Gibeonites. Whether or not Saul was aware of the covenant between Israel and the Gibeonites is unknown to us, but tragedy struck when he tried to destroy them. Saul's violation of the covenant between Israel and the Gibeonites compromised the integrity of the land—the Lord released a curse.

David's willingness to own the offense and repent of it was necessary for reconciliation with the Gibeonites, and the necessary step for the healing of the land.

The healing of the land was uniquely tied to the healing of the Gibeonites, and it was up to David on whether or not he would participate in their healing. If he had not, I am almost sure that the famine would have continued. The land was cursed, not because the Gibeonites were unbelievers, or had cursed it, but because a covenant had been violated. The land was suffering the consequences of that broken promise. That clearly shows us how God's law of covenant cannot be violated. 2 Chronicles 7:14 illustrated the process to which David had committed himself.

David realized that there was only one thing to do. The only way he and his nation would be released from the famine was to heal the breach of covenant. He approached the Gibeonites, and asked,

> 'What shall I do for you? How shall I make amends so that you will bless the Lord's inheritance?'
>
> 2 Samuel 21:3

Notice the position of humility David took, even in the asking. He did not dictate a solution or social program. He did not offer compensation. He did not come up with strategies not to ever let this happen again. He did not demand a blessing. (All of which would easily replace faith.) He put himself at the mercy of the Gibeonites in the fear of God, knowing God was the only one who could bring the necessary healing and reconciliation. David realized that God is serious about covenants and promises made. He trusted God for the outcome.

"Identificational repentance," a phrase coined by John Dawson in his book, *Healing America's Wounds,*[5] is the position David chose to take. David's saying, *"What shall I do for you? How shall I make amends so that you will bless the Lord's inheritance?"* was an admittance to the offense. The choice he made was to **identify** with the wounds created by his own countryman, Saul. David's willingness to **own the offense** and repent of it was necessary for reconciliation with the Gibeonites, and the necessary step for the healing of the land. Identificational repentance does just that, for those who willingly submit to it. They receive God's heart first, identify with the wounds, i.e. offenses, and then take the necessary steps of repentance.

Likewise, in chapter nine of Ezra, also of Nehemiah and Daniel, you can find the prayers of these three men who also, like David, chose to stand in the gap for their nation. They took a posture of humility, took ownership of their nation's sin, and repented before the Lord. God hears and responds to such prayers.

When David made sincere efforts to bring reconciliation between Israel and the Gibeonites, God once again answered prayer in behalf of the land. The famine was lifted.

Once the land is healed, God's people are once again able to receive the Lord's fullest blessings—harvest. For David, the natural circumstance was his window to the spiritual reality.

The spiritual did not come first, but the natural, and after that the spiritual.

1 Corinthians 15:46

It was what God used to reveal His purposes, just like it can be for you and me.

ARE WE THE ONES?

"Fill up, then, the measure of the sin of your forefathers!"

—Jesus, Matthew 23:32

Could we be the generation that could reverse the tragic flow of blood in this nation and bring the glory of God's presence into the land? If so, we must break the tendencies and patterns of fallen humanity. How can we steward a land if we continue to pollute it?

If we want to move from a *visitation* of God to a *habitation*, then we must assume responsibility to open the doors of repentance and make a way for the Lord to come in and heal us. We are His ambassadors. He's making His appeal through us. Let's call on Him to raise a standard of righteousness so that we can cleanse and heal the land and its people.

History is waiting for men and women with a heart like King David, William Penn, Christian Fredrick Post and so many others to restore and release this land and its people, to be all that God intended us to be.

I pray that we will take a serious look into the necessary steps to be a people with hearts like David's, after God's heart. We can make a difference. As overwhelming as the process of healing seems, the wonderful thing about it is that whatever God requires, he enables. Everyone can be healed. Everyone can be a healer.

ENDNOTES

1. Loewen, James W., *Lies My Teacher Told Me*, (A Touchstone Book, Simon & Schuster, New York, N.Y., 1995), p. 319.
2. *Ibid.*, pp. 12-13.
3. Notice what God commands regarding oaths; "This is what the Lord commands: When a man makes a vow to the Lord or takes an oath to obligate himself by a pledge, he must not break his word but must do everything he said" (Nu. 32:1-2).
4. It is not known why Saul was unable to annihilate the Gibeonites but it could be that God had intervened and sovereignly honored and protected the covenant between Israel, the Gibeonites, and the Lord.
5. Dawson, John, *Healing America's Wounds*, (Regal Books, Ventura, California, 1994), p. 15.

1 6

KEEPING COVENANT

Ask for the ancient paths, ask where the good way is, and walk in it, and you will find rest for your souls.

Jeremiah 6:16

I believe Penn, as a forerunner, has passed the baton to this generation. History has preserved what is necessary. He proved by virtue of the Holy Experiment that only God is sovereign and that His blessings would follow those who would but put themselves into His hands and see each other through His eyes. Penn made this manifest by his decrees and actions. Men and women were not property to possess or oppress but were, each and all, created in God's image—free to be an expression of His love, if they would so choose.

Accomplishing this kind of release, however, can only happen as our focus remains centered in God. What lies within the depths of the human heart is where God begins looking, and is what He will test to prove its character. God is looking for a people who want what He wants, giving Him freedom to uncover every area of doubt and fear. Allowing God to produce a clean and pure heart is an open door to the freedom we long for. But we can only get to that place if we allow Him to take us on an eternal walk with Him.

When Jeremiah speaks of asking for the ancient paths, I find it hard to relate and difficult to understand how any of that has power over my "todays" and the choices I make. But they do. Here's how: when the Bible speaks of His plan for me, it speaks of a path on which the Lord directs me because of His purposes for my life. He has planned for my life before I was born (see Ephesians 2:10). His plan for me doesn't change, even if I choose not to walk in it. But if the day comes when I realize I am not walking in that plan, I must ask for it and make the necessary response to adjust my life to it, to return to His path and keep going into the future. He will take me to where I could never go on my own. It is present and is revealed from one place of glory to the next because God's path eventually leads all the way to Him. It is ancient in the sense that God is and was and has always been. He knew me, the Bible says, before the foundations of the earth (see Ephesians 1:4; Romans 8:29). His plan for me is ancient—as it is for any individual, family, or nation. This is too awesome to fathom, but true.

What are our nation's ancient paths and where are they found? They relate to the past in the context of God's divine purposes. It is not found in retreating, freezing time or rehearsing the past. What William Penn envisioned was a path in which God would be remembered and sought, continually, where righteousness would be the standard, and where people would be embraced. His government, he hoped, would allow that. It was as up to date as any culture could be, on the cutting edge of the glory of God: a place where God's desire to be glorified and people's desire to be fulfilled could coincide. A land brought up to remember and fear God.

Isaiah 50:10,11 gives fair warning to those who try to follow God in their own wisdom and strength.

Who among you fears the Lord and obeys the word of his servant? Let him who walks in the dark, who has no light, trust in the name of the Lord and rely on his God. But now, all you who light fires and provide yourselves with flaming torches, go, walk in the light of your fires and of the torches you have set ablaze. This is what you shall receive from my hand: You will lie down in torment.

God's "ancient paths" speak of a way of living that is conducive to His righteousness and will ultimately lead us to a place of rest and peace.

LESSONS FROM ISRAEL

Israel has had to face many tragic losses in their history. Many of those losses were due to their own rebellion and rejection of God. God could never honor His own people when they acted independently of His leadership. It was always important for the Lord to remind Israel how their past defeats and successes were all related to how much or how little they put their trust in Him. As it was for Israel, so it is with anyone standing on God's Word to heal the breach. We not only have to reconcile with God but must keep His promises. We too, like Israel, must remember what the Lord is able to accomplish when we trust Him and the tragic results when He is forgotten. One such event forever changed the course of Israel's life and history.

After God delivered Israel from Egypt He guaranteed their place in the Promised Land. It would require, however, their participation. The obstacles, so it seemed, were too large a task and they refused the challenge. The consequence of their rebellion was the forfeiture of the Promised Land—a heavy price for their lack of trust. An entire generation lost the promise of the land flowing with milk and honey, buried in the desert sands of the wilderness. Even Moses, a friend of God (see Exodus 33:11), the most humble man on earth (see Numbers 12:3), and God's anointed leader, never received the gift of the Promised Land. God would not tolerate, even from Moses, being misrepresented before His people (see Numbers 20:1-13).

Forty years later, in keeping with His covenant promise, God brought them back to the edge of their inheritance once again. *His plan for them hadn't changed.* In Deuteronomy 8:2 Moses said,

> 'Remember how the Lord your God led you all the way in the desert these forty years, **to humble you and to test you in order to know what was in your heart**, whether or not you would keep his commands.' (emphasis mine)

Reaching the fulfillment of God's promise could only be proven in one place, and that was in the hearts of His people. His purpose for testing them was to find a people who would believe and trust Him for what He promises. God knew what He was capable of; He wanted His people to believe it also.

The Lord hasn't changed since then. He's still searching to strengthen hearts that are fully committed to Him.

For the eyes of the Lord range throughout the earth to strengthen those whose hearts are fully committed to him.

2 Chronicles 16:9

He will not release into our hands that with which we cannot be trusted. A. W. Tozer wrote, "God is looking for men in whose hands his glory is safe."[1]

REMEMBER, AND DO NOT FORGET

Just before the Lord took this new generation into the land, He cautioned them in Deuteronomy 8 always to remember what He had done for them and to never forget. There, on the banks of the Jordan River, was their divine opportunity to renew their covenant with the Lord their God. Here, in part, is what God said to them through His servant Moses.

Be careful to follow every command I am giving you today, so that you may live and increase and may enter and possess the land that the Lord promised on oath to your forefathers. Remember how the Lord your God led you all the way in the desert these forty years, to humble you and to test you in order to know what was in your heart, whether or not you would keep his commands.

Deuteronomy 8:1-2

When you have eaten and are satisfied, praise the Lord your God for the good land he has given you. Be careful that you do not forget the Lord your God, failing to observe his commands, his laws and his decrees that I am giving you this day. Otherwise, when you eat and are satisfied, when you build fine houses and settle down, and when your herds and flocks grow large and your silver and gold increase and all you have is multiplied, then your heart will become proud and you will forget the Lord your God, who brought you out of Egypt, out of the land of slavery.

Deuteronomy 8:11-14

But remember the Lord your God, for it is he who gives you the ability to produce wealth, and so confirms his covenant, which he swore to your forefathers, as it is today.

Deuteronomy 8:18

As we shall see, some lessons, are sorely learned.

CONTINUED WARNINGS

During the days of Samuel the prophet, (see 1 Samuel 8) Israel saw that Samuel had aged and that his sons were not walking in their father's ways. Consequently, they asked for a king to be appointed to rule over them.

They said to him (Samuel), 'You are old, and your sons do not walk in your ways; now appoint a king to lead us, such as all the other nations have.'

1 Samuel 8:5

God knew their hearts and knew what it was they were demanding. Their sin did not consist merely in any inherent evil for wanting a king. Their sin was also in the *reason* for asking—they said, "such as all the other nations have."

The Lord had always been the One to provide and protect His people. Their desire for a king "such as all the other nations have" broke covenant with the Lord, Who had pledged to be their King. Their request was an overt denial of that relationship. God had set them apart from all other nations to be His people; He, their King, pledged to be their Savior and Deliverer. Now they were rejecting everything God had been for them by asking to follow a man rather than God, and the world's system of government instead of His.

After Samuel had prayed to the Lord about what the people demanded, the Lord said to Samuel:

'Listen to all the people are saying to you; it is not you they have rejected, but they have rejected me as their king. As they have done from the day I brought them out of Egypt until this day, forsaking me and serving other gods, so they are doing to you. Now listen to them; but warn them solemnly and let them know what the king who will reign over them will do.'

1 Samuel 8:7-9

Even after Samuel shared with the people the Lord's warning, they rejected the warning and continued to demand a king like the other nations.

But the people refused to listen to Samuel. 'No!' they said. 'We want a king over us. Then we will be like all the other nations, with a king to lead us and to go out before us and fight our battles.'

1 Samuel 8:19, 20

Thus, Israel experienced a sad change in the way she would be governed. Without God as the head, Israel's leadership would be drastically limited to men and the consequences that would follow.

God's desires are to be personally connected to his people. His fullest blessings are intrinsic to our fidelity with Him and our following through with whatever He commands. History is replete with stories of civilizations who missed their destiny by failing to respond to the voice of the Lord, and by failing to be intimate with Him. God wants to be known by His people. Trust is the issue.

For many years Israel's refusal to repent continued, in spite of the continued warnings. They continued to reject their covenant relationship with the Lord, choosing rather a life of rebellion and apostasy. But God was not finished with His people. As a loving Father, He would not allow them to continue in their rebelliousness.

In keeping with the covenant He had established with Abraham, Isaac and Jacob, God raised up a foreign nation, Babylon, to discipline His people. In 586 B.C., Babylon invaded and destroyed the city of Jerusalem. Many of Jerusalem's citizens were taken captive.

Babylon, in turn, was eventually overthrown by Persia. Cyrus, king of Persia, showed compassion on the Exiles and allowed them to return to their beloved city.

THE CALL OF NEHEMIAH

Seventy years after Jerusalem's destruction, on March 12, 516 B.C., worship was restored to the city by the rebuilding and dedication of the temple through Zerubbabel and Ezra. However, full restoration was not yet complete. The walls and gates around the city lay in ruins. News reached Babylon of the condition of Jerusalem.

> *The wall of Jerusalem is broken down, and its gates have been burned with fire.*

Nehemiah 1:3

Nehemiah, one of the Jews taken captive into Babylon, became God's special candidate for a very special mission. He heard that Jerusalem's walls and gates still lay in ruins. The protective walls and gates around a city such as Jerusalem were their strength and security. The prophet Isaiah had already prophesied,

> *'No longer will violence be heard in your land, nor ruin or destruction within your borders, but you will call your walls Salvation and your gates Praise.'*

Isaiah 60:18

...as long as the city of the Great King remained in its present condition, the enemies of God had access to the city any time they desired.

Nehemiah knew that as long as the city of the Great King remained in its present condition, the enemies of God would have access to the city any time they desired. Startled and broken-hearted, Nehemiah agonized before the Lord throughout many days of weeping, fasting and prayer.

This action of Nehemiah's started one of Israel's great transformations. Nehemiah chose to take ownership by identifying with the sins of Israel's forefathers. He stood in the gap on behalf of his people and cried out to God with prayers of repentance.

> *'I confess the sins **we** Israelites, **including myself and my father's house**, have committed against you. **We** have acted very wickedly toward you. **We** have not obeyed the commands, decrees and laws you gave your servant Moses.' (emphasis mine)*

Nehemiah 1:6b-7

Nehemiah, favored in the courts of Babylon as King Artaxerxes' cup-bearer, was shown mercy and compassion to go and rebuild his beloved city.

After arriving in the city and examining the damage, Nehemiah approached the people and said to them:

> *'You see the trouble we are in: Jerusalem lies in ruins, and its gates have been burned with fire. Come, let us rebuild the wall of Jerusalem, and we will no longer be in disgrace.'*

Nehemiah 2:17

> *The people replied with **one voice** and said, 'Let us start rebuilding.'* (emphasis mine)

Nehemiah 2:18

This was the beginning of one of Israel's great revivals as the restoration to the city began. Fifty-two days later, on October 2, 445 BC, the walls that had lain in ruins for one hundred and forty-one years were rebuilt and dedicated to the Lord. That began not only the rebuilding and rehanging of the city's walls and gates, but more significantly, it foreshadowed the rebuilding of a people who were returning to God through confession, repentance and purification of themselves from their sins.

REBUILDERS OF THE WALL

It is God's desire for us to be a people who, like the people of Nehemiah's day, rehang the gates and rebuild the walls of our lives. If we do this, then we will deny the enemy access. For as a people are healed and changed, so is the family or nation of those people. Only God can cause this. You can almost hear the words of the prophet Isaiah echoing to us through the corridors of time:

> *Your people will rebuild the ancient ruins and will raise up the age-old foundations; you will be called Repairer of Broken Walls, Restorer of Streets with Dwellings.*

Isaiah 58:12

This valuable piece of history demonstrates the necessary restorative process. History provides for us a window of insight into discoveries about our past, telling us who we are today and what's needed for full recovery. It is possible to rebuild—to have new points of reference.

As we see from this wonderful illustration from Nehemiah, who is an Old Testament type of the Holy Spirit, the plan of redemption always begins at the place of injury and, if we are willing, continues when we allow God to complete the restoration. The "ancient paths" begin in our hearts. This is good and necessary because as we receive a revelation of the heart of God, He will also give us a revelation of ours. God knows we need Him; He just wants us to get to the same place He is; where we agree that everything He says about us is true. The Holy Spirit's task is to convict and convince, and how repentance is the necessary bridge that keeps us connected. God made the way through Jesus, the new and living way (see Hebrews 10:19-22).

THE SUCCESS OF REBUILDING

At the State Library in Harrisburg, above the door to the Department of Law, inscribed in granite, are these words:

LAW IS THE SCIENCE
OF HUMAN CONDUCT
DERIVED FROM THE PAST

REGARD FOR THE PUBLIC WELFARE
IS THE HIGHEST LAW

It is true that the highest law, as it has been developed through trial and error in our past, is regard for human conduct and the welfare of all mankind. People should be our highest regard. But so often, as history has proven, there are breaches along the way that prevent us from moving on in God's plan, breaches that we may feel, in the natural, as insurmountable.

The greatest task any man or nation can undertake, requiring the most courage, is not only to look at what successes may be achieved in the future but

THE SEED OF A NATION

also to look at whatever successes we can find when we face the woundings of our past—success through rebuilding. This truly takes great courage, for a wounded heart can be the most serious of injuries, though healing it is the greatest joy.

THE FIG LEAF PRINCIPLE

God's desire is that we become an expression of His love to each other. There has been, however, a problem with our connecting with God about this issue, a problem that has plagued mankind since the dawn of time—the ongoing problem illustrated in what I call "The Fig Leaf Principle." To see this for all its worth, we must return to the Garden of Eden.

After God had created the Garden, and had put Adam and Eve in it to care for it, the Lord would often come and visit them in the cool of the day. However, on one particular day, the Lord's visit met with something foreign and unfamiliar—a cold, dark enmity and distrust hung in the air that had never been experienced there before. Adam and Eve had disobeyed the Lord, and had sinned.

> *Then the eyes of both of them were opened, and they realized they were naked; so they sewed fig leaves together and made coverings for themselves.*

> *Then the man and his wife heard the sound of the Lord God as he was walking in the garden in the cool of the day, and they hid from the Lord God among the trees of the garden.*

> Genesis 3:7,8

The Lord already knew what had happened, but He came into the garden to see them anyway, just as he had always done. The Lord came asking Adam a question never before asked anywhere, one I'm sure Adam never wanted to hear or have to answer. Adam knew that there had been preemptive warnings given regarding this day. The Lord had told Adam that the day of his disobedience would bring death (see Genesis 2:17).

Here, in God's question to Adam, lies an amazing picture of the Lord's incredible mercy. After Adam and Eve sinned, the Lord did not come into the garden to kill them. In Genesis 3:9 God came asking them a heart provoking,

"Where are you?"

Of course, the Lord knew where Adam was all along, just as He knows where you and I are, just as He knows all that happened here in Pennsylvania, and in this nation. But God wanted to hear from Adam. He wanted to know if mending broken trust was more important to Adam than the shame and guilt he now had to live in. It's the same with us.

I believe the key in the Lord's question to Adam was not so much in the question, but in the manner in which the Lord was providing for Adam to answer. Could it be that God in His infinite mercy and grace was giving Adam the opportunity to confess *what he had done*? Could it have been that the Lord was waiting to minister forgiveness in order to restore them? In Genesis 3:10 Adam said to the Lord,

'I heard you in the garden, and I was afraid because I was naked; so I hid.'

Adam had never feared the Lord's presence before, nor had he ever had any reason to hide. But now, as the result of his sin, Adam's shame and fear were greater than his understanding of the Lord's ability to love and forgive.

TO CONFESS OR NOT TO CONFESS

If we confess our sins, he is faithful and just and will forgive us our sins and purify us from all unrighteousness.

1 John 1:9

Sadly, failing to recognize the true heart of God's love and mercy, Adam exchanged accusation and blame for confession and repentance. Instead of accepting God's love and assuming personal responsibility for his disobedience, Adam blamed both God and Eve for his failure. Adam said,

*'The woman **you** put here with me—**she** gave me some fruit from the tree, and I ate it.' (emphasis mine)*

Genesis 3:12

This response caused both Adam and his wife to forfeit the full blessing of God's restorative provision. What a tragedy for them to forfeit everything that

God had created for them to enjoy. But what else could God do? Adam and Eve were judged by their own confession. Jesus tells us in Matthew 12:34 that out of the heart the mouth speaks and that we would be judged accordingly. Jesus continues to speak about the condition of man's heart when He says,

> *'The good man brings good things out of the good stored up in him. But I tell you that men will have to give account on the day of judgment for every careless word they have spoken. **For by your words you will be acquitted, and by your words you will be condemned.'** (emphasis mine)*

Matthew 12:35-37

But, how often we too forfeit the full blessings of God when we, like Adam and Eve, find ourselves responding as they—hiding from God and passing the blame onto someone else for our failures.

God in his wisdom knows that in order for us to be properly oriented to Him, we must be aware.

As our eyes are opened to the painful reality of this, we begin to understand that where we've been is inherently tied to the *"Where are you?"* question. We cannot know where we are unless we know which path we used to get there. We become disoriented and the sad part about it is, we aren't aware. We're trying to make sense of a life we've been dropped into, never knowing why some parts of it just don't work well. God in his wisdom knows that in order for us to be properly oriented to Him, we must be aware. But, like Adam and Eve, we try to hide from God and each other. We use all manner of fig leaves to cover our shame and substitute something else for His presence instead of confessing our vulnerability and nakedness to Him. We don't trust Him and are afraid of what He may reveal. Our lack of trust reveals our ignorance of His love that heals. Romans 10:11 says,

> *Anyone who trusts in him will never be put to shame.*

No one can hide from God! Thinking we can just for the sake of feeling protected is illogical and violates our God given conscience. When we become exposed in our nakedness, our tendency is to run to the nearest fig leaf and try to hide our shame and guilt instead of making confessions that could heal and restore. We were never created to hide from a merciful and loving God. We replace transparency and vulnerability with selfishness and self-centeredness, and a need to make life work without God—the age-old cry of sinful and fallen man.

STANDING IN THE GAP

'I looked for a man among them who would build up the wall and stand before me in the gap on behalf of the land so I would not have to destroy it, but I found none.'

Ezekiel 22:30

God is always looking for those who are willing to stand in the gap. Standing in intercessory prayer requires sacrifice and courage. There are multiplied injuries we've committed against God and each other that have resulted in the defiling of the land. Healing that requires walking away from the altar of convenience—we've worshipped there far too long—and stepping into the fire of God's love. God wants the gaps filled with those who desire, like Him, to see people healed and set free, thus making real and practical our devotion to one another (see 2 Corinthians 7:12). We must cleanse ourselves from all worldly influences, purify our hearts and be willing to lay down our lives, our reputations, our positions and place in order to be used as a vessel of *God's heart* spilling into the hurting gaps of peoples lives. He sees and will use those who are willing to pay the price.

Before we can be the kind of people who bridge the gap, we must remember to commit ourselves to reach the "good way," as Jeremiah 6:16 suggests. "Ask for the ancient paths, ask where the good way is, and walk in it, and you will find rest for your souls." There are necessary steps of recognizing, confessing and repenting for wandering from God's truth that must happen. That is the "good way," and only God can show us how to get there. The incredible stories from the Word of God show us how different people wandered from the "ancient paths" and how God by His great mercy called them back to the "good way." I believe God wants to use these stories to illustrate to us, not only an understanding of how our fallen nature separates us from everything divine but also how we are so dependent on Him. God invites us to join Him in the restorative process.

ENDNOTES

1. Rowell, Edward K., *Quotes and Idea Starters for Preaching and Teaching*, (Baker Books, Grand Rapids, MI, 1996), p. 68

1 7

REPLANTING THE SEED

You cannot see things till you know roughly what they are.

—C.S. Lewis

E ven though it appears our freedom has been exploited, the seed that planted America has not gone uncultivated or been completed by the history books. The Lord has sent many to proclaim His glory and freedom. I believe we can re-discover America's "ancient paths" (Jeremiah 6:16) that have been in God's mind and heart all along. We don't have to start over, only to realize what these past three hundred years have taught us—that we need Him! After all, that is the primary message of the Gospel.

We can begin by recognizing every misrepresentation of the nature of God that we have made. C.S. Lewis said, *"You cannot see things till you know rough-ly what they are."* This is true. Nor can we pray effectively until we "roughly" know to what purpose we are applying our faith. God has shown us so much already and will show us the next step too. I believe it.

The Lord is bringing His people together in this nation as never before. Many are responding to the unction of the Holy Spirit and are recognizing the times and seasons of our day. We long for God to move.

It is unreasonable to think that William Penn could control all the elements that came into his beloved province.

Are we desperate for God? Most likely we're more desperate than we realize. In Ephesians 1:17 Paul prayed that we would receive a "Spirit of wisdom and revelation, so that we may know him better." Prayer opens us to the heart of God. My prayer is that we will be willing to obey once we know what the Father wants. He has already laid out strategies for overcoming. He's waiting for us to get involved. He is the Equipper for all He calls.

THE BIG PICTURE

It is unreasonable to think that William Penn could have controlled all the elements that came into his beloved province. However, as long as Penn was the proprietor, a high standard of righteousness was maintained within his administration. Because of his conviction that God is the only one who can draw men, change their lives and provide true liberty, he had an open door policy, which has gained him much criticism. Freedom could not be legislated, only demonstrated. Penn knew it was worth the risk even if others might abuse the freedom he allowed. William Penn didn't come into Pennsylvania blind or naive.

History has tried to teach us that America's conflicts were merely a chronological political evolution. Not so. God has always had a greater purpose for this nation. His purposes are large, bigger than our own, encompassing hundreds, even thousands of years. If we don't see His plan, we will never see the breach, thereby negating any need for Him at all. If history doesn't bring us to this place, then it is useless and our destiny is forfeited. But make no mistake; God will ultimately get the glory. As men find out, through time and process, He will have it no other way. One day, every knee will bow and He will get the last word.

WHAT'S IN A NAME?

It was no mistake that Pennsylvania was nicknamed The Keystone State. "Keystone" refers to the wedge-shaped, central keystone in an arch that holds all the other stones in place. Pennsylvania has been the key to many events that have birthed and changed the course of this nation politically, socially, economically and religiously.

I believe the season of this nation's greatest prophetic opportunity (perhaps in an entirely different way) is yet to come. Perhaps, the Keystone State may become the archway to a mighty move of God throughout this land, bringing healing and deliverance to many people. And let's pray that the Holy Experiment, which has seemingly failed, be seen as only postponed; waiting for the necessary ingredients of a people who realize that the great purpose of this nation was His all along.

William Penn was more than a Quaker and Pennsylvania more than just a refuge for them.

A TIME FOR HARVEST

For the nations want a precedent and my God will make it the seed of a nation. That an example may be set up to the nations.

In these prophetic words Penn stated what his province was to become. Penn was more than just a Quaker and Pennsylvania more than just a refuge for them. The vision with which God inspired Penn had far greater potential than merely reaching Pennsylvania and The United States. To think that the Holy Experiment was solely about one people would be narrow-minded. There is a bigger picture.

Ultimately, God's desire for America was for her to become a vehicle to reach the nations and to be an example for others who would have the same desire. Nations are people, which is where God is, knocking on the hearts of men, women and children. God hasn't changed His mind. It is still His desire for all men to be saved (see 1 Timothy 2:4), not willing that any should perish (see 2 Peter 3:9). God wants to bring America into her destiny so she can offer true freedom to all people.

Can a place, a state, a nation have such a destiny? Of course! America was intended to be an example to the nations—a nation of true unity and freedom. The nations did come and the seed was planted. The forces of darkness, however, have moved mightily to uproot and destroy it. We must fight back with humility, faith, repentance and prayers of intercession, against these forces that would try to overwhelm us.

THE PROMISE OF UNITY

Division in America, as the result of broken covenants, has produced a catalyst for major conflict in the heavens—paralleled here on earth—making unity one of the most evasive conditions America has ever known. This is why racism and segregation have become such malefactors for us. Racism separates human beings and prevents the glory of God from being revealed. It violates some of God's most fundamental commandments and is more revealing of our arrogance and independence from God than of our rationalized separation. Psalm 133 tells us:

Walking in unity is the greatest challenge the people of God face.

How good and pleasant it is when brothers live together in unity! It is like precious oil [anointing] poured on the head...For there the Lord bestows his blessing and life forevermore.

Covenants like the *Great Treaty* represent God's desires for this nation. Unity, not sameness, is what allows the glory of God to be revealed and the anointing of God to be manifest. Unity through diversity is a most beautiful representation of God. What an example America would have been if through the diversity of its culture, righteousness, peace and joy (the very nature of the Kingdom of God, Romans 14:17), could have been evident to all that would and did come here! I don't know where else in the world this kind of opportunity was so available. But it did happen here, once—even if only in seed form.

The dynamic of unity consists in imperfect people loving *in* His perfect love, which is not of this earth—it's supernatural. "Love is of God." (1 John 4:7) That is why it takes a supernatural people to achieve it. Walking in unity is the greatest challenge the people of God face.

If Jesus could have left us with a single most important message, I believe it was the prayer that He prayed to His Father in John 17:21. His last prayer for us was that we would be one as He and the Father are one. One in purpose—one in heart. Oh, how we need the anointing of God to be what we are called to be, to do what we are called to do. The more love we have the more anointing we will carry.

CAN WE REALLY WALK IN UNITY?

You and I can start right now. Does this mean we can walk in unity with everyone? What about unbelievers? What about those with whom I disagree? Yes! As far as it depends on you, you absolutely can. We have been deluded into thinking that we can only live in unity with those with whom we agree, or those with whom we find common ground. Unity is bigger than that. It is bigger than agreements we must have to work hand in hand with others to accomplish given purposes. The beginning of unity is a degree of faith that enables us to see that all men and women are created by God. His love and will for us is always greater than

Our faith can always be checked by our ability to love.

what we see. God is the one who draws men and women to Himself. As a matter of fact, no one can come to Him unless He first draws them. Only He can change an individual. I must relinquish control and judgment. If we do not have this kind of faith, then people become a threat. We also forfeit our ability to speak light into darkness.

However, if we gain security in God, we can love inclusively, without altering convictions or being defensive. In fact we grow stronger in our convictions because we become secure as God supernaturally pours His love into our lives for others, even those I would never love on my own. You find out that nothing can contaminate you, not even chaos. Our faith can always be checked by our ability to love. Remember,

"The only thing that counts is faith expressing itself through love." (Galatians 5:6) Also, "Without faith it is impossible to please God." (Hebrews 11:6)

Ask yourself these questions:

1. Do I arrange my life exclusively, so as only to be with people like me, or people who advance my goals?

2. Do I *need* to give my opinion? Do I give my opinion, even when not asked? (Arrogant opinions separate)

3. Do I resort to rules and regulations to feel safe? (Legalistic, Religious)

4. Can I handle chaos? (Things out of my control)

5. Can I move forward in love in the midst of chaos? ("None of these things move me"—see 1 Corinthians 15:58).

6. Do I compare critically? (Myself, my family, my church, my nation)

7. Am I content with the measure of faith God has given to my family, my church, and me?

8. Do I pride myself in having more "truth" than others?

9. Do I serve?

10. Do I love?

If you are exclusive, opinionated, legalistic and religious, if all your ducks need to be in a row before you can move forward, if you scrutinize every move of God, if you think you or others are missing out just because you see differences, then you are far from the liberty in Christ that is yours and what will ultimately give God the most glory. He can keep you safe no matter what the cost to live in His righteousness. That's what William Penn knew. That's what gave Penn courage to live with a clear conscience. That's why Penn heard God. And you can too!

HEALING TO THE NATIONS

Write down the revelation and make it plain on tablets so that a herald may run with it. For the revelation awaits an appointed time; it speaks of the end and will not prove false. Though it linger, wait for it; it will certainly come and will not delay.

Habakkuk 2:2,3

I believe that the words of William Penn in the state capitol's rotunda at Harrisburg were inspired by God. His prophetic message to the nations still lingers not only in the capitol's rotunda, but awaits its appointed time, when by God's grace a chosen generation will take the baton handed down to us from history. Not for some political end, but that men and women of all cultures, races and nations may experience the wonder of knowing the living God who was and is and is to come. That is when America will take her place to lead in humility and love—an example to the nations.

I'll never forget the day the I first stood in Penn Treaty Park in Philadelphia, where the purposes of this state were first heard by men and by God. I was overwhelmed as I learned, in almost tragic symbolism, how on a stormy Saturday night March 3, 1810, the great elm tree that overshadowed the covenant made between William Penn and the Delaware blew down. Standing throughout two hundred and eighty-three years, eight feet in diameter and twenty-four feet in circumference, this great patriarch of the forest stood as a testimony to the strength of the two nations that met here in a gracious and grace-filled commitment of love, respect and unity. And then, as one tried to dominate the other, forces

Perhaps, as Pennsylvania was the seed for the birthing of this great nation some three hundred years ago, she may become a seed to America's healing as well. I pray.

stronger than they could withstand forced these two nations apart, and the great elm came crashing to the earth in a collision of bloodshed and heartache.

Near the sight of the original treaty, another elm tree grows. May it be a prophetic seed to the vision of William Penn as its branches reach out over the walls of hostility and its leaves become healing to the nations (see Revelation 22:2).

CAPTURED BY THE BREATH OF GOD

What happens next is up to us. Will we be those who wipe away the tears of the American Indian, along with all those who followed and reaped much the same, and accomplish their healing? History is still in the making—our story is not yet over. Perhaps, as Pennsylvania was the seed for the birthing of this great nation more than three hundred years ago, she may become a seed to America's healing as well. I pray.

As I pause and reflect on William Penn, the freedoms he bequeathed this nation, the Delaware, the covenant made between the two and its destruction thereafter, there rises inside of me something I cannot deny, something that changed me during that drive home from Virginia Beach in July, 1995. There lies within me a sound testimony that cannot be debated, the unmistakable cry of God's heart resounding in the chambers of my own—the place where God speaks to us all. Something of the Spirit of God that keeps me praying, keeps me writing, keeps me searching. The undeniable truth that I have not been able to walk away from tells me, *"God wants and is waiting to do something here!"* But, in the same breath as I cry *"How?"* and *"When?"* I'm drawn to the words of John Wesley, who said, "God does nothing but in answer to prayer."

A fire burns in my heart to see God wake this slumbering nation. Let's covenant with the Lord and let the rain of our prayers and the demonstration of our commitment to honor one another be poured out upon the seed; that the life of unity may come back again to this nation; that His Holy Spirit may breathe into William Penn's prophecy and make America an example to the nations once again; that healing and reconciliation may come and put an end to hostility and restore the friendships that we made here so long ago. I believe He will raise up many for this great task. Prayers of humility reach the heart of an all-merciful God. Let's repent of our nation's sins, repent of our own racist hearts for the atrocities committed against the people of this land—and watch the enemy's strongholds fall one by one, as people are set free.

Within the entrance to the East Wing of the capitol building in Harrisburg there lies a plaque that reads:

WITH GOD'S GUIDANCE MAY ALL THE MEN AND WOMEN WORKING WITHIN THESE WALLS DEDICATE THEMSELVES TO PERPETUATE THE HOLY EXPERIMENT OF WILLIAM PENN WITH INTEGRITY, FRUGALITY, COMPASSION AND RESPECT FOR ALL MANKIND.

Governor Dick Thornburgh
(Pennsylvania's Governor from 1979-1987)

He who began a good work in you will carry it onto completion.

Philippians 1:6

ENDNOTES

1. C. S. Lewis, book 1, Out of the Silent Planet, from The Space Trilogy

Map of the Pennsylvania Region
Showing Fort Locations

Printed in the USA
CPSIA information can be obtained
at www.ICGtesting.com
JSHW082155140824
68134JS00014B/249

9 781600 372049